Poetic Inclinations
Ethics, History, Philosophy

Dorthe Jørgensen

Poetic Inclinations

Ethics,
History,
Philosophy

To my beloved Willy with eternal gratitude

Willy Aastrup (1948–2019)

Contents

Introduction 9

Attuned to Wonder 17

Philosophy at a Crossroads 29

The Relevance of Aesthetics 49

Aesthetic Thinking as a Common Humanist Concern 69

The Dialogue of Experience 75

History as a Work 97

***Felix Aestheticus* and the Good Life** 117

Toward an Aesthetics of Well-Being 141

Immanent Transcendence 155

Limit and Threshold 177

Hospitality and World Poetry 197

Bibliography 221

Acknowledgments 231

Introduction

It is common to identify aesthetics with the philosophy of art, but this notion of aesthetics is ripe for revision. In *Poetic Inclinations*, I introduce a metaphysics of experience developed with a foothold in philosophical aesthetics and hermeneutic phenomenology. This philosophy is about sensitively expanded aesthetic thinking, as well as the mind-opening and world-transformative experiences related to such thinking and traditionally called 'aesthetic' or 'religious' experiences. In *Poetic Inclinations*, I present my metaphysics of experience with a specific emphasis on the practical implications of this philosophy. I disclose the constructive critical nature of aesthetic thinking, a quality of crucial relevance to any theory or analysis of contemporary culture and institutions. Pitching the formative consequences of sensitively expanded thinking, I reveal its importance for not only academic research but also contemporary culture. In addition to explaining what it means to think in an aesthetic way, *Poetic Inclinations* attests the relevance of such thinking by showing its implications for human action and the choices we make in life. The book demonstrates, for instance, how sensitively expanded thinking can foster human well-being and improve our understanding of human history and the lives we lead.

Presenting the ethical significance of sensitivity, transgressive experience, and expanded thinking, the texts included in *Poetic Inclinations* explain the benefits of applying an experience-metaphysical approach to many practical issues. For example, they show the consequences of aesthetic thinking for the understanding of what it means to be a critical intellectual, including what philosophy and universities essentially are or should be. In its choice of texts, the book also makes evident that aesthetic thinking and the notion of the artwork can contribute to the philosophy of history by developing our ability to encompass both the historical and the ahistorical, rather than feeling forced to choose between them. Similarly, the book demonstrates how aesthetic thinking, due to its sensitively expanded nature, can contribute innovatively to current disciplines such as border studies, the study of human well-being, and social studies.

In *Poetic Inclinations*, I introduce and apply new interpretations of prevailing concepts of, for example, poetry, philosophy, experience, truth, thinking, beauty, aesthetics, history, borders, hospitality, and transcendence. The first chapter deals with the wonder in which philosophy originates, including the significance of wonder, experience, and memory for both literary and biographical storytelling. The second chapter addresses the intellectual crisis caused by the fact that few people today dare to prioritize *philosophia*, the search for wisdom that philosophy originally was. However, in this chapter, I suggest that a metaphysics of experience nourished by philosophical aesthetics and hermeneutic phenomenology can revitalize philosophy and enhance the humanities. The third chapter explains the contemporary relevance of philosophical aesthetics not only for the study of art but also for the humanities and society in general. This chapter rejects the usual identification of philosophical aesthetics with the philosophy of art, as well as the current focus on physical corporeality and sensuousness to the neglect of sensitivity and sensitively promoted insight. The fourth chapter consists of ten theses on the essence of aesthetic thinking and its importance for academic research, culture in general, and society as a whole. In discussing what it means to be a philosopher, the fifth chapter further pursues the question concerning the nature and meaning of philosophical thinking, and the connection between such thinking and the good life. Being a philosopher means being an intellectual, that is, someone who thinks critically owing to a sensitive awareness of the ambiguity of the immanent and a desire and ability not to contrast the particular and the universal.

The sixth chapter follows up on the question of literary and biographical storytelling by discussing how philosophical aesthetics, including the concept of the artwork, can contribute innovatively to historiography and the philosophical notion of history, which demands aesthetic thinking. The seventh chapter, devoted to *felix aestheticus*, interprets the good life aesthetically as the life of free philosophical thought and proposes a broad outlook, which is currently much needed in both the academic world and society in general. The eighth chapter develops the content of the short fourth chapter. In particular, it explains the significance of aesthetic thinking for human well-being and challenges current interpretations of the notion of the 'beautiful soul' by interpreting it as the capacity to perceive something as intrinsically valuable and surpass dichotomies in thought. The content of the short fourth chapter is also developed in chapter nine, which, by distinguishing between transcendence and the transcendent and between divinity and the divine, contemplates the transcending quality of aesthetic thinking interpreted as sensitively expanded thinking. The tenth chapter translates the mindset presented in the previous chapters into reflections on the notions of the limit and the threshold, thus contributing innovatively to current border studies and more specifically to contemporary border aesthetics. Finally, the eleventh chapter contributes innovatively to current social studies by interpreting hospitality as an expression of aesthetic sensitivity and world poetry as the multidimensionality of immanence perceived in transgressive experiences.

*　*　*

Poetic Inclinations is part of a duology that also includes the book *Imaginative Moods: Aesthetics, Religion, Philosophy*.[1] Together these books represent the first comprehensive presentation in English of what I term the metaphysics of experience, and which,

---

1 Dorthe Jørgensen, *Imaginative Moods: Aesthetics, Religion, Philosophy* (Aarhus: Aarhus University Press, 2021).

owing to my monographs in Danish, is well known and widely used in the Nordic countries. Aesthetics plays an important role in both books, but each book has its own scope and can therefore be read as an individual work. As is evident from the description of *Poetic Inclinations* presented in the previous paragraphs, this book includes a focus on ethics, history, and philosophy (for example, the ethical significance of aesthetic thinking, in the sense of its formative consequences). *Imaginative Moods*, on the other hand, includes a focus on aesthetics, religion, and philosophy (for example, the potential contribution of aesthetics to the understanding of prayer). Nevertheless, the two books are interrelated due to their shared task as introductions to the metaphysics of experience and their mutual cross references. They genuinely supplement and complement each other.

Poetic Inclinations makes the metaphysics of experience available to beginners and introduces practitioners in various professions, fields, or occupations to the implications of this philosophy. It proves the relevance of the metaphysics of experience by emphasizing the significance of aesthetic thinking in fields such as education, politics, and social work. Besides appealing to scholars and students, this book may also appeal to practitioners such as teachers, pedagogues, and social workers. *Imaginative Moods*, on the other hand, provides further knowledge about and insight into the metaphysics of experience. This book is slightly more demanding, since it focuses on the aforementioned metaphysics as such and its theoretical implications in aesthetics and theology. *Imaginative Moods* may appeal to scholars, students, pastors, psychologists, and artists, as well as those who have read *Poetic Inclinations* and who are thus already familiar with the relevance of the metaphysics of experience.

Poetic Inclinations and *Imaginative Moods* give an international readership access to innovative work that includes the reinterpretation of established concepts, the introduction of new notions, and the presentation of the practical and theoretical implications of both. They also offer new ways to conceive of and apply aesthetics, hermeneutics, and phenomenology, which includes groundbreaking theoretical work in the form of a unique integration of these disciplines, as well as a unique integration of aesthetics and theology. Phenomenologists and hermeneutic philosophers generally reject or diminish aesthetics in favor of the philosophy of art. Traditionally, Protestant theologians also rejected aesthetics, and contemporary theological attempts to include aesthetics mostly confuse it with the study of art. Finally, *Poetic Inclinations* and *Imaginative Moods* present numerous practical (critical, ethical, pedagogical) as well as philosophical and theological implications of contemplating contemporary phenomena within the framework of the metaphysics of experience. They expose the importance of sensitive contemplation that has an eye for transgressive experience and acknowledges both the existential relevance of such experience and its significance for the production of knowledge, for contemporary culture, and for society in general.

Both books consist of collections of texts written in various contexts but revolving around the aforementioned topics. The texts I have selected for publication together constitute two monographs thanks to their thematic kinship, common terminology, and common introduction and application of the metaphysics of experience; I edited and organized them for their present release, in English and in book form. I was motivated to produce these monographs by my international colleagues, who have often lamented that the majority of my research, including my major presentation of the metaphysics of experience—that is, the 965-page monograph *Den skønne tænkning* (Beautiful Thinking)—is only available in Danish.[2] Many scholars and artists from various backgrounds have requested a comprehensive English introduction to the metaphysics of experience, including the research in which this philosophy originates, the way of thinking of which it is a product, and its practical and theoretical implications. It is my great hope that *Poetic Inclinations* and *Imaginative Moods* will fulfill this request, at least

---

2   Dorthe Jørgensen, *Den skønne tænkning: Veje til erfaringsmetafysik. Religionsfilosofisk udmøntet* (Beautiful Thinking: Pathways to the Metaphysics of Experience. Religio-Philosophically Implemented) (Aarhus: Aarhus University Press, 2014).

partly, and I am deeply grateful for the interest that has motivated their publication.

The editing of the present material was guided by a wish to avoid unnecessary repetition but also to enable the reader to approach and understand each text and each book without prior knowledge of the others. A certain amount of repetition was thus unavoidable, but, as a teacher and knowledge disseminator, I have learned that repetition is far from harmful for educational purposes, especially when the content being mediated is philosophical and thus potentially difficult to access. Some of the texts presented in *Poetic Inclinations* and *Imaginative Moods* have been published previously, in various books or journals and in Danish or English, while others represent hitherto unpublished material produced with a foothold in my Danish monographs. Precise details can be found in the acknowledgements, where I also express my deep gratitude to the journal editors and publishers who have authorized me to reproduce previously published work. The editorial organization of the texts makes it possible, as mentioned, to favor an anarchistic way of reading in which one jumps between the texts and books, or perhaps only reads a single text or book. However, it also entails that one benefits from reading the books from beginning to end, starting with *Poetic Inclinations* and finishing with *Imaginative Moods*. At the end of the day, reading with an open mind is the most important premise of the outcome, and such a mindset aligns perfectly with the moral implication of the metaphysics of experience and thus with the ethos of the books.

***

The texts included in the present publication were translated into American English by me, in close cooperation with various copyeditors and proofreaders, and edited following the Chicago Manual of Style. Each text constitutes a chapter. To make it easier to use the chapters on an individual basis, I provide full bibliographic information in a footnote about texts I refer to the first time they appear in a chapter. All quotations follow current translations into English; in cases where there is no available translation, I have made one myself. Numbers and letters in references to Plato's texts refer to the Stephanus pagination, and in references to Aristotle's texts to the Bekker numbering. Citations and quotations from Kant's texts refer to page numbers in the Cambridge Edition of the Works of Kant, followed by volume and page numbers in the Academy Edition.

Attuned to Wonder

"From a very young age, I suspected there was more to my world than I could see."[3] Such are the opening words of Orhan Pamuk's beautiful memoir *Istanbul*, and they make me think that, from a very young age, he was attuned to wonder. Writing the aforementioned words, Pamuk is referring to his belief as a child that "somewhere in the streets of Istanbul, in a house resembling ours, there lived another Orhan so much like me that he could pass for my twin, even my double."[4] Pamuk does not remember where this idea came from. "It must have emerged from a web of rumours, misunderstandings, illusions and fears."[5] We later learn from his memoir—which deals not only with his childhood and youth but also with the city of Istanbul, the West's view of the East, the Europeanization of Turkey, the relationship between art and society, and a mood called *hüzün*—that the word 'illusion,' or rather the related word 'imagination,' is particularly important for him. The 'more' that Pamuk refers to, which he could feel but not see, belonged to a world that imagination gave him access to, and this world of imagination became a lifelong companion. Even his first reflections describe how "the ghost of the other Orhan in another house somewhere in Is-

---

3 Orhan Pamuk, *Istanbul: Memories and the City*, trans. M. Freely (London: Faber and Faber, 2006), 3.

4 Pamuk, *Istanbul*, 3.

5 Pamuk, *Istanbul*, 3.

tanbul" never left him.⁶ Later he discovers that his father, to whom the book is dedicated and who understood his daydreams without reservation, also had a double. Having found his father's hideout, Pamuk's deceived mother describes it to Pamuk, and he in turn describes it to us: "A pair of pyjamas that my father wore at home was sitting on the pillow in this other bedroom, and on the bedside table stood a tower of bridge books, just like the one he'd built on his side of the bed at home."⁷ Pamuk shudders at his mother's words, not because of his father's infidelity but because: "it was as if he had done what I had never managed—he'd found his double, his twin, and it was this creature, not his lover, he went to this other house every day to be with."⁸ This thought reminded Pamuk that "something in my life, in my very soul, was wanting," and he decided to become a writer: to devote his life to the imagination, to the trips into another world where he could meet his twin.⁹

The double motif appears not only in Pamuk's memoir but also in his novels, which confirms an experience shared by many people, namely that no human being can say with certainty what is only narrative and what is life itself. This relationship between life and narrative is what the columnist Celal in the novel *The Black Book* explains to the junk dealer Aladdin when he asks if he can write about him in his column,¹⁰ and it is further confirmed by the interrelation between the memorial work *Istanbul* and the novel *The Black Book*, especially, perhaps, if one reads the memoir first. Admittedly, in *Istanbul*, when introducing his first love, Pamuk says that "because this is a memoir, I must hide her name, and if in naming her I offer a clue in the style of the Divan poets, I must also hint that this clue, like the rest of this story, might also be mislead-

---

6   Pamuk, *Istanbul*, 4.

7   Pamuk, *Istanbul*, 325.

8   Pamuk, *Istanbul*, 326.

9   Pamuk, *Istanbul*, 326.

10   Orhan Pamuk, *The Black Book*, trans. G. Gün (New York: Farrar, Straus, and Giroux, 1994).

ing."[11] Perhaps everything he says about himself and his city is just fiction. Perhaps the reason is not only that writers fantasize but also that the mind is a garden—as we are told in *The Black Book*—in which imagination flowers abundantly. Nevertheless, having first read Pamuk write about 'the other Orhan' in *Istanbul*, it is thought-provoking and even a little disconcerting to experience the fictional character Galip being transformed into 'someone else' in *The Black Book*. This novel not only shows that the art of narration has a transformative quality; it also retrospectively sheds light on Pamuk's memoir and problematizes everything in it. Because Pamuk decided to become a writer at a young age, his life has become a story and his memory a confirmation of the characters in his novels. Literature may thus in fact be truer than life, and perhaps even the only reality we can recognize? No, says Italo Calvino, who, in the book *Mr. Palomar*, also conducts a thoughtful self-portrait.[12] In the lecture series *Six Memos for the Next Millennium*, Calvino more specifically claims that the idea of literature as more real than reality would carry him too far from the use of words, as he understands it, namely as "a perpetual pursuit of things, as a perpetual adjustment to their infinite variety."[13] Similarly, Pamuk does not try to elevate literature at the expense of life. On the contrary, in *The Black Book*, he lets Galip conclude that "nothing can be as wondrous as life. Except for writing."[14]

The wondrous nature of life or reality is confirmed by Calvino's alter ego, Mr. Palomar. Calvino's indirect self-portrait describes a philosophical man's futile attempt to maintain reality. Reality might not surpass the fantasy into which, according to Calvino, images rain down, but it does exceed our rational concepts and thus the philosopher falls short. Calvino takes the idea of images rain-

11   Pamuk, *Istanbul*, 293.

12   Italo Calvino, *Mr. Palomar*, trans. W. Weaver (San Diego, New York, and London: Harcourt Brace Jovanovich, 1985).

13   Italo Calvino, *Six Memos for the Next Millennium*, trans. P. Creagh (Cambridge, MA: Harvard University Press, 1988), 26.

14   Pamuk, *The Black Book*, 400. Translation modified.

ing into fantasy from Dante's *Divine Comedy*, but, in his fourth lecture in the *Six Memos for the Next Millennium*, he asks where the rain comes from.[15] According to Calvino, no one has written more insightfully on this topic than Jean Starobinski, who, in his essay "L'empire de l'imaginaire" (The Empire of the Imaginary), shows that there are two different conventional understandings of imagination.[16] Imagination is either identification with the world soul, or an instrument of knowledge that follows a path different from—yet a path that can coexist with or form a necessary phase of—the path to scientific knowledge. Calvino himself considers literature to be a cognitive quest, but he does not view imagination as a means to acquire scientific knowledge. On the contrary, he understands imagination in a third way: as "a repertory of what is potential, what is hypothetical, of what does not exist and has never existed, and perhaps will never exist but might have existed."[17] This is what rains down into fantasy, and it rains from "processes [epiphanies] that ... go beyond our intentions and our control, acquiring—with respect to the individual—a kind of transcendence."[18] According to Calvino, this hypothesis-forming, evocative imagination is the source of literary activity. Because imagination unfolds differently in literature than in science, literature can say something different about reality than science can. With imagination—and literature—there is a possibility of "flying to another world," which Calvino considers anthropologically necessary.[19] In his lectures, he encourages us to fly into the new millennium, albeit "without hoping to find anything more in it than what we ourselves are able to bring to it."[20] Yet we

15   Dante's idea of an image rain is expressed in *Purg.* 17.25. See Dante Alighieri, *Purgatorio*, trans. J. Hollander and R. Hollander (New York: Doubleday, 2003), 345.

16   Jean Starobinski, "L'empire de l'imaginaire," in *La relation critique: Essai* (L'oeil vivant II) (Paris: Gallimard, 1972).

17   Calvino, *Six Memos for the Next Millennium*, 91.

18   Calvino, *Six Memos for the Next Millennium*, 87.

19   Calvino, *Six Memos for the Next Millennium*, 27.

20   Calvino, *Six Memos for the Next Millennium*, 29.

can bring a great deal, according to Pamuk and Calvino—and also according to Walter Benjamin, whom Pamuk and Calvino both take after in spirit.

One thing we can bring into the new millennium is our memories (unless, like Celal, we suffer from a loss of memory or, like the Prince [another character in *The Black Book*], we deliberately try to empty the world of meaning by destroying all things and all memories). In memory, we are led from one garden to the next, inevitably, and, in the flowers of imagination, we find possibilities that were not yet actualized, and perhaps never will be. For as Pamuk demonstrates in the form of the novel, and as Benjamin and Calvino confirm philosophically, one can become someone else in imagination and things can transform into things of another world, one more in the midst of the existing world. The imagination lets us see new possibilities that are not just the products of imagination itself and which therefore are not arbitrary. Memory brings possibilities to imagination in the form of seeds; in the imagination, these seeds grow into flowers in the gardens of memory; and, in literature, these flowers are hand-tied in bouquets brought by us to those we wish we were. We all do this because we must narrate to live: we must make life meaningful, interpret it. Authors in particular do this—by means of literature, they cultivate the existential necessity that one must become someone else in order to be oneself. Literature gathers the flowers from the gardens of memory in the bouquets we call stories. In these stories, the possibilities that imagination displays by disclosing the seeds as flowers are actualized. By this flower arranging, life is interpreted, meaning is added to it, and literature thus not only confirms the past but also shows what could have been, what will be, or what will never be. As underlined by Giorgio Agamben's concept of potentiality, which is evocative of Benjamin's philosophy of history, if we only perceive possibilities from the perspective of what was actualized, we never see what was *not* actualized. We never see the negativity that possibilities must contain in order to be possibilities and not necessities: that the possibility of x must also be the possibility of not-x. We lose our sense of the possibility as *possibility* and therefore we lose half of history:

all the histories of the nonactualized possibilities. However, unlike the majority of philosophy, literature has a sense of possibilities, namely thanks to the imagination and to memory.[21]

Benjamin might also be the source of Pamuk's effort in *Istanbul* to write about his city, too, and what it has become and what it has not become, when he writes about himself. In the introduction to his memoir *Berlin Childhood around 1900*, Benjamin explains that, in this book, he is trying "to get hold of the *images* in which the experience of the big city is precipitated in a child of the middle class."[22] This is a historical task, he thinks. For centuries, there have been creative forms available for the memories of a childhood set in the country, but no customary forms await the memories of a childhood set in a city. Perhaps the images of his metropolitan childhood "are capable, at their core, of preforming later historical experience."[23] This is exactly what they may have done for Pamuk, albeit in a slightly different situation, since Pamuk encounters a lack of forms available for the memories of a childhood set in an Eastern city that is partially transforming into a Western city. Pamuk himself points out that, until the twentieth century (in literature right up to his own novels), the writing of Istanbul's history was left to Westerners. At the same time, he quotes from Benjamin's book review "The Return of the Flaneur": "if we were to divide all the existing descriptions of cities into two groups according to the birthplace of the authors, we would certainly find that those written by natives of the cities concerned are greatly in the minority."[24] According to Benjamin, this is because the excitement of seeing a city from the outside is located in the exotic or picturesque perspective; to the city's natives, by contrast, the attachment is always mediat-

---

21 Giorgio Agamben, "The Dictation of Poetry," in *The End of the Poem: Studies in Poetics*, trans. D. Heller-Roazen (Stanford: Stanford University Press, 1999), 76–86.

22 Walter Benjamin, *Berlin Childhood around 1900*, trans. H. Eiland, in *Selected Writings, Volume 3: 1935–1938*, eds. H. Eiland and M.W. Jennings (Cambridge, MA and London: The Belknap Press of Harvard University Press, 2002), 344.

23 Benjamin, *Berlin Childhood around 1900*, 344.

24 Pamuk, *Istanbul*, 216.

ed by memories. Pamuk thinks that this observation is particularly valid for Istanbul (and similar cities), not only because of the (perhaps common human) absence of a perception of the homeland as exotic and picturesque, which allows one to study the alien more intensely than the domestic, but also because, unlike Europeans, the people of Istanbul (and others like them) lack a tradition of introspection: of making themselves, including their city, subjects of consideration. They have no tradition of the kind of storytelling that self-contemplation forms, and which, for example, manifests itself in memoirs. Such a tradition is present in the West—but here, however, we now lack something else.

Traces of the Western tradition of self-contemplation are evident from Augustine's *Confessions* to works such as *Mr. Palomar*.[25] However, in the West, we also have a tradition of opposing life and literature. As early as Plato, truth and fiction were in opposition, though not truth and poetry. For Plato, fiction was not a natural feature of poetry, but something poets indulge in when they do not follow the nature of poetry: its ability to come close to metaphysical truth. If the life lived is not *noumenon*, but *phainomenon*—more physical than metaphysical—there is, according to Plato, already in this a contradiction between life and literature, but this is because there is *no* such contradiction between truth and literature. After the 'sweet style' of the Middle Ages, which Dante cultivated and in which life and literature melted together completely, life and literature were radically torn apart, says Agamben in "The Dictation of Poetry," which also set literature and truth in opposition. However, since early German Romanticism, many authors have been reluctant to do this; they have insisted on the connection between writing and lived experience. Life and literature are indeed different, but, as Galip acknowledges in *The Black Book*, they are both wondrous, and this is due to their common openness: they can be interpreted in several ways. In both the variegated universe of fiction and in life there is not just one but many truths. For example,

---

[25] Saint Augustine, *The Confessions of St. Augustine*, trans. E.B. Pusey (Auckland: The Floating Press, 2008).

there is at least one truth for every person in the form of what each person has the potential to become, and which Benjamin refers to as "the wish."[26] "The fairy in whose presence we are granted a wish is there for each of us," he writes, adding: "But few of us know how to remember the wish we have made; and so, few of us recognize its fulfillment later in our lives."[27] As modern humans, we do not appreciate what we have and we therefore cannot identify what we lack. We see the world of the fairy tale and our own world as opposed to one another, and therefore we see far too little. We have emptied the existence of fairies and flying carpets, clinging to the empiricism and logic that we have elevated to the foundation of science. As if true discoveries do not require the ability to create hypotheses and anticipate what is not yet available; as if science needs no imagination.

When we shorten reality and science, the dimension in which our 'twins' live fades out and we become poorer in insight into ourselves. As such, it is not only *istanbullus* but also Westerners who may face difficulties becoming themselves. The transformation to someone else that self-contemplation comprises is a prerequisite for insight into oneself, but it is not the fulfillment. It also matters how one looks upon oneself. This is precisely what Benjamin was aware of: that we also have other eyes to see with than those used in the modern world; that we can have other experiences than the experiences we prioritize today. There is another world in the world, there is transcendence in the immanence, and the future depends on whether we wake up to this. However, Benjamin would most likely not say that Martin Heidegger had an eye for this immanent transcendence. After reading Heidegger's thesis on Duns Scotus, he wrote to Gershom Scholem: "it is incredible that anyone could qualify for a university position on the basis of such a study. Its execution requires *nothing* but great diligence and a command of scholastic Latin, and, in spite of all its philosophical packaging, it

---

26 Benjamin, *Berlin Childhood around 1900*, 357.

27 Benjamin, *Berlin Childhood around 1900*, 357.

is basically only a piece of good translating work."[28] There are nevertheless many opportunities to connect the two thinkers. They both despised 'scholastic' philosophy, and Heidegger's thoughts on attunement and understanding are related to Benjamin's reflections on experience and knowledge. With the word 'attunement,' Heidegger means being in a mood, and, as stated in § 29 of *Being and Time*, moods are neither objects of the world nor psychological states in humans.[29] The interest in a level of experience prior to the emergence of subject and object that Heidegger thus exhibits also motivated Benjamin's experience-theoretical considerations. According to Heidegger, moods do however tell us more about ourselves than about things. We realize the being of things by watching them, or we experience it in our use of them, depending on whether they are something present-at-hand or something ready-at-hand, but, in attunement, it is our own being that reveals itself to us, and this being is our being thrown into the world. Attunement "*discloses Dasein in its thrownness*"—'discloses' means that it makes it available to experience.[30]

This disclosure is fundamental; it is "*before* all cognition and willing and *beyond* their scope of disclosure."[31] The experience provided by attunement of our own being is not a product of cognition and we cannot control it; we are ourselves controlled by it. "Mood assails. It comes neither from 'without' nor from 'within,' but rises from being-in-the-world itself as a mode of that being."[32] Therefore, although we most often turn away from it and although it is thus foreign to us, nothing is more familiar and everyday than

---

28   Benjamin, "92. To Gerhard Scholem," in *The Correspondence of Walter Benjamin 1910–1940*, eds. G. Scholem and Th.W. Adorno, trans. M.R. Jacobson and E.M. Jacobson (Chicago and London: The University of Chicago Press, 1994), 168.

29   Martin Heidegger, *Being and Time*, trans. J. Stambaugh, rev. D.J. Schmidt (Albany: State University of New York Press, 2010), 130–136.

30   Heidegger, *Being and Time*, 133.

31   Heidegger, *Being and Time*, 132.

32   Heidegger, *Being and Time*, 133.

attunement. Something similar applies to the *hüzün* mentioned by Pamuk in *Istanbul*: nothing is as celebrated yet as incomprehensible as *hüzün*—because of the lack of memoirs. In the Qur'an, the word *hüzün* refers to pain and grief caused by loss, but, over time, two different understandings of *hüzün* have gradually developed. According to the first understanding, a person experiences *hüzün* when he or she has invested too much in worldly pleasures and material gain, and, according to the second, *hüzün* is the spiritual anguish one feels because one cannot do enough for Allah in this world. Sufism is the source of this second understanding, and it is the absence of *hüzün*, not the presence of it, that makes the Sufi feel it. "He suffers because he has not suffered enough," that is, he suffers because he has not been close enough to Allah.[33] Istanbul and its residents are dominated by *hüzün* in the Sufi sense of the word, states Pamuk.[34] However, this is mainly due to the way that, following the destruction of the Ottoman Empire, history has been reflected in "the city's 'beautiful' landscapes and its people," namely as a way of looking at life and as a state of mind that is "ultimately as life affirming as it is negating."[35] Unlike melancholy, this *hüzün* is not the feeling of the individual person but rather something collective like *tristesse*. Both *hüzün* and *tristesse* are reminiscent of "a communal feeling, an atmosphere, and a culture shared by millions."[36] Nevertheless, they are not identical. In Istanbul, where *hüzün* dominates, one sees everywhere "the remains of a glorious past and civilization" that "inflict heartache on all who live amongst them."[37] In Delhi or São Paolo, where one can experience *tristesse* because life is uncertain, the impression of a ruined civilization is missing and so is, thus, the metaphysical background of *hüzün*.

33 Pamuk, *Istanbul*, 81.

34 Pamuk, *Istanbul*, 81.

35 Pamuk, *Istanbul*, 82.

36 Pamuk, *Istanbul*, 90.

37 Pamuk, *Istanbul*, 91.

In Berlin, Benjamin also witnessed civilizational weathering, and he, too, cultivated the ruinous. To him, the melancholy feeling was not just negative and it was hardly just personal. When he transformed "A Berlin Chronicle" into *Berlin Childhood around 1900*, he deleted everything autobiographical.[38] He wanted to create something of a more general validity than a testimony merely of his own life: a work about the mood in Berlin retrospectively considered, about a melancholy common to at least some, perhaps a Western *hüzün*. Somewhat in the same spirit, Roland Barthes opens his self-portrait *Roland Barthes by Roland Barthes* with the words: "It must all be considered as if spoken by a character in a novel."[39] Barthes does not write about himself as an individual subject, but as writing subjectivity—engulfed and guided by the writing and its "floating" moves.[40] The writing works with a "mana-word" that is not selected and pigeonholed but gradually appears and takes the place of every signified (*signifié*).[41] "In an author's lexicon, will there not always be a word-as-mana, a word whose ardent, complex, ineffable, and somehow sacred signification gives the illusion that by this word one might answer for everything?"[42] Perhaps the history of the mana-word is precisely what is described by autobiographical authors—in the work of Barthes represented by the word 'body'; in the works of Benjamin, Calvino, and Pamuk perhaps by the words 'image,' 'lightness,' and 'the double.' In any case, many authors have an experience of not being masters of their stories. They may pave the way by grasping the pen, but the tale tells itself when it begins. Similarly, it is not we but life that is living when

---

38 Walter Benjamin, "A Berlin Chronicle," trans. E. Jephcott, in *Selected Writings, Volume 2: 1927–1934*, eds. M.W. Jennings, H. Eiland, and G. Smith (Cambridge, MA and London: The Belknap Press of Harvard University Press, 2001).

39 Roland Barthes, *Roland Barthes by Roland Barthes*, trans. R. Howard (New York: Hill and Wang, 1977), 1.

40 Barthes, *Roland Barthes by Roland Barthes*, 129.

41 Barthes, *Roland Barthes by Roland Barthes*, 129.

42 Barthes, *Roland Barthes by Roland Barthes*, 129.

it begins in life: life lives itself out through us. Even in 'the age of technology,' we do not simply determine life and death, and therefore we still wonder; how did *this* become my life? We keep understanding 'backwards': through memory and thus in the wonder-arousing form of stories. We are attuned to wonder, but often we turn our back on it and must therefore practice being prepared for it. Wonder is the first step toward wisdom, and thinking constitutes the path between these poles, and it is on this path that things take place. It is on this path that we narrate in order to live. We narrate because we do not understand that life is what is living, while we ourselves are present in life, and never more present than when we tell our wondrous stories.

Philosophy at a Crossroads

> We are told that the 'state of emergency' that thought is in is the rule rather than the exception. But the task is to provoke the real state of emergency: the expansion of thought.[43]

The Consolation of Philosophy

Anicius Boethius was in prison, sentenced to death for treason and witchcraft. Noticeably aged, he was lost in sad thought and found his only comfort in the Muses of Poetry. But suddenly he saw a woman whose "burning gaze was indescribably penetrating," unlike anyone he had ever met.[44] It was Philosophy paying him a visit in his cell and giving him inspiration for *The Consolation of Philosophy*. In this book Boethius says that "her complexion was as fresh and glowing as that of a girl, [though] she was ancient and … nobody would mistake her for a creature of our time. It was impossible to estimate her height, for she seemed at first to be of ordinary measure, but then, without seeming to change, she appeared to be extraordinarily tall, so that her head all but touched the heavens. I was certain that if she had a mind to stretch her neck just a little,

---

43 Thanks to Walter Benjamin's thesis VIII in "On the Concept of History," trans. H. Zohn, in *Selected Writings, Volume 4: 1938–1940*, eds. H. Eiland and M.W. Jennings (Cambridge, MA and London: The Belknap Press of Harvard University Press, 2003), 392.

44 Anicius Manlius Severinus Boethius, *The Consolation of Philosophy*, trans. D.R. Slavitt (Cambridge, MA: Harvard University Press, 2008), 2–3.

her face would penetrate the skies, where it would be utterly lost to human view."[45]

Boethius further states that Philosophy at first listened to his grievances, but then declared that this was not the time for complaint, but for treatment. Had she not nourished him with her rich milk and fed him on her diet as he was growing up? Had she not prepared him with such weapons as he could now use in his difficulties if he had not chosen to discard them? Did he even recognize her? Why did he keep his silence; was he ashamed or just dumbstruck? But Philosophy also realized that Boethius was stupefied and unable to answer. She therefore placed her hand on his chest and said comfortingly: "He is in no real danger. He merely suffers from a lethargy, a sickness that is common among the depressed. He has forgotten who he really is, but he will recover, for he used to know me, and all I have to do is clear the mist that beclouds his vision."[46] With these words she gathered the skirt of her dress and gently dried the tears from his eyes.

Philosophy is the Art of Interpretation

Very few people nowadays have any idea of what philosophy actually is. As early as a century ago, Walter Benjamin realized this problem, which in his time manifested itself in the neo-Kantian identification of philosophy with epistemology, and lives on today in the form of a widespread predilection for cognitive science. "Knowledge is possession," Benjamin wrote in *The Origin of German Tragic Drama*.[47] The acquisition of knowledge is an intention-

---

45   Boethius, *The Consolation of Philosophy*, 3.

46   Boethius, *The Consolation of Philosophy*, 6.

47   Walter Benjamin, *The Origin of German Tragic Drama*, trans. J. Osborne (London and New York: Verso, 2009), 29. In German: "Erkenntnis ist ein Haben," that is, "Cognition is to possess." Generally I prefer to translate 'Erkenntnis' as 'cognition,' but here I follow John Osborne in using the word 'knowledge.' This way specific wording problems in English are solved (in the last sentence of the paragraph, for instance) without altering the meaning of the German original (since cognition results in knowledge, whereas philosophy cares for wisdom). Moreover, Benjamin's terms 'philosophy' and 'knowledge' specifically refer to a

al act carried out by a consciousness that functions as a subject, and for whom the known is an object. The object of knowledge is thus something that consciousness possesses as its property. Philosophy, on the contrary, is not intentional, and does not have an object; instead it is oriented toward ideas that are not intentional objects about which certain and complete knowledge can be achieved. For the same reason philosophy does not strive to *know* ideas; on the contrary it strives to *present* them.[48]

According to Benjamin, this presentation is the 'method' of philosophical thinking, provided that the word is not understood as in the modern sciences, where method determines thought from its very beginning.[49] The method of philosophical thinking corresponds more to the old Greek *methodos*—'the road on which'— whose path has not been determined in advance but arises gradually as the object is expounded, and whose direction is only seen in retrospect. This philosophical method, which according to Benjamin takes shape as a presentation of ideas, he also called "digression."[50] Whereas knowledge aims directly at its target, philosophy concentrates upon the phenomenon, even though it is the idea it seeks to present. Philosophy digresses and is characterized by renouncing the "uninterrupted purposeful structure."[51] Not only does it digress to the phenomenon in order to approach the idea, but it also keeps returning to the phenomenon to start again: "This

---

hermeneutic way of thinking and the approach of modern science, respectively. Therefore, I write not only 'philosophy' and 'knowledge' but also 'philosophical thinking' and 'scientific knowledge,' and the latter I use interchangeably with not only 'knowledge' but also 'conceptual knowledge.'

48 *Darstellung* is the German term for philosophy's ambition. It has the double meaning of both presentation and representation that was important to Benjamin, but is lost in Osborne's translation. According to Benjamin, the task of philosophy is to present the ideas—not to represent them.

49 Benjamin, *The Origin of German Tragic Drama*, 28. Benjamin opens his epistemo-critical prologue by stressing the treatise as a philosophical genre and defines presentation as the method of the treatise.

50 Benjamin, *The Origin of German Tragic Drama*, 28.

51 Benjamin, *The Origin of German Tragic Drama*, 28.

continual pausing for breath is the mode most proper to the process of contemplation."⁵²

Philosophical thinking settles on the phenomenon because it is interested in the idea, and this happens not in order to map the phenomenon but to interpret it. For philosophy seeks to present the idea, which with regard to the phenomenon means that it seeks not to explain it but to understand it. Thus philosophy is the *art of interpretation*. It is through the interpretation of the phenomenon that philosophy seeks to present the idea, and for this purpose it involves the concept. With the concept the phenomenon is broken down into its constituent elements; but far from destroying the phenomenon this analytical "disintegration" actually "rescues" it because here the concept is no longer in the service of knowledge, but appears in philosophical thinking that is oriented toward the idea.⁵³

Aided by the concept, philosophy leads the phenomenon back to the idea, thus letting it 'partake' of the idea's being and rescuing it from the existence to which phenomena are otherwise condemned. This transfer of being—and thereby of meaning—to the phenomenon is also what makes it possible for philosophy to present the idea through philosophy's conceptually mediated interpretation of the phenomenon.⁵⁴ So in philosophical interpretation, the phenomenon is expounded in the light of the idea, and the idea is presented in the world of phenomena, both aided by the concept. The interpretation of the phenomenon and the presentation of the idea are thus two sides of the same coin;⁵⁵ they cannot be separated without there being neither interpretation nor presentation. The phenomenon cannot be interpreted without an orientation toward the idea, and the idea cannot be presented without interpreting the phenomenon. The phenomenon needs the idea to reach gen-

52   Benjamin, *The Origin of German Tragic Drama*, 28.

53   Benjamin, *The Origin of German Tragic Drama*, 33–34.

54   Benjamin, *The Origin of German Tragic Drama*, 34.

55   Benjamin, *The Origin of German Tragic Drama*, 34.

uine unity, that is, the meaning that arises with the idea—which is different from the superficial unity that is added when it is merely categorized under some concept by knowledge.[56] The phenomenon needs the idea to be understood, whereas the idea needs the phenomenon to be presented, and they both need the concept. The phenomenon needs the concept to become rescued by approaching the idea, and the idea needs the concept to approach the phenomenon so that it can be presented.

However, there is a principal distance between the phenomenon and the idea, which philosophy cannot abolish despite the mediation of the concept. Phenomenon and idea can never be united completely, because the idea exists at another ontological level than the phenomenon. The presentation of the idea is therefore a never-ending task for philosophy. It must start afresh all the time, and return to the phenomenon in order to look for the idea again. Philosophy is obliged to shuttle between phenomenon and idea; it must take shape as a dialectic thinking that will never find rest in any synthesis.

Many Kinds of Metaphysics

Benjamin was concerned for philosophy, but today there are even fewer possibilities than in his time to practice the hermeneutics described by him. The obstacles today are not just the demands made by politicians and administrators for speedy and popular results, immediate social relevance, and so on. Nor do the obstacles only include the wish, shared by many players in this field, and many humanities scholars, for all humanist research to take shape as some kind of social science and include something about cognition and so on. The possibility of thinking philosophically is also weakened by the aversion to metaphysics that has been widespread for so long. However, this remark should *not* be understood as a defense of the traditional metaphysics criticized by Martin Heideg-

---

56   See the sections titled "Knowledge and truth" and "Division and dispersal in the concept" in the epistemo-critical prologue.

ger. On the contrary, in analogy with Heidegger's criticism it should be seen as a defense of thought understood as *meditative thinking*.[57]

For a long time we have had an eye for only two possibilities: either to do metaphysics (which is seen as problematic) or to reject all metaphysics (meaning that there is really only one way forward, and that is *away* from metaphysics). This attitude to metaphysics rests on a widespread idea that the word 'metaphysics' covers a historically invalid understanding of two worlds, one that is immanent and one that is transcendent. Either that, or the attitude mentioned rests on the idea that metaphysics is identical with theoretical-scientific thinking, so criticized by Heidegger, which reduces Being to a being.[58] However, the word 'metaphysics' can also be used in a third way, one which aims at something as important as 1) opening up to experience of another kind than sensory/empirical experience; 2) being willing to deal with this different experience systematically; 3) doing so in a meaning-seeking way that demands interpretation and thus also openness to something that transcends the experience itself (something more universal, a wider context, an idea).

According to this third definition of metaphysics, philosophical thinking has been metaphysical from the very beginning—and this is understood not as a problem, but as a mark of distinction. If we stay with this definition, the metaphysical character of philosophical thinking does not exist in the tendency, criticized by Heidegger, to objectify everything, but rather in the expansion of the horizon that Benjamin depicted. Precisely the expansion of the horizon is a prerequisite for philosophy to take shape as an art of interpretation, instead of sinking to a level of pure description or concept analysis without insight. As shown by Benjamin, philosophy understood as the art of interpretation demands openness to

---

57 Heidegger distinguished between "meditative thinking" (*das besinnliche Nachdenken*) and "calculative thinking" (*das rechnende Denken*), see his "Memorial Address" in *Discourse on Thinking: A Translation of Gelassenheit*, trans. J.M. Anderson and E.H. Freund (New York: Harper and Row, 1966), 46.

58 'Theoretical-scientific thinking' is synonymous with 'calculative thinking' (see footnote 57).

something else and something more than the phenomena in our experiences. Philosophical thinking also demands openness to the ideas without which it is impossible to interpret phenomena. It is essential to show this openness in case one is not satisfied with only describing and explaining what one observes, as modern science does, but also wants to understand it—that is, to gain an insight into the meaning of its presence.

It follows from this that the art of interpretation described by Benjamin constitutes a metaphysics—but of a kind that differs from the theoretical-scientific thinking so criticized by Heidegger. This can be translated into a distinction between *traditional* and *modern* metaphysics, as also lies between the lines of one of Benjamin's early works: "On the Program of the Coming Philosophy."[59] In this text Benjamin introduced the concept of 'higher experience,' which refers to a phenomenon that differs from empirical experience and which he thus also called metaphysical experience.[60] The coming philosophy should be the philosophy of this experience. Such a philosophy of experience was the new and different metaphysics that should replace traditional metaphysics from the time before Immanuel Kant, as well as the scientism that resulted from Kant's criticism of metaphysics.

Philosophy and metaphysics are thus in fact the same, however not because philosophy is 'essentialistic' by nature, but because it was originally introduced as *philosophia*, that is, thinking in the form of striving for wisdom, and because this thinking demands not only concepts but also ideas. Philosophy has however manifested itself in various ways in the course of history and for the same reason there are different forms of metaphysics, for example, both traditional and modern. Heidegger and Benjamin both distanced themselves from traditional metaphysics at the same time as they contributed to the development of new metaphysics. In their op-

---

59   Walter Benjamin, "On the Program of the Coming Philosophy," trans. M. Ritter, in *Selected Writings, Volume 1: 1913–1926*, eds. M. Bullock and M.W. Jennings (Cambridge, MA and London: The Belknap Press of Harvard University Press, 2002).

60   See Benjamin, "On the Concept of the Coming Philosophy," 102. Benjamin writes "higher experience" and "a deeper, more metaphysically fulfilled experience."

position to traditional metaphysics they did not jeopardize thinking; they formulated a new and different kind of metaphysics rather than becoming antimetaphysical.[61]

The Prerequisite for Understanding

The modern metaphysics of Benjamin can be profiled through a further presentation of his understanding of ideas. It is well known that Plato considered ideas to be what truly exists, and which as normative archetypical images precede the appearances we spontaneously take to be reality, but which according to Plato are in fact just shadow pictures. It is this understanding of ideas that lies behind the doctrine of static essences that is so unpopular today, and whose problematic character invites an antimetaphysics. Kant, on the other hand, saw ideas as concepts of reason which we think of necessity but which do not correspond to any concrete object of experience; for him it was especially the idea of God, of the immortality of the soul, and of the world as a whole. In Kant's philosophy ideas are thus not, as in Plato, of a constitutive but only of a regulative importance for cognition. Ideas are not present in advance as metaphysical entities that make the phenomena into what they truly are. On the contrary, ideas are the products of human consciousness, and they do not let the consciousness realize anything about the phenomena, but only facilitate its orientation in the world, that is, in its own recognitions of various objects.

Although phenomenon and idea are found at different ontological levels, not only in Plato but also in Benjamin, and although according to Benjamin the phenomenon can only be understood in the light of the idea, his understanding of ideas is nevertheless at variance with Plato's. At the same time it also differs from Kant's,

---

61   This interpretation of Benjamin and Heidegger has been developed in my book *Den skønne tænkning: Veje til erfaringsmetafysik. Religionsfilosofisk udmøntet* (Beautiful Thinking: Pathways to the Metaphysics of Experience. Religio-Philosophically Implemented) (Aarhus University Press, 2014). Alongside a comprehensive religio-philosophical implementation of philosophical aesthetics and hermeneutic phenomenology, this work also contains twenty-four chapters on A.G. Baumgarten, Kant, Benjamin, Heidegger, and contemporary aesthetics theorists.

though Benjamin's concept of presentation does in fact include that consciousness contributes to the idea. Like Plato, Benjamin understood ideas as metaphysically given, as ontologically different from phenomena, and as the truth of the phenomena. Unlike Plato, however, he did not consider ideas as already finished entities about which we can and must acquire knowledge; the task does *not* lie in pushing an untrue world of phenomena aside. At the same time, like Kant, Benjamin understood ideas to be a product of an effort of consciousness and a prerequisite for orienting oneself in the world, that is, in the knowledge acquired by consciousness about various phenomena. But unlike Kant, he did not see ideas as solely the responsibility of consciousness and thus as completely subjective; nor did he consider them to be without constitutive importance for phenomena.

All in all Benjamin considered ideas to be metaphysically given but in the special way that they are not finished and ready entities, but rather *potentials to be actualized*. Despite their metaphysical status ideas are also a product of consciousness, namely because of the latter's efforts to actualize the metaphysically given potentials that ideas essentially are; they are also a product of the philosophical attempt to present them. Thus it is not just the metaphysical character of the idea that keeps philosophy busy, but also the fact that it is only given as a potential, which needs philosophical reflection in order to be actualized. This effort, that is, the attempt to present the idea, manifests itself as a dialectically structured and phenomenological thinking aimed at understanding. According to Benjamin, it is with this kind of thinking that we approach truth, since with the word 'truth' he was referring not to the empirical truths of scientific knowledge, but to truth of a metaphysical character.[62]

Benjamin called the aforementioned metaphysical truth a "unity of being" (*Einheit im Sein*); a unity whose elements are ideas, meaning that they themselves are unities essentially linked to be-

---

62   Concerning the term 'scientific knowledge,' see footnote 47.

ing.[63] It is a question of a truth inaccessible to scientific knowledge, which only has the many phenomena as its object and which is not aimed at any unity.[64] Since philosophy is engaged in ideas, it is, in contrast to scientific knowledge, aimed precisely at truth understood as a unity of being, that is, metaphysical truth. This unity is not just a product of the activity of the concept, but something given, and it is therefore outside the reach of any questioning. Or, as Benjamin formulated it: "Knowledge is open to question, but truth is not."[65]

This means firstly that we can question the regional 'truths' of an empirical nature that the sciences postulate with their knowledge. This knowledge can be queried, but truth cannot, because as metaphysical truth—as a unity of being—it is absolute. Secondly, it means that philosophy, which moves at the level of the concept but aims at the idea, is constantly thrown back to the phenomenon, thanks to the inaccessibility of metaphysical truth. The idea brings philosophy to the phenomenon in a roundabout way, but at the same time asks it not only to deal with the phenomenon, but to do so with an eye for something that knowledge does not know and which is a "direct and essential attribute."[66] It is this genuine unity (different from the superficial unity of conceptual knowledge) that the phenomenon is supplied with when it is taken back to the idea and borrows some of its being. Instead of just being categorized, the phenomenon is endowed with metaphysical significance, that is, meaning. It is being interpreted and understood when it appears as part of something larger that is the prerequisite of understanding.

---

63   Benjamin, *The Origin of German Tragic Drama*, 30, 37.

64   If there were a unity for knowledge, it would, according to Benjamin, only be something general (*The Origin of German Tragic Drama*, 30). It would only consist in a coherence of a mediated character—a collocation of singular cognitions, each of which would fade in this collocation. It would be merely general, rather than universal.

65   Benjamin, *The Origin of German Tragic Drama*, 30.

66   Benjamin, *The Origin of German Tragic Drama*, 30.

Back to Philosophy

Philosophy has healing powers, Boethius told us. She gives us the necessary insight, helps us to see things in perspective. Perhaps the humanities, which Philosophy once "nourished with her rich milk and fed on her diet," should consider asking Philosophy for help? The humanistic disciplines today are in a situation similar to that of Boethius, and like him they are in crisis. For a long time they have been the object of a criticism that has paralyzed their scholars and let newspeak and trendy ideas gain popularity—not because the criticism has hit the mark, but because the humanities themselves have forgotten what they are. Just as Boethius lost his awareness of himself as a philosopher while in prison, so do the humanities suffer from a lack of awareness of themselves—their history and their value. Hence, perhaps the humanistic disciplines should call on Philosophy in the hope that she will assist them as she assisted Boethius in his cell.

Among the problems of the humanities today, however, is that Philosophy herself needs help. She is impressive in her stature, as Boethius wrote, and her dress is a "miracle of fine cloth and meticulous workmanship."[67] But already in his day the beauty of the dress had "darkened like a smoke-blackened family statue in the atrium as if through neglect and was dingy and worn."[68] "Some ruffians had done violence to her elegant dress, and clearly bits of the fabric had been torn away."[69] And today, after centuries of scientific narrowing of Philosophy's horizon, a comprehensive restoration of her dress is needed to make its beauty visible again. Washing and ironing is no longer enough; something new must be added, in the form of interpretation fulfilling potentials not yet actualized.

Philosophy has internalized the demand from the surrounding world to carry out 'proper' science (follow the ideal of the method of the natural sciences) and to be 'oriented toward applicability'

---

67 Boethius, *The Consolation of Philosophy*, 3.

68 Boethius, *The Consolation of Philosophy*, 3.

69 Boethius, *The Consolation of Philosophy*, 3.

(to result in concrete products as technical science does). That is why analytical philosophy is pushing hermeneutics and phenomenology out of the German universities, and Scandinavian philosophers are competing among themselves to develop 'applied philosophy'—just to mention a couple of examples. However topical this tendency may be, it reactivates the old antithesis between *bios theoretikos* and *bios politikos*, which in the Middle Ages became an antithesis between *vita contemplativa* and *vita activa* and in recent times has ended up as the antithesis between *theory* and *praxis*. Philosophy has traditionally represented the *theoria* or *contemplatio* that is now the subject of renewed suspicion and is being put under an ever-increasing pressure from practical life to be practical itself.

The aforementioned demand reveals a conspicuous lack of knowledge of what it means to think philosophically. Thinkers such as Benjamin, Heidegger, and Hans-Georg Gadamer have demonstrated that philosophical thinking is precisely *not* a theoria estranged from *praxis* and *poiesis*. On the contrary, philosophical thinking, this theoria, constitutes in itself a kind of *poietic praxis*.[70] Therefore, to ask philosophy to become practical is to ask for something completely unnecessary. Philosophy is *already* practical, but in another way than the technical sciences, namely one that is more like poetry. Philosophy is not just productive, but creative, and it is precisely as *thinking* that it is creative—it is as *theoria* that it is poietic—and that is its praxis. But this praxis cannot blossom when philosophy is ordered to follow the methodological ideal of the modern sciences instead of its own *methodos*, that is, the presentation discussed by Benjamin.

The methodological ideal of the sciences presents philosophy to a demand of 'sound science,' understood as limiting itself to description and concept analysis without insight. If we follow this ideal, only 'pure' knowledge is true, and so we support the preju-

---

[70] Since Philosophy chased the Muses of Poetry away on her arrival in Boethius' cell and discussed them with contempt, it is evident that my reference to her is conditional. I share her love for the contemplative life, but defend this life based on an understanding of the relationship between poetry and philosophy that is different from hers. To her it was dichotomous, whereas I consider it to be chiastic. This, too, is an expression of the previously mentioned difference between traditional and modern metaphysics.

dice that philosophy is theory unconnected to praxis. It is precisely when professional philosophers do not strive for insight that the relevance of philosophy becomes vague for others. If philosophy today appears a meaningless relic, it is not because it is philosophical, but because it is *not* so. For in philosophy it is not sufficient to describe phenomena accurately, nor merely to analyze and use concepts with precision. As outlined by Benjamin, thinking in a way searching for understanding presupposes an openness to *ideas*. It is necessary to orientate oneself to a level in thought that transcends the levels of both phenomenon and concept. An element of *spirit* is required, and the emergency of both the humanities and philosophy is in the end primarily the reservations about spirit, ideas, and insight that follow from rejecting metaphysics *as such* (not just traditional metaphysics). The result is that *philosophia* is sacrificed—the free, open, questioning reflection that Benjamin actualized as the art of interpretation, and which Heidegger pursued with his hermeneutic phenomenology.

Narrowing the Horizon

Thanks to Gadamer, hermeneutics has become known as the philosophy of the possibility and the necessity of a fusion of horizons. We bring along a horizon of prejudgment when we read a work, but if the reading results in understanding, a fusion has taken place. The reader's and writer's horizons have met in the understanding of the work. However, such a fusion presupposes, and is in itself, an expression of an expansion, not least of the reader's horizon, that is, a transcendence of his or her prejudgment. The question as to how this is possible has become even more relevant today than it was in the time of Gadamer, because with globalization we are now facing intensified demands for cross-cultural understanding. Is a fusion of culturally, that is, not only historically, different horizons possible? Can we actually understand one another globally? Intercultural hermeneutics has considered this issue, but philosophical aesthetics can also make a contribution.

This last statement may cause surprise, not only in an analytical philosophical context, but also in a hermeneutic phenomenological framework. Analytical philosophers persistently confuse philosophical aesthetics with art theory or philosophy of art; therefore, genuine philosophical aesthetics is rare in the UK, in the US, and in Scandinavia.[71] Continental philosophy has also treated philosophical aesthetics unfairly, either by mistaking aesthetics for philosophy of art and doing the latter instead; or by identifying aesthetics with aestheticism and the study of art (by Heidegger called metaphysics), thus (also) not doing aesthetics, but philosophy of art (possibly called phenomenology or hermeneutics).

Heidegger's and Gadamer's negative opinions of aesthetics—their rejection of aesthetics in favor of art and hermeneutic phenomenology—are examples of the latter.[72] They met philosophical aesthetics with a prejudgment determined by the aestheticism and the study of art in the nineteenth and twentieth centuries. This historically conditioned baggage prevented them from seeing the original philosophical aesthetics as the philosophy of experience, in the form of which it was introduced by Alexander Gottlieb Baumgarten and partially continued by Kant.[73] Like many others, Heidegger and

---

71   Art theory and philosophy of art deal with *art*, that is, art theory focuses on the formal aspects of art, while the philosophy of art deals with questions concerning the nature of art. Philosophical aesthetics, on the other hand, deals with the aesthetic *experience*. See the chapter "The Relevance of Aesthetics" in the present volume, and the "English Summary" in *Den skønne tænkning*, 947–965.

72   See, for example, Martin Heidegger, *Nietzsche, Volume 1: The Will to Power as Art; Volume 2: The Eternal Recurrence of the Same*, ed. and trans. D.F. Krell (San Francisco: HarperSanFrancisco, 1991), 77ff., and Hans-Georg Gadamer, "Part One," in *Truth and Method*, trans. J. Weinsheimer and D.G. Marshall (London and New York: Bloomsbury Academic, 2013).

73   Baumgarten introduced philosophical aesthetics with *Meditationes philosophicae de nonnullis ad poema pertinentibus* (1735) and *Aesthetica* (1750–1758). See Alexander Gottlieb Baumgarten, *Reflections on Poetry: Meditationes philosophicae de nonnullis ad poema pertinentibus*, eds. and trans. K. Aschenbrenner and W.B. Holther (Berkeley: University of California Press, 1954), and *Ästhetik, Volume 1–2*, trans. D. Mirbach (Hamburg: Felix Meiner Verlag, 2007). Kant rejected Baumgarten's aesthetics (see Kant's *Critique of Pure Reason*, eds. and trans. P. Guyer and A.W. Wood [Cambridge, UK: Cambridge University Press, 1998], A 21/B35, footnote, and his *Critique of the Power of Judgment*, eds. and trans. P. Guyer and E. Matthews [New York: Cambridge University Press, 2000], § 15 [5: 226–229]), but as shown in *Den skønne tænkning* he continued and developed it further in a number of ways.

Gadamer remained blind to the experiential philosophical potential in aesthetics, and thus overlooked a decisive condition for the fusion of horizons: the *expanded way of thinking* linked to the aesthetic power of judgment understood as the ability to apprehend something as being beautiful.[74]

As it appears in his Nietzsche lectures, Heidegger mistook the sensitivity mentioned by Baumgarten for sentimentality. He therefore rejected Baumgarten's aesthetics as an expression of psychological sensualism, at the same time as devaluing in "A Dialogue on Language between a Japanese and an Inquirer" the concept of beauty as an expression of traditional metaphysics (although he linked beauty with truth understood as *aletheia* in "The Origin of the Work of Art").[75] In fact Heidegger had an understanding only for art, and this influenced Gadamer's approach to aesthetics. In *Truth and Method* Gadamer made Kant responsible for the so-called aesthetic consciousness (aestheticism and scientism), although Kant saw beauty as a symbol of the good and regarded judgment's expanded way of thinking as a prerequisite for acting morally.[76] At the end of the same work, however, Gadamer acknowledged the similarity of the experience of beauty with the hermeneutic experience. Nevertheless, he insisted on the precedence of hermeneutics over

---

74 For the notion of an aesthetic and, as such, expanded way of thinking, see Kant, *Critique of Judgment*, § 40 (5: 293–296). Paul Guyer and Eric Matthews translate Kant's term *die erweiterte Denkungsart* as 'the broad-minded way of thinking,' which causes an unfortunate narrowing of the term's meaning, limiting it to something moral and associating it with the primarily sociological and psychological approach of our day. John Henry Bernard and James Creed Meredith made better choices in their translations of Kant, using the expressions 'enlarged thought' and 'enlarged mind,' respectively; but it is even better to translate the term in question as 'the expanded way of thinking.'

75 Martin Heidegger, "A Dialogue on Language between a Japanese and an Inquirer," in *On the Way to Language*, trans. P.D. Hertz (New York: HarperOne, 1982), 14 (beauty as the shine of something suprasensuous), 43ff. (beauty in the sense of grace); Martin Heidegger, "The Origin of the Work of Art," in *Poetry, Language, Thought*, ed. and trans. A. Hofstadter (New York: Harper Perennial Modern Thought, 2013), 44.

76 For Gadamer's interpretation of Kant, see "Transcending the Aesthetic Dimension," in "Part One" in *Truth and Method*; for Kant's own thought, see the *Critique of Judgment*, 227, 173–175 (5: 353, 293–295).

aesthetics, because he reproduced the accustomed identification of aesthetics with the philosophy of art.[77]

Expanding the Horizon

According to philosophical aesthetics itself, as formulated by Baumgarten, aesthetic experience differs from both sense perception and intellectual cognition by being *sensitive*, which here means neither sensory nor sentimental, but emotional, perceptive, and suggestive, that is: not conceptual.[78] The aesthetic concept of truth is therefore something different from the truth-concept dominating in the modern sciences and in philosophy turned into science. It is a question of insight, traditionally called wisdom and originally considered by philosophy to be the highest form of knowledge. Philosophical aesthetics is thus an expression of thinking that has *not* jeopardized love for wisdom. However, unlike the ancient wisdom-seeking philosophy, aesthetics does not revolve speculatively around general concepts, but concentrates upon human experiences. It explores our experiences with questions, in order to bring forth the experientially felt truth about us and the world— bring it forth from the aesthetic ideas that structure our aesthetic experiences. This is the signature of modernity in the *philosophia* that aesthetics is by nature.

Thus philosophical aesthetics can provide systematic insight into, and a philosophical language for, a substantial part of our experiences: all those that transcend sense perception and intellectual cognition. In philosophical aesthetics this realm of experience has given rise to considerations in which beauty has played an es-

---

[77] Gadamer, *Truth and Method*, 493ff., and "Aesthetics and Hermeneutics," trans. D.E. Linge, in *The Gadamer Reader: A Bouquet of the Later Writings*, ed. R.E. Palmer (Evanston: Northwestern University Press, 2007).

[78] The word 'sensitive' (*sensitivus*) in Baumgarten is often seen as a term for something sensuous. However, this reception is not in agreement with his understanding of aesthetics as philosophy of an independent kind of *cognition* (sensitive cognition as a contrast to intellectual cognition), and it was explicitly rejected by him in his introduction to the third edition of his *Metaphysics*. See Alexander Gottlieb Baumgarten, *Die Vorreden zur Metaphysik*, ed. and trans. U. Niggli (Frankfurt am Main: Vittorio Klostermann, 1998), 53–55.

sential part. Here it is not about beauty seen as a quality of objects, but beauty understood as *experience*. Furthermore, it is not about experience of beauty understood as an experience of something being nice and neat. On the contrary, it is about the experience of something having *value in itself*, and of us being *part of something larger*. The experience of beauty is therefore an experience of cohesion and meaningfulness. According to Kant it is about something as fundamental as our "feeling of life" (*Lebensgefühl*) and what this feeling says about us, including our relationship to each other and to the world.[79] The humanities without philosophical insight into this feeling of life are only a shadow of themselves, and historically precisely philosophical aesthetics was introduced as the 'place' for this insight.

Kant must also be credited for having demonstrated that experiences of beauty are individually manifested, but common to all people, and thus not private but universal. We can communicate our experiences, and we do so in the hope of meeting understanding, and we are not actually hoping in vain. No two people can experience exactly the same, but we can understand the importance of one another's experiences, because we share their 'organ,' called by Kant not only the aesthetic power of judgment, but also *sensus communis*.[80] As already mentioned, this power of judgment is associated with an expanded way of thinking, and according to Kant this way of thinking follows the principle of "putting [oneself] into the standpoint of others."[81] The expanded way of thinking is thus marked by empathy: it considers many views without submitting to any of them, and thus has an eye for the common weal.[82] In other

---

79   Kant, *Critique of Judgment*, 90 (5: 203).

80   See Kant, *Critique of Judgment*, § 40 (5: 293–296).

81   Kant, *Critique of Judgment*, 175 (5: 295).

82   For the same reason, according to Kant, it is necessary to think in an expanded way in order to practice reason's consistent way of thinking, thus never doing anything oneself that one would not be willing to allow everyone else to do as well. We would not be able to act morally if we did not own an aesthetic power of judgment, and therefore ethics rests on aesthetics. See Kant, *Critique of Judgment*, 173–175 (5: 293–295).

words, philosophical aesthetics is philosophy about a way of thinking that excels by gathering without reducing what is different to the same—a thinking already thematized by Baumgarten, though he called it "beautiful thinking" (*ars pulchre cogitandi*).[83]

This beautiful and as such expanded thinking is, in Baumgarten's thought, characterized by a comprehensive sensitivity to the many impressions contained in the realm of experience, but also to its content of meaning. What is expanded in beautiful thinking is found precisely in both of these, which in Baumgarten's terminology means that perfect sensitive cognition, that is, the experience of beauty, is characterized by both diversity and unity—or rather by a nonreductive form of unity in diversity. The experience of beauty thus excels not only by its palpability, but also by giving us insight. It gives insight into that which neither sense perception nor intellectual cognition has any access to—by Benjamin called ideas, without which thinking does not move beyond pure description and barren concept analysis.[84]

The Use of Philosophy

Philosophy is to have an eye for what is big in the smallest things. Physically sensing, we are swallowed up by what is sensuous, and rationalizing we are lost in abstractions, but thanks to sensitivity we sense the connections between what is big and what is small, so inaccessible to a dualist way of thinking. We sense that what is universal is not to be found somewhere else, but in the particular; that what is thought-provoking in the particular comes from what is universal about it. Ideas do not hover in the firmament; neither

---

83   Baumgarten, *Ästhetik*, § 1.

84   As demonstrated in *Den skønne tænkning*, hermeneutic phenomenology is thus not so different from or more fundamental than philosophical aesthetics. On the contrary, Heidegger and Gadamer reinvented philosophical aesthetics in new clothes. To the detriment of aesthetics this happened without any admission by hermeneutic phenomenology of its own debt to aesthetics. However, the 'reinventors' made all kinds of conscious efforts to move beyond the dualist philosophy of mind. Baumgarten's aesthetics, which by nature was a dualist philosophy of mind, also committed such a transgression, but only as an unplanned consequence of his interest in sensitivity.

are they merely a figment of the imagination. They reside in the things of the world, but not as static entities. They are present as the surplus of meaning that we sense when things appear irreplaceable and are called beautiful. This explains why philosophy, and therefore the humanities as well, are in trouble today. We are not supposed to think of anything as irreplaceable, to hear the universe in a bird twitter, and to thank anyone other than ourselves for our existence. We are not supposed to be able to link what we observe in such a way that we gain a kind of overview. We are simply expected to produce—the more unconsciously and faster the better, no matter which profession and industry we are in.

As Philosophy said to Boethius, this is however not the time for complaint, but for treatment. Anybody who wants her dress to regain some of its previous glory must 'strike' to defend the meditative thinking—resist the constant demand to act, and contemplate instead, alone or with others, for instance, in order to write out of inner necessity rather than for the benefit of merit; or to take part in projects and conferences out of personal desire rather than to please the boss or improve one's CV. Philosophy's biggest emergency is precisely that too rarely do we say no to what does *not* further it—that we do not say no by saying yes to what *does*: quietude and stillness, the common conversation, the delight in writing, in being thought, in experiencing "es denkt in mir" (it thinks in me).[85]

The humanities need philosophy, and philosophy needs a rehabilitation of the contemplative life—not understood as abstract theorizing, but as a creative praxis. This is also what society needs. If thinking is to have an important societal value, it must be rele-

---

85   Friedrich Wilhelm Joseph von Schelling: "Es denkt in mir, es wird in mir gedacht" (It thinks in me, thinking is happening in me). See Friedrich Wilhelm Joseph von Schelling, *Zur Geschichte der neueren Philosophie: Münchener Vorlesungen*, ed. M. Buhr (Leipzig: Phillipp Reclam jun., 1966), 28. Previously Georg Christoph Lichtenberg had written, *"Es denkt,* sollte man sagen, so wie man sagt: *es blitzt"* (*It thinks,* we should say, just as one says, *it lightnings*), see Georg Christoph Lichtenberg, "[76], Notebook K: 1793–1796," in *Philosophical Writings*, ed. and trans. S. Tester (Albany: State University of New York Press, 2012), 152, which Friedrich Nietzsche elaborated on in Part I, 17 of *Beyond Good and Evil: Prelude to a Philosophy of the Future*, trans. A.D. Caro, in *The Complete Works of Friedrich Nietzsche, Volume 8: Beyond Good and Evil; On the Genealogy of Morality*, eds. A.D. Schrift and D. Large, first organized in English by E. Behler (Stanford: Stanford University Press, 2014).

vant not just for the experts, but for ordinary people too. But it is not so in the form of abstract theorizing, nor is it so when its protagonists merely reproduce given tendencies and countertendencies and thus confirm the 'policy of necessity.' Thinking is relevant for those who are not experts when it interprets our experiences in ways that create meaning for us. Philosophy can do so when it is not competing with the natural sciences to be the most 'methodical' and with the technical sciences to be the most 'productive,' but when it is open to its own inherent poiesis, the creative element of philosophy itself, and believes in the value of the inherent *methodos* of this poiesis. It may then turn out that it is not the contemplative life that is antiquated. On the contrary, another way of thinking has outlived its role, namely the one that ignores the sensitivity, the creative receptivity, the aesthetic quality of philosophy.

The Relevance of Aesthetics

From Aesthetics to the Study of Art

In the introduction to his lectures on fine art, Georg Wilhelm Friedrich Hegel said that he would term their topic "aesthetics."[86] According to Hegel's own statement, he only applied this designation because the name of the discipline in question did not mean much to him and because it had become common to refer to it as aesthetics. Nevertheless, he did not consider the designation 'aesthetics' to be especially adequate as aesthetics was "the science of sensation" whereas he himself wanted to discuss "the philosophy of fine art."[87] In this connection, Hegel did not mention Alexander Gottlieb Baumgarten, but only referred to 'the Wolffian school.' However, Baumgarten is considered the founder of philosophical aesthetics, and to him aesthetics was *not* the science of sensation (sense perception), but the philosophy of *cognitio sensitiva* (sensitive cognition). Translated into a more recent idiom, Baumgarten thought of aesthetic experience as a kind of true cognition and saw aesthetics as philosophy about this experience. Since antiquity, art theory dealing with the form of the artwork had constituted one tradition, while the metaphysics of beauty, whose object was the idea of the beautiful, had formed another tradition. In Baumgarten, the two traditions fused into a new and different way of relating to

---

86 Georg Wilhelm Friedrich Hegel, *Aesthetics: Lectures on Fine Art, Volume 1,* trans. T.M. Knox (Oxford: Clarendon Press, 1988), 1.

87 Hegel, *Aesthetics, Vol. 1,* 1.

'the aesthetic' that constituted an independent philosophical discipline, which he named *aesthetica*, and which had neither the form of the artwork nor the idea of the beautiful as its central object. In Baumgarten's philosophical aesthetics, it was all about aesthetic experience conceived as a kind of true cognition, that is, aesthetics was therefore starting out as a kind of epistemology, but thanks to Hegel, among others, it changed into philosophy of art at the end of the eighteenth and the beginning of the nineteenth century. Hegel demanded that aesthetics should give back cognition to logic and concentrate on art, and as he himself did not require a formal analysis from aesthetics, his demand did not send it back to art theory. On the contrary, Hegel raised the philosophical question about what art is, that is, about the essence of the work of art, and with him, philosophical aesthetics consequently took shape as the philosophy of art.[88]

The unfortunate consequences of this development would have been limited if only posterity had followed in Hegel's footsteps. Even though his aesthetics essentially belongs to the philosophy of art, it does contain elements of the metaphysics of beauty as well as elements of philosophical aesthetics from which potential attempts to resume the study of aesthetic experience might have found nourishment. For example, Hegel's aesthetics presents art as a sensuous manifestation of the idea of the beautiful and the experience of beauty as one out of several potential paths to knowledge. However, posterity did not continue to reflect philosophically upon art, as Hegel had taught his students to do. His philosophy was popular in the first half of the nineteenth century, but subsequently it aroused opposition thanks to its idealistic nature, and this opposition is still alive. Since the second half of the nineteenth century, it

---

88 The distinctions applied here between 'the metaphysics of beauty,' 'art theory,' 'philosophy of art,' and 'philosophical aesthetics' derive from my book *Skønhedens metamorfose: De æstetiske idéers historie* (The Metamorphosis of Beauty: History of Aesthetic Ideas) (Odense: Odense University Press, 2001). It appears from the introduction to the book that the metaphysics of beauty and philosophical aesthetics deal with the idea of the beautiful and aesthetic experience, respectively. Against this, art theory and philosophy of art both have art as their object, but whereas art theory deals analytically with the form of the artwork, the philosophy of art is concerned with the question of the essence of the work of art.

has thus been a widespread opinion that idealism is too speculative and that one must assume a more scientific approach to things. As far as Hegel himself was concerned, he certainly demanded a scientific approach in philosophy. However, in continuation of the philosophical tradition of antiquity, his idea of knowledge was closer to wisdom than to knowledge, if we apply the narrow concept of knowledge of our time. His demand for scientific philosophy was thus a demand to deal with true—that is, spiritual—reality instead of just having an eye for reality as it appears. It expressed criticism of the imitation practiced, according to Hegel, by Immanuel Kant in his *Critique of Pure Reason* of the way of thinking in the modern natural sciences.[89] However, when nineteenth-century critics of idealism demanded a scientific approach, they began with the narrow concept of knowledge and the methodological ideal of modern natural science. They did not endeavor to develop philosophy but wanted to replace philosophy with science. This transformation of humanist self-conception, which was inspired by the natural sciences, also had consequences as far as aesthetics was concerned, changing it from the philosophy of art into the study of art.

The establishment of the study of art as a substitute for philosophical aesthetics can be seen at different levels. First, it can be read in the creation of a number of disciplines with a scientific approach to art, such as art history and literary history, which are relatively new. Art and literature have been the objects of intense studies since Aristotle's *Poetics*, but it was not until the nineteenth century that disciplines such as art history and literary history were introduced as independent units at European universities and defined as bound by the modern methodological ideal.[90] According to this ideal, scientific results can only be considered true if others can reach the same results by repeating the analyses they derive from, and such a repetition is only possible if the analyses themselves are

---

89 Immanuel Kant, *Critique of Pure Reason*, eds. and trans. P. Guyer and A.W. Wood (Cambridge, UK: Cambridge University Press, 1998).

90 Aristotle, *Poetics*, trans. I. Bywater, in *The Complete Works of Aristotle: The Revised Oxford Translation, Volume 2*, ed. J. Barnes (Princeton: Princeton University Press, 1984).

methodical. As the new disciplines with their scientific approach to art saw themselves as sciences that were bound by this methodological ideal, their formation resulted in the development of a number of methods for the analysis of the works of art under scrutiny. At the same time, the attempt to make the relation to art and literature scientific also affected the way philosophy reflected upon aesthetic questions, since philosophical thinking itself assumed a more scientific nature. By the end of the nineteenth century, this manifested itself in a new kind of psychological theory of aesthetics, in particular, while in the twentieth century it entailed, for example, that aesthetics was shaped according to the sociologically orientated social sciences.[91] The result is a contemporary situation characterized by much study of art, but hardly any philosophical aesthetics, and thus the creation of disciplines with a scientific approach to art gave birth to further new disciplines, but at the expense of a differentiation in thinking. Instead of letting philosophical aesthetics and the study of art be mutually complementary and inspiring, philosophical aesthetics has been replaced by the kind of technical scholarship that the study of art essentially is.

Truth or Method

No tradition of philosophical aesthetics is in fact visible in the English-speaking world and in the countries that are oriented to-

---

91 By way of examples of psychological aesthetics at the end of the nineteenth century, Claudius Wilkens, *Æsthetik i Omrids* (Aesthetics in Outline) (Copenhagen: Gyldendalske Boghandels Forlag, 1888), and George Santayana, *The Sense of Beauty: Being the Outlines of Aesthetic Theory* (New York: Charles Scribner's Sons, 1896), may be mentioned, among others. Of contemporary aesthetics of the sociologically orientated, social-scientific cut there are numerous examples, ranging from Jürgen Habermas's integration of the aesthetic in *The Theory of Communicative Action. Volume One: Reason and the Rationalization of Society; Volume Two: Lifeworld and System: A Critique of Functionalist Reason*, trans. T.A. McCarthy (Boston: Beacon Press, 1984–1987), and Jean Baudrillard's *Symbolic Exchange and Death*, trans. I.H. Grant (London: Sage Publications, 1993), through Niklas Luhmann, *Art as a Social System*, trans. E.M. Knodt (Stanford: Stanford University Press, 2000), or Pierre Bourdieu, *Distinction: A Social Critique of the Judgement of Taste*, trans. R. Nice (Cambridge, MA: Harvard University Press, 1984), and *The Rules of Art: Genesis and Structure of the Literary Field*, trans. S. Emanuel (Stanford: Stanford University Press, 1996), to *The Ideology of the Aesthetic* (Oxford and Cambridge, MA: Basil Blackwell, 1990) by Terry Eagleton.

ward Anglo-American thought, for instance, Denmark and other Nordic countries.[92] In Denmark, disciplines practicing the study of art, for example literature or art history, are referred to as *the aesthetic disciplines*, and it is left up to them to define what is to be understood by aesthetics. In consideration of the fact that the word 'aesthetics' was introduced as a designation for the philosophy of aesthetic experience, conceived as a kind of true cognition, only disciplines dealing philosophically with aesthetic experience should be regarded as *aesthetic* disciplines. Disciplines such as literature and art history do not have the aesthetic experience but literary or artistic works (or other artifacts) as their central object, and their approach to their objects is scientific rather than philosophical. They do not reflect philosophically on what art and literature essentially are; they subject works of art and literature to analyses that are intentionally methodical. Consequently, the disciplines currently referred to as aesthetic disciplines are neither aesthetic nor philosophical in their approach to art but scientific, and accordingly their scientific analyses rely primarily on art theory, not on philosophical aesthetics. Therefore, it is hardly surprising that in these disciplines aesthetics is identified with art theory. As these disciplines are left to define what is to be understood by aesthetics, due to the lack of a tradition of philosophical aesthetics, the conception that aesthetics is art theory also dominates the rest of academia and is widespread in the population as a whole.[93] The establishment of the study of art as the institutionalized form of aesthetics has implied a return to art theory, without any aware-

---

92   In many places in the US and UK something called *aesthetics* or even *philosophical aesthetics* is practiced, and there are big societies for aesthetics, such as the "American Society for Aesthetics." However, these designations typically refer to art theory (as is the case with George Dickie) or maybe the philosophy of art (which is partly the case, as far as Arthur C. Danto is concerned). The same holds true in Scandinavia, and Denmark is no exception to the rule. On the other hand, in Germany and Italy there is a tradition of philosophical aesthetics, though in Germany it has been gradually reduced to a niche existence.

93   Today, the word 'aesthetics' is applied very widely to all kinds of aesthetic phenomena (art, design, organizations, life style, self-presentation, etc.) and theories about these phenomena. I am alluding to the circumstance that the latter are generally of an art-theoretical character: they deal with the forms of the aesthetic phenomena.

ness of the fact that originally philosophical aesthetics was neither art theory nor philosophy of art but epistemology.

The intention of my critical remarks is not to reject disciplines with a scientific approach to art. Thanks to the way of relating to art that they represent, there now exist a number of highly developed methods for the analysis of the aesthetic forms found in and outside art. However, as pointed out by Hans-Georg Gadamer in his *Truth and Method*, the scientific approach is not without expenses.[94] If the natural sciences did not demand a methodical way of working from themselves, we would have every reason to feel endangered. We would not know if their results were true or false in a scientific sense and, consequently, we would have no idea how to react to them. Nevertheless, it is also a well-known fact that scientists may be mistaken if they do not rise above the level of experimental work. They run the risk of drawing conclusions from their knowledge that they might be able to avoid had they seen things from a wider perspective. This question about possessing both knowledge and wisdom is even more precarious to humanists than to medical scholars, for instance, for humanists do not only have to have an eye for the universal in the particular, as indeed we all ought to have. It is an open question whether it makes any sense, at all, to humanists to ask about cause and effect, that is, to insist on a method modelled according to the natural sciences. Via a methodical approach humanists may scientifically analyze the aesthetic forms inside and outside art, but will doing this make them realize anything *essential* about art and the world? According to Gadamer, the answer must be no. Methodical thinking provides various kinds of knowledge, but it prevents humanists from experiencing what is philosophically true and thus also true in a humanistic sense. At any rate, it is not meaningful *only* to treat humanistic topics in such a way that they are subjected to scientific studies modelled according to the natural sciences. Understanding humanistic topics also requires philosophical questioning.

---

94 Hans-Georg Gadamer, *Truth and Method*, trans. J. Weinsheimer and D.G. Marshall (London and New York: Bloomsbury Academic, 2013).

For example, we would obtain greater insight into contemporary art if we approached it with philosophical reflection about this art and about the concept of art. Contemporary art is characterized by great diversity. Like the historical avant-garde, many contemporary artists are trying to influence society by means of politically committed artworks. At the same time, other artists are cultivating a lyrical, fairy tale-like kind of painting that is far from the avant-garde's orientation toward action. Many art historians think that the current diversity, which also includes many other tendencies apart from the aforementioned, renders it impossible to say anything in general about contemporary art, and they thus reject all universals about art. However, in doing this they fail to see that the relationship between concept and empirical reality was always a relationship between unity and variety, and that it makes no difference as to the validity of the concept if there are more artistic expressions now than before. Concepts seem by nature to be simple compared to empirical reality, but philosophical reflection about concepts can set them in motion so that they are not simplifying. This art of reflection is not possible within the framework of the analytical discourse of science, but it is the primary task of philosophical thinking. Add to this that art historians who reject the concept of art, instead of considering it carefully, still cannot refrain from applying one or several concepts of art, and that the lack of consideration as to the meaning of the concept of art has the effect that its nature and consequences remain unknown to them. Therefore, in contemporary art, such academics only see what is pointed out by the theories of art on which they are leaning, so that they can practice their study of art rather than drown themselves in empirical observations. Consequently, their unwillingness to reflect on the concept of art philosophically will *not* get them closer to empirical reality; they will rather become insensible to empirical differences, otherwise so urgent to them. The particular fades out of sight upon the altar of the antiphilosophical scientific spirit, and simultaneously the predominant theories are repeated and confirmed uncritically.

The Humanities without Humanitas

The loss of differentiation depicted in the previous section is not unique to the disciplines with a scientific approach to art, for they are not the only ones professing to adhere to the modern methodological ideal. As a whole, the humanities are characterized by the same scientific approach and thus face similar problems. When the studies of art are blindly groping their ways toward their conclusions, this is not only due to the variety of different artistic expressions that is often mentioned as the reason, but due in particular to the lack of philosophical reflection on this variety. Similarly, the humanities as a whole are in a state of crisis even though humanists have adhered to the scientific commandment since the nineteenth century; consequently, students of the humanities of our day think that philosophy is the same as the theory of science. The surrounding world does not honor the endeavors of the humanities, but only calls for still more scientific results modelled according to the natural sciences, and, among these, immediate applicability. The outcome of this scientific approach is that the humanities have become fragmentary to such a degree that there is no intrinsic cohesion anymore, and no ability to take the offensive, because there is no common humanist self-conception. Not only the surrounding world but also the humanities themselves often mention the lack of immediate applicability in humanistic scholarship as the reason behind the skepticism of the surrounding world, though the source is actually a different one. In fact, the lack of immediate applicability is only a problem because contemporary humanists do not know how to argue in favor of it, and the lack of this ability is due to the lack of consciousness about what the humanities are. By imitating the natural sciences, the humanities have been lost as humanities, and this problem will only be solved if humanists reconsider *what* constitutes the humanities instead of only being interested in *how* humanist scholarship is performed (that is, as science). Not only for the study of art but for the humanities as a whole, the problem is thus the aforementioned scientific approach, and the solution consists in philosophical reflection. Of course, a more questioning treatment of the subject matter will not instantaneously make humanistic scholarship more applicable, but it is the prerequisite for the recognition of *what* is actually called for in its applicability and thus also for an evaluation of *how* this demand can and should be addressed.

This lack of philosophical thinking on the part of the humanists is the background of the kind of criticism worded by Martin Heidegger in his "Letter on 'Humanism.'"[95] In this text, Heidegger does not reject humanistic thought as such, but he questions the technical version it has achieved over the course of history. According to Heidegger, thinking in a humanistic way should be the same as considering *humanitas* in *humanum*, that is, the essence of the human, and what is specific to the human is not being the rational animal, *animal rationale*, otherwise claimed since antiquity.[96] On the contrary, what is specifically human about humans is that they are always in a relation to something larger than the human, that is, to being, without which human being-there would not be, at all. Or what is specifically human about humans is, more closely defined, that by way of being humans we relate to this relation in a particular way, that is, in openness, which means with the possibility of experiencing being. However, thanks to the technical version that humanistic thought has achieved over the course of history, this possibility of genuine experience, which it is otherwise precisely the task of the humanists to cultivate, has been forgotten. Instead of thoughtfully absorbing themselves in this possibility of experience, thus being both protective and enlightening about it in its different forms, for example, as the experience of art, the humanities have become humanities without *humanitas*. The reason is that where we *might* have had thinking characterized by both knowledge and wisdom, we are now left with a scientific outlook that results not in insight but in narrow-mindedness. The humanities of our time

---

95   Martin Heidegger, "Letter on 'Humanism,'" trans. F.A. Capuzzi, in *Pathmarks*, ed. W. McNeill (Cambridge, UK: Cambridge University Press, 1998).

96   Phrased differently, Heidegger calls for 'meditative thinking' as opposed to 'calculative thinking.' See Martin Heidegger, "Memorial Address," in *Discourse on Thinking: A Translation of Gelassenheit*, trans. J.M. Anderson and E.H. Freund (New York: Harper and Row, 1966), 46

with their scientific approach do not reflect upon vital human experiences in a questioning way, including aesthetic experiences. The way the humanities look today, they are rather controlled by arbitrary whims in the shape of new methods and by the pragmatism to which the criticism of idealism can be boiled down.

However, many people both inside and outside academia are aware that today we are in need of a transverse outlook. If the historians of ideas took it seriously that ideas are or should be the central object of their studies, they would be able to provide us with this outlook, for ideas transverse borders, including those that divide the sciences.[97] However, many historians of ideas actually reject ideas, by referring to their own lack of belief in the existence of such static, metaphysical entities modelled on Plato, as ideas apparently by necessity are, according to their conception. Thus, the discipline of the history of ideas is marred by the same kind of scientific approach as the rest of the humanities, and for this discipline the consequences may, if possible, be even worse. For the aforementioned rejection of ideas is first of all an expression of a remarkable lack of historic consciousness. The term and the concept of the idea have a long history, which tells us that ideas cannot only be 'static, metaphysical entities.' Secondly, the rejection of ideas is the expression of a tremendous lack of knowledge as to the history of philosophy. That is to say, it is rather difficult to decide what ideas actually meant to Plato, and one does *not* solve the problem by saying 'static, metaphysical entities.' Thirdly, the aforementioned rejection is an exact expression of the lack of philosophical reflection from which the rejection of the concept of art in the study of art and the lack of *humanitas* in the humanities emerge. Fourthly, the rejection of ideas is a textbook example of how humanists lose their object when they are unwilling to relate to it philosophically, thereby losing hold of their own discipline, too.

---

[97] The international founder of the discipline called 'the history of ideas,' Arthur O. Lovejoy, already emphasized the element of interdisciplinarity in its viewpoint, and it was also stressed by the founder of the history of ideas in Denmark, Johannes Sløk. See the chapter "Hvad er idéhistorie?" (What is History of Ideas?) in my book: *Historien som værk: Værkets historie* (History as a Work: The Work's History) (Aarhus: Aarhus University Press, 2006).

Philosophical reflection is a prerequisite for knowing what ideas are, and without such knowledge, wanting to practice the history of ideas makes no sense. Historians of ideas who do not know their object are really practicing something other than the history of ideas, for example, political science or history of science, and then the surrounding world will ask in vain for a well-argued connection between the designation 'the history of ideas' and what claims to be the history of ideas. When this happens, we are all at risk of missing out on the transverse outlook that is needed today and that the viewpoint of history of ideas could provide us with. This problem can only be solved by the historians of ideas finding their way to the philosophical component in the history of ideas. Only in this way can the history of ideas help the humanities to think about the common and the universal, that is, by delivering a philosophically and historically well-reflected understanding of what ideas are and how they can be studied.

The Importance of Aesthetics

Philosophical thinking is the prerequisite for conceiving what ideas are, for wording a common self-conception as humanists, and for meaningful reflection on the aesthetic world of forms, but it is not identical with philosophy as a discipline. For example, logical positivism would not take us further, despite all its other credits, but philosophical aesthetics can because it is philosophy about aesthetic experience conceived as a kind of true cognition. Furthermore, it is not only a kind of epistemology but also a special theory about cognition because it deals with *aesthetic experience*, precisely. Today, Baumgarten's terms *sensitivus* and *aesthetica* are often misinterpreted, in the sense that many people believe they testify to the aesthetic experience being especially characterized by sensuousness. However, the verb *aisthanomai*, from which the Greek term *aisthesis* and thus also the Latin term *aesthetica* have been derived, does not only mean to perceive in the sense of registering through the senses, but also to conceive in a wider and more comprehensive sense. This appealed to Baumgarten because in his work on poetry he had become aware that there is not only sense perception and intellectual cognition; there is also a hitherto neglected kind of experience, albeit only through feelings, sensations, and presentiments, but containing an element of cognition, nevertheless.[98] That is the experience Baumgarten called "sensitive cognition" (*cognitio sensitiva*), and he did so to bring out the emotional aspect as well as the cognitive aspect in it.[99] To him, 'sensitive' was therefore not just sensuous but rather emotional, and for the same reason an aesthetic experience does not distinguish itself so much by sensuousness as by sensitivity, he thought. That is the reason why Baumgarten—schooled in rationalistic philosophy by, among others, the writings of Christian Wolff, as he was—could argue that there is cognition in this kind of experience. He rejected the rationalist, dualistically conditioned prejudice that everything aesthetic is also irrational, by definition, and made the aesthetic accessible to philosophical analysis. By founding philosophical aesthetics in this way he established a new and different kind of epistemology, that is, epistemology conceived as theory of *experience—aesthetic experience*.[100]

As the object of Baumgarten's aesthetic epistemology is the aesthetic experience, this epistemology is occupied by something

---

98   Alexander Gottlieb Baumgarten, *Reflections on Poetry: Meditationes philosophicae de nonnullis ad poema pertinentibus*, trans. K. Aschenbrenner and W.B. Holther (Berkeley and Los Angeles: University of California Press, 1954).

99   Alexander Gottlieb Baumgarten, *Ästhetik, Volume 1-2*, trans. D. Mirbach (Hamburg: Felix Meiner Verlag, 2007), § 1.

100   Unlike many people who see the terms 'sensitivus' and 'aesthetica' as proof that Baumgarten considered the aesthetic experience to be especially sensuous, Robert Dixon thinks that Baumgarten betrayed the original meaning of the word *aisthanomai*, as is clear in his book *The Baumgarten Corruption* (London and East Haven: Pluto Press, 1995). According to Dixon, Baumgarten's concept of aesthetics has nothing whatsoever to do with sense perception because his aesthetics is only about High Art, to which people relate at a purely intellectual level. However, Dixon's reduction of *aisthanomai* to sense perception is philologically incorrect. Moreover, Baumgarten did not strip the aesthetic experience of all sensuousness, as Dixon thinks, even though he did not simply identify aesthetic experience with sense perception. It is also erroneous to present Baumgarten's aesthetics as a philosophy of art; on the contrary, it is a philosophical aesthetics, which *also* deals with art. Likewise, it is doubtful to claim that people only relate to so-called High Art at a purely intellectual level, as this art also contains shapes and colors that appeal to the senses.

different from what rationalist and empiricist epistemologies typically were. As mentioned earlier, Baumgarten saw the aesthetic experience as a kind of true cognition, and consequently another concept of truth is operative in his theory than was the case in rationalism and empiricism. In fact, the element of true cognition that Baumgarten identified in the aesthetic experience is more related to insight than to knowledge in the scientific sense of the word. However, it was precisely insight—or in other words, wisdom—that philosophy originally considered to be the most sublime kind of knowledge, but which has been ignored or even rejected by much modern philosophy. In our time, philosophical aesthetics may therefore be the closest we will get to genuine philosophy conceived as *philosophia*. It constitutes a kind of thinking that has not lost its love of wisdom—this wish for real insight—nor will it merely circle around in analytical or speculative approaches to universals, as traditional philosophy often did. Philosophical aesthetics is thus not only philosophical but must be regarded as a *modern* kind of philosophy that proceeds along phenomenological and hermeneutic lines, even though this trait was only nascent in the aesthetics of Baumgarten, with his rationalist schooling. As Kant later emphasized, the aesthetic experience is always the individual human being's experience of a singular object, and philosophical aesthetics is precisely philosophy about the experience of the particular. In philosophical aesthetics, we are dealing with a kind of thinking that devotes itself to studying the world of our experiences in order to pick up the emotionally experienced truth about ourselves and the world through the aesthetic ideas that structure our aesthetic experiences. Consequently, it is most unfortunate that philosophical aesthetics is hardly anywhere to be found today. This shortage means that we are missing out on systematic insights and philosophical terms, as far as an essential part of the world of our experiences is concerned, that is, the many experiences that are not just sense perceptions or intellectual cognitions.

In the philosophical aesthetics that *has* been developed, this phenomenological field of aesthetic experiences has given occasion to reflections in which beauty has played an essential part. For to philosophers like Kant, for example, beauty is not a quality appertaining to the object but an experience, and this experience is not reserved for our relation to art but also known from encounters with nature, in particular. According to Kant, beauty is more closely defined as something that profoundly affects our "feeling of life" (*Lebensgefühl*) and enlightens us about ourselves and our interrelationship with each other and with the world.[101] It tells us, for example, that we and the world may be less alien to one another than we tend to believe because the world is not just our surroundings, but also our origin. The humanities without philosophical aesthetics are lacking as to philosophical insight into this feeling of life, and consequently these humanities are but a shadow of themselves. Thus, it is urgent that we retrieve philosophical aesthetics, and this can only be done by studying and teaching it. Moreover, the lack of philosophical aesthetics does not only mean that the phenomenological field of aesthetic experiences remains unstudied. It also means that the art of reflection, which aesthetics by nature is, is not cultivated and that the potentialities of this art are not released, either. When most philosophy has become a science and thus nonphilosophical, as is today the case because it aims only at knowledge and is not seeking wisdom too, it is philosophical aesthetics that can teach us the necessity of philosophy and that the philosophy we should not reject is not so much philosophy as a discipline, but thinking freely. In other words, philosophical aesthetics does not only expand the horizons of the study of art by opening it to philosophical questioning. It can also create a consciousness of and thereby contribute to the development and preservation of the autonomous reflexivity that is the foundation of all kinds of research, and to which knowledge is not just a means to an end in the shape of more growth, but an end in itself.

---

101   Immanuel Kant, *Critique of the Power of Judgment*, eds. and trans. P. Guyer and E. Matthews (New York: Cambridge University Press, 2000), 90 (5: 203).

Aesthetic Experience

If we are to actualize the potential of philosophical aesthetics, we must explore aesthetic experience philosophically, and such an exploration requires a clarification as to what experience is and what it means to think philosophically. According to Baumgarten aesthetic experience consists neither in sense perception nor in intellectual cognition, but in feeling, sensation, and presentiment. Even though Kant criticized Baumgarten on other points, he adopted the notion that aesthetic experience is sensitive rather than sensuous, and later the early German Romantics, Heidegger, Gadamer, and Theodor W. Adorno, among others, elaborated upon this view. However, recently the body and sensuality have been focused upon to such a degree that they are now cultivated rather thoughtlessly, both by artists and by theorists. Consequently, it is no surprise that today many people see aesthetic experience as particularly sensuous and do not consider it a kind of experience that has any connection to truth; thus, aesthetic experiences are considered devoid of cognition. This reduction of the aesthetic experience—a reduction that by its advocates is seen as a liberation of aesthetics—arises out of a postmodern animosity to anything that may be characterized as metaphysical, especially the concept of truth, and to all cognition that is true in more than just a purely empirical sense. The topical cult of the body and sensuality is thus connected to a kind of pragmatism that collides with what aesthetics originally was, namely a philosophy about aesthetic experience, conceived as a kind of true cognition. Furthermore, this pragmatism ignores the realization by a number of modern philosophers that we should not reject every possibility of true cognition just because the concepts about truth and cognition handed down to us are insufficient. It makes more sense to develop new concepts of truth and cognition that are in a better harmony with the experiences we have.

    The topical reduction of aesthetic experience to sense perception is also promoted by the fact that far too many people do not distinguish between mere impression and experience proper.[102]

---

102 The distinction between impression and experience I am applying here is a trans-

Much of what is today referred to as aesthetic experience and seen as proof that this kind of thing has no metaphysical qualities is actually not aesthetic *experience,* but aesthetic *impression.* Aesthetic impressions may very well distinguish themselves by being particularly sensuous, without possessing any special cognitive potential, whereas it makes no sense to say the same thing about aesthetic experiences. Although aesthetic experiences are not a product of conceptual thinking, they are different from impressions in that they are reflective. True, there is no denying impressions, since as a starting point we always relate to ourselves and to the world via impressions, and because experiences rely not only on reflexivity but also on impressions. However, an impression does not leave any lasting trace in the subject, apart from the recollection of the dent it may have left behind, whereas the experience affects the subject in such a way that he or she is no longer what she was before. Experiences bring about changes and they occasion wondering and thus reflection, too, although the subject (he or she) may not be conscious about 'thinking.' In other words, experiences do not differ from impressions only by including reflexivity, in the sense that they are impressions adapted in reflection. They also trigger off reflection, and therefore they contain a cognitive potential, in themselves, and for the very same reason they are a source of development. Unlike impressions, experiences are thus essential to what, since the eighteenth century, has been termed 'liberal education,' which is still the prerequisite for a social condition in which society truly is a society, that is, where the individual will not only satisfy his or her own needs and desires, but also appreciate the common weal.

Unlike pragmatic experiences, aesthetic experiences distinguish themselves by being metaphysical, and therefore they do not differ from sense perceptions only by being more sensitive than sensuous; they also differ thanks to the element of cognition of metaphysical truth that sensitivity makes possible. When an

---

lation, by way of experiment, of the Danish distinction between 'oplevelse' and 'erfaring,' which is equivalent to the German distinction between 'Erlebnis' and 'Erfahrung.'

aesthetic experience is indeed an aesthetic experience, as distinct from an aesthetic impression—that is, in a Kantian perspective, when we are not dealing with mere sensuous pleasure, but with an experience of beauty—it constitutes an experience of cohesion and meaningfulness. As modern humans, we rely predominantly on understanding, by which we appropriate positive knowledge and which is thus a must in our practical lives, as well as in the sciences. Understanding is analytical, and from its point of view the world is not cohesive and thus devoid of meaning.[103] However, this absence of cohesion and meaningfulness is not absolute, although it is a pragmatic and scientific fact. The aesthetic experience testifies to some other possibility, even though it only happens momentarily and the experienced cohesion and meaningfulness is unintelligible and hard to talk about. Aesthetic experiences allow for an intuition of meaning that is more comprehensive than the kind of meaning known from the cognitions produced by understanding. This different meaning does not constitute a metaphysical truth in the traditional sense but it is both true and metaphysical, only in a different way. The cohesion and meaningfulness exposed by aesthetic experience is not a fact in the empirical sense but just a suggestion: in aesthetic experience, one feels something that *could* be. It is a hypothetical interpretation of what is, placing the already given in an unaccustomed light. In our aesthetic experiences we thus intuit a harmony otherwise inaccessible, while the actual disruptions of the world are not dissolved. The experienced cohesion and meaningfulness are only symbolic, and so they call for interpretation.

Aesthetic Thinking

Philosophical aesthetics is needed because human beings have aesthetic experiences, and they call for interpretation, and philosophical aesthetics was created for the very purpose of providing this in-

---

103   The word 'understanding' here denotes the faculty of concepts and intellectual reasoning, that is, the *Verstand*. Modern humans who predominantly rely on understanding in this sense of the word miss understanding in the hermeneutic sense of it described in the chapter "Philosophy at a Crossroads."

terpretation. In aesthetic experience, we take in something we feel certain about, but actually do not understand, and which we consequently find it hard to express. However, philosophical aesthetics provides us with the means and terms that render a thoughtful absorption in this experience and sensible communication of it possible, without losing the feeling of cohesion and meaningfulness. Between early philosophical aesthetics (for example, Baumgarten's contribution) and the much later philosophical aesthetics we find in the work of, for example, Heidegger and Walter Benjamin, there is considerable difference, however. Baumgarten founded philosophical aesthetics, but more recent philosophers have moved on with regard to taking thoughtful care of the experience. This is much more successfully done with an increasingly phenomenological approach in philosophy, and in so far as the philosophical exploration of the experience practices a kind of thinking that is reflecting freely in the sense of letting the faculties of cognition assist one another, as is the case in aesthetic experience. Philosophical aesthetics must mime the kind of 'thinking' going on in aesthetic experience itself, but it must be done within the framework of the conceptual discourse appertaining to philosophy. Philosophical aesthetics must adopt the reflective structure of aesthetic experience, the free and harmonious interplay between understanding and imagination, and transform this interplay into the kind of adaptation of the concepts needed to give cognitive deliverance to the feeling of cohesion and meaningfulness. Philosophical aesthetics itself must think aesthetically to succeed in its philosophical interpretation of the aesthetic experience.

Such philosophical interpretation of aesthetic experiences is not only a qualitative asset in dealing with 'the aesthetic'; it also represents a cultivation of thinking and thus also of the practical life of action. This is not only due to the expansion of the philosophical field, by way of the aesthetic elasticity of the interpretation; it is also due to what, in this way, will be accessible to philosophical thinking. The feeling of cohesion and meaningfulness connected to the aesthetic experience that philosophical aesthetics sheds light on is not only individual but also common to humankind. When philosophical aesthetics gives this feeling a cognitive deliverance, it is thus not something private but, on the contrary, something of universal validity that is recognized. Of course, personal experiences of cohesion and meaningfulness manifest themselves individually, as they present themselves at definite moments in definite places and are occasioned by something specific, for example, a special natural scenery experienced on a particular day in a summer marked by a special love or a certain loss. However, the very feeling of cohesion and meaningfulness experienced by the individual in such a specific situation is not different from the one that others have experienced in other situations. Different people have the experience in common *that* a feeling of cohesion and meaningfulness is possible, however different the individual manifestations of the feeling they memorize may be. When philosophical aesthetics furnishes this feeling with a language that is tuned in to it, as it thinks in a different way from other kinds of philosophy, that is, in an aesthetic way, it will thus articulate an experience of existential significance to the individual human being that is not private but common. In its interpretation of the aesthetic experience, philosophical aesthetics makes it possible to recognize, articulate, and discuss something of universal validity, and that has not only theoretical but also practical implications.

A certain dose of knowledge about philosophical aesthetics is required in order for the individual person who practices aesthetics as a science to get a clear conception of the concepts applied. Furthermore, philosophical aesthetics may add perspectives to the scientific analyses of artworks so that they will seem less technical and more constitutive of meaning (including to people who are not acquainted with the scientific knowledge of art). However, philosophical aesthetics is capable of more than just supplementing the art theory that already supports the study of art. When philosophical aesthetics implements the *philosophia* that philosophy was originally conceived as, by giving the feeling of cohesion and meaningfulness a philosophical cognitive deliverance, it will ascribe a role to philosophy in which it is not an alien superstructure but the experiential basis of everything we do. It is in the form of such an underlying element of common reflexivity that philosophical aesthetics may strengthen the humanities by establishing cohesion without removing the differences. In this way, aesthetics can also tie together the university as a whole and, by and large, strengthen the cohesive force of society, something that is often called for. That is to say: the philosophical aesthetics in question will not merely repeat older philosophy, although it will find inspiration in this. Thanks to its concept of aesthetic experience and its phenomenological procedure, philosophical aesthetics has put the dualism of traditional philosophy between sense perception and intellectual cognition in the past. It shows that we can deal seriously with the world of our experiences in all its variety without giving up the philosophical quest for truth, and the feeling of cohesion and meaningfulness as to which it conveys an insight is of invaluable significance to our practical lives. This is the feeling that turns the epitome of aesthetic experience—the experience of beauty—into the experience that something is of value, in itself. Without this experience, society is in distress, for where it is not to be found everything becomes instrumental, even the most precious relations between humans. The experience of beauty reminds us where the limit goes, and philosophical aesthetics provides this reminder with a language.

Aesthetic Thinking as a Common Humanist Concern

The humanities are in lack of intrinsic cohesion and humanist self-conception. Consequently, we need to consider *what* constitutes the humanities. It is not enough to be interested in *how* humanist scholarship is performed. Hence, we have to reintroduce philosophical thinking into the humanities. As things stand today, there is too much theorizing and too little philosophizing. This does not mean that we are in need of more philosophy, considered as a discipline. What is needed is reflection that is open, free, and questioning. Thinking that is not determined by outward circumstances, but has its purpose in itself and is reflecting upon what this means. Without this thinking, we shall not be able to understand what is human about human beings and preserve the humanities by way of being humanities. It is necessary in order to avoid narrow-mindedness and to practice enlightenment, which is the task of the humanities. It is a prerequisite for the humanities to help the surrounding world to understand the complexity of matters of, for example, a global, political, and ecological nature.

This free, open, and questioning reflection has a name. It is called not only philosophical thinking, but *aesthetic thinking*. Here, I am not aiming at the philosophy of art or theories about the aestheticizing of anything from politics to consumption. On the contrary, it is all about the special way of thinking that is connected to judgment and to the specific, aesthetic experience. The experience of beauty is the experience that something has a value of its own and of being part of something greater. It conveys the feeling of belonging to the world, and, consequently, it is an existentially important experience of cohesion and meaningfulness. The experience of beauty throws an unaccustomed light upon what is a given, it is hard to comprehend, and it is thought-provoking. However, it may be communicated to others, and although it is always manifested individually, it is not a private but a common human experience. Likewise, the way of thinking appertaining to judgment is characterized by being expanded, that is, marked by empathy, and, consequently, it has moral significance. It adheres to the principle of being able to identify oneself with others and take many views into consideration, without submitting to any one of these. With the expanded way of thinking, it is possible to elevate oneself above individual interests and consider the common weal. This way of thinking is, according to Kant, a prerequisite for fulfilling reason's principle of universalizability: "act only according to that maxim through which you can at the same time will that it become a universal law."[104] Without judgment, it would not be possible to act in a moral way, and, consequently, ethics is based on aesthetics.

However, this expanded way of thinking is also the prerequisite for thinking philosophically in the free, open, and questioning way that is crucial to the humanities. As Ernst Cassirer has put it, philosophical thinking is aiming at the cognition of unity in diversity.[105] This does not mean that it will obliterate all the empirical differences to replace them with a single, common denominator. It does not aspire to simplification, but, on the contrary, to finding something that unites. Philosophical thinking aims at a harmony between items that are different from one another—and not similar to one another. However, as modern human beings controlled by intellectualism, we think in an unphilosophical way. We are liable to view

---

104 Immanuel Kant, *Groundwork of the Metaphysics of Morals*, eds. and trans. M. Gregor and J. Timmermann (New York: Cambridge University Press, 2011), 71.

105 Ernst Cassirer, *An Essay on Man: An Introduction to a Philosophy of Culture* (New Haven and London: Yale University Press, 1974), 222–223.

unity and variety as contrasts. Often, we end up in either/or and not both/and. Due to the expanded way of thinking, aesthetic judgment may help us to reflect in a less theoretical, but more philosophical way. Then, in our thoughts, we may be in several places at the same time, thinking what is not, otherwise, to be reflected upon, for example, the connection between what is historical and what is suprahistorical, between rupture and continuity, between tradition and what is new, between transcendence and immanence, or between what is local and what is global. Today, we are in sore need of a kind of thinking that can dissolve rigid contrasts. The humanities can satisfy this need, but only in so far as aesthetic thinking will become a common humanist concern.

So what the humanities need is to recall the ability to see things in their interrelationship. Consequently, we need aesthetic thinking to be a common humanist concern, and this is why philosophical aesthetics can contribute substantially to the future development of the philosophy of science. *In this way*, the humanities will find themselves in a stronger position when confronted with the surrounding world, without cutting the latter off. *In this way*, we can preserve the link to tradition without losing sight of our own age. Or in a summary of ten points:

1. Concepts must be clarified in such a way that they are clearly comprehensible, and this requires philosophical thinking. Scholarship, as well as communication, will gain by the clarification, and this will not result in a kind of essentialism, as is often feared. When you are trying to define concepts, they are put in motion. On the other hand, essentialism occurs when you refuse to consider the meaning of the concepts.

2. When conceived of as the free, open, and questioning reflection, which philosophy originally was, aesthetic thinking can change philosophy into something different from and more than just a tool or an alien superstructure. Instead, such philosophy may be constitutive of an experiential basis of what we are saying and doing by way of being humanists. In this way, an intrinsic cohesion may be established within the humanities, without removing the differences among the individual disciplines.

3. The lucidity of aesthetic thinking may promote an understanding from the surrounding world as to the necessity of the freedom of scholarship and research and as to the importance of not reducing knowledge into a means to an end of growth, but seeing it as an end in itself. Aesthetic thinking is, in itself, a creative praxis, which by its own way of working demonstrates that the demands of applicability from the surrounding world are really needless.

4. If humanist scholarship is to exert an influence, it must be relevant not just for the experts, but for ordinary people too. It will not achieve this by paying lip service to the *Zeitgeist* or by becoming more mechanized, but by interpreting human experiences in ways that are meaningful to human beings themselves. Such initiatives will hardly convince technocrats. However, the humanities will also be of greater service to themselves and to society, as a whole, by focusing on their alliances in the population rather than by being hypnotized by their enemies.

5. By reflecting aesthetically, that is, freely—phenomenologically and hermeneutically, and in other ways—philosophical aesthetics will provide a world of experience that is of crucial existential significance with systematic insight and a philosophical language. In doing so, aesthetics will promote a central task of the humanities— the free, interpretative aspiration toward meaning-making—and fulfill the most essential criterion of relevance: to give human beings something they need.

6. There is danger to society when we forget that something is of value in itself; if it were not, everything would be instrumental, even the relation to the other. The experience of beauty reminds us as to where the limit goes, philosophical aesthetics provides this reminder with a language, and aesthetic thinking converts it into practice. The general educational potential is enormous. Here, the intrinsic cohesion does not only apply to the humanities, but to society, as a whole.

7. Philosophical aesthetics is, for example, of great importance to pedagogy as well as politics, which both have or ought to have the good life as their purpose. Aesthetics explores the moments when life *is* already good, mind you, in a radical and not just a comfortable sense. This calls for reflection upon what is, in fact, the meaning of pedagogical and political efforts.

8. The expansion characterizing the aesthetic way of thinking consists in the ability to be in several places at the same time in your thoughts, that is, to reflect upon something at different levels simultaneously without contrasting it. It is all concerned with thinking about what is general or universal without losing your sense of what is unique in what is singular or particular. This art of aesthetic reflection is the best safeguard against barren and prejudiced polemics, and it ought to be common know-how, not only within the humanities, but within society as a whole.

9. Thanks to its expanded nature, aesthetic thinking will gather, without reducing what is different to being the same. That is what we need in a society marked by fragmentation and globalization. It is through this expanded way of thinking that, as human beings, we may elevate ourselves above our private needs and desires to pay regard to the common weal. This is what is needed at a time characterized by individualism.

10. Aesthetic thinking is, for example, a prerequisite for actualizing the ideal of cosmopolitan citizenship. If this expanded way of thinking is lacking, the local and the global, the national and the cosmopolitan, will be contrasted, as so often happens in sociology, for instance. Aesthetics is the road to the cosmopolitan city; general education in expanded thinking is a prerequisite for the actualization of the cosmopolitan citizen.

The Dialogue of Experience

Contingency and Necessity

"One isn't born a philosopher," Gianni Vattimo writes in *The Responsibility of the Philosopher*, "it's something one becomes."[106] The process of becoming a philosopher is a random one, so the profession of the philosopher is also associated with contingency. Since the philosopher could have become something else, the connection between him and his employment is not inevitable. It would not ruin his life were he to practice another profession, which does not mean, however, that nothing matters, for as Vattimo also writes: "Fortuitous circumstances, though, are mostly just the start of a trajectory that is driven much more by necessity, in form and in detail, than it may appear to be at the outset. There is a *contingency* in every professional vocation that transforms in part, or may transform, into *necessity*. For example there is a certain determinism in the affinities that one goes on to discover, or forge."[107]

Ultimately, it would thus still be a problem if a philosopher could no longer practice philosophy—for example, because of increasing difficulties finding the right words to use. He might have become something else, but has now become one with thought. Thinking has become his way of being in the world, and if it were taken from him, not much else would be left. However, I am not re-

---

106 Gianni Vattimo, *The Responsibility of the Philosopher*, ed. F. D'Agostini, trans. W. Mccuaig (New York: Columbia University Press, 2010), 112.

107 Vattimo, *The Responsibility of the Philosopher*, 112.

ferring to the philosopher's vocation as a professional philosopher, his position as an employee at a university. On the contrary, I am referring to philosophical thinking and the way of life associated with this thinking. It is not the profession, but this thinking and this being in the world that become constitutive of someone who ends up as a philosopher. That is what becomes necessity, even if it started in contingency.

Even the philosopher's *profession* is associated with necessity. Not in the sense of the duties imposed on professors as university employees, but in the sense of the commitment permeating their performance of these duties, provided they are 'intellectuals.' 'Intellectuals' is Edward W. Said's designation, in *Representations of the Intellectual*, for people who think about things, ask questions, and side with the weak in society; such is the responsibility of the intellectual.[108] In contrast, 'professionals' is what Said calls academics who prioritize their careers, value their competence more highly than universal values such as truth and freedom, and cultivate a postmodernism that is nothing but one big concession of their own "lazy incapacities, perhaps even indifference."[109] For the sake of their careers, professionals are busy "not rocking the boat, not straying outside the accepted paradigms or limits, making [themselves] marketable and above all presentable, hence uncontroversial and unpolitical and 'objective.'"[110] According to Said, this mentality has spread from academia to the media and to the cultural sphere, where we are presented with positivist knowledge and subjective opinions, but no reflection on key issues. Much would be gained if more people refused to do as expected, and asked why one

---

108   Edward W. Said, *Representations of the Intellectual: The Reith Lectures* (New York: Vintage Books, 1994). This meaning of the word 'intellectual' differs from its established philosophical meaning, applied in other chapters of the present volume and according to which 'intellectual' is synonymous with 'logical' and 'conceptual.' But Said's idea of what it means to be an intellectual is partly comparable to my interpretation of this issue in, for example, Dorthe Jørgensen, *Viden og visdom: Spørgsmålet om de intellektuelle* (Knowledge and Wisdom: The Question of the Intellectuals) (Frederiksberg: Det lille forlag, 2002).

109   Said, *Representations of the Intellectual*, 18.

110   Said, *Representations of the Intellectual*, 74.

does what one does, and whom it benefits. If only it were not the need to bask in the limelight that made their mouths run, but "love for and unquenchable interest in the larger picture, in making connections across lines and barriers, in refusing to be tied down to a specialty, in caring for ideas and values despite the restrictions of a profession."[111]

Whereas Said's book is about the responsibility of the *intellectual*, Vattimo's is about the *philosopher's* responsibility; but expressed in Said's terminology, Vattimo speaks precisely as an *intellectual* when he speaks of the teaching and communication that are part of his job as a *philosopher*. "I have to perform well as a philosophy professor, because it's my job," he writes. "But ultimately 'because it's my job' just means: because I am of service to someone."[112] His occupation involves more than the job, and is not actually work, but doing, which expresses itself in his way of understanding and managing his job. The job, his position as a philosophy professor, is contingent, but the doing is necessary, and it serves the salvation of others, rather than of himself—that is, of the students, the general public, the European community. His doing is not for the benefit of the institution or his career, but for something larger that demands *dialogue* and *thinking*. "Actually, in my considered view, there is no difference between what I do when I am teaching in the university, and what I do when I write a column for a newspaper," he says.[113] Moreover, as a teacher and columnist he not only educates; he also engages in *Bildung* (formation), for "in philosophy I believe that some political good is always at stake, some question of political community. That is what justifies philosophy as teaching, philosophy in the newspapers, and philosophy in politics too."[114]

---

111   Said, *Representations of the Intellectual*, 76.

112   Vattimo, *The Responsibility of the Philosopher*, 102.

113   Vattimo, *The Responsibility of the Philosopher*, 101.

114   Vattimo, *The Responsibility of the Philosopher*, 105.

The Importance of Dialogue

Vattimo thinks of "the philosophical vocation as profoundly grounded in the *polis*," from which the hermeneutical idea of the importance of dialogue was inherited.[115] Socrates is the classic example of the conversational philosopher who, in dialogue with other people, explores questions aroused by wonder, and to whom conversation is the medium for his thinking. Here, we find the source of the idea that not only does thinking take place *through* conversation but also thinking *is* conversation—an idea that has taken on various forms throughout the course of history. Socrates had conversations not only with his fellow citizens but also with both the goddess Diotima and with himself, his own daemon. As a writer of philosophical dialogues, Plato was in conversation with both the historical Socrates and Plato's literary manifestation of Socrates, and thus also with a whole gallery of other people. To Christian philosophers, thinking has unfolded as a conversation with God, and for this same reason it has been difficult to distinguish it from prayer. Therefore, it is perhaps unsurprising that not only religion but thought, too, got into trouble when philosophers such as Immanuel Kant reduced prayer to foolish monologue.[116] The conversation became one that was based on the premises of the modern sciences. Previously, it was characterized by a desire for religious and philosophical insight; now it took the form of a quest for scientific knowledge, and the art evaporated from the art of conversation, as it turned into knowledge sharing.

The foregoing development was not only applauded but also thwarted—by the early German Romantics, Søren Kierkegaard, and Friedrich Nietzsche, among others. To them, Socrates was not necessarily exemplary, but their philosophical forms of presentation were related to Plato's, thanks to the literary devices they used. Since then, especially the philosophical hermeneutics of the twen-

---

115 Vattimo, *The Responsibility of the Philosopher*, 107.

116 Immanuel Kant, *Religion within the Boundaries of Mere Reason: And Other Writings*, eds. and trans. A. Wood and G.D. Giovanni (Cambridge, UK: Cambridge University Press, 1998), 186 (6: 194–196).

tieth century has tried to save the art of conversation, in hermeneutics through the dialogue with tradition in particular, with which Martin Heidegger and Hans-Georg Gadamer were concerned, which they practiced, and whose importance they also articulated. However, in recent years the academic world has been unfavorable to hermeneutics. Professorships in philosophical hermeneutics are being discontinued in favor of something that is often of an analytic philosophical or cognitive-scientific character. At the same time, hermeneutics is also being discredited in other humanistic disciplines, for example by literary scholars who—misled by polemicists such as Hans-Ulrich Gumbrecht—reject it on the basis of a reductionist understanding of what hermeneutics is.[117] They see hermeneutics as 'passive reception'—as distinct from the creative practice in the form of 'creative writing,' for example, which they regard as the opposite of hermeneutics, and which they believe should be prioritized in the curriculum. Students do not need to interpret texts or other phenomena, but to express themselves—no matter how they are to become good at this, including in having something to say, if they do not learn how to 'read the world.'

The humanist rejection of hermeneutics is fatal to the humanities. This rejection has been facilitated by too little and too poor dialogue between professional philosophers and other humanist scholars, but it cannot be explained solely with reference to philosophical introversion. The rejection is also due to a general contemporary humanist aversion to genuine philosophical thinking, and that is why it is dangerous. The humanities can do without philosophy as a discipline, at least in principle, but they cannot do without philosophical thinking. Besides wonder, philosophical thinking requires the creation of a connection between the part and the whole. Without an eye for the universal in the particular,

---

[117] Gumbrecht's polemical-reductionist approach to hermeneutics disfigures his *Production of Presence: What Meaning Cannot Convey* (Stanford: Stanford University Press, 2004). See my discussion of Gumbrecht in the chapter "Nærvær og somaæstetik" (Presence and Somaesthetics) in my book *Den skønne tænkning: Veje til erfaringsmetafysik. Religionsfilosofisk udmøntet* (Beautiful Thinking: Pathways to the Metaphysics of Experience. Religio-Philosophically Implemented) (Aarhus: Aarhus University Press, 2014). See also footnote 123.

it is not possible to gain insight into what things mean to us; one is confined to simply registering what is before us. Insight requires interpretation, and interpretation demands the gaze that both Vattimo and others have described as characterized by totality understood as an orientation toward the whole.

The Orientation Toward the Whole

"The life of the spirit is a unity that specificates in the individual vocations and yet maintains a certain continuity," Vattimo writes, referring to Wilhelm Dilthey and Luigi Pareyson.[118] Whatever one does, one expresses all one's spirituality, and thus the task is to "maintain the unity of the spiritual life while knowingly accepting one's own finiteness, and therefore choosing and accepting one's own specialization."[119] However, in extension of this, Vattimo also writes that "it is sometimes said that the characteristic of philosophers is that they have a certain rapport (which may even be critical) with totality. Georg Simmel depicted the philosopher as 'he who possesses an organ that perceives and reacts to the totality of Being' ... the philosopher has 'a sense for the wholeness of things and life.'"[120]

Vattimo's statement that one is not born a philosopher probably concerns not only the profession but also this sense of wholeness. That is, no one is born thinking holistically, but one may learn to think this way, and that is why the activities of teaching and communication associated with the job of a philosophy professor are so important. The task is not just to share one's knowledge with others, and to make sure that they acquire more knowledge of the things about which it is possible to have knowledge, for example the history of philosophy, the characteristics of various positions, the meanings of concepts, and the use of logical formulas. The task

---

118 Vattimo, *The Responsibility of the Philosopher*, 110.

119 Vattimo, *The Responsibility of the Philosopher*, 110.

120 Vattimo, *The Responsibility of the Philosopher*, 111–112.

is also to help others develop their ability to think holistically, so that they can connect varied knowledge rather than just archiving what they know, and so that they can interpret their knowledge rather than resorting to subjective opinion-making. Moreover, if the point is not only to educate but also to form, it must be because there *is* something to form—to cultivate. There *is* something that is innate—and this is true of not just some, but all—namely, the *possibility* of becoming someone who knows how to think holistically, also called a philosopher.

It is the aforementioned possibility that is ignored by the 'professionals.' The intellectual not only masters a profession but also manages to rise above the knowledge she gains through her profession, and therefore she is not limited by her knowledge, but is able to use it to serve the common good. As a cultural-analytical literary scholar at an American university in the 1990s, Said could not refer to intellectuals as *philosophers*, and probably could not see them in this light either. However, this shortcoming is merely an expression of historical contingency. If he had been living a century earlier in Central Europe, his vocabulary would have been different, but the object would have been the same: holistic thinking, without which we are only producers of knowledge and opinion makers. Vattimo expresses this clearly when he writes that "nobody can seriously 'specialize' unless they are permanently alive to the totality of spiritual life: that is what's 'philosophical' in every human life."[121]

According to Vattimo, the desire to practice the kind of thinking made possible by the sense for wholeness, and to pursue the goals it implies—namely, to focus on the salvation of others, to side with the weak—is what motivates the philosopher, and according to Said, it is what drives the intellectual. This desire is not only the precondition of philosophical thought but also what justifies it: "I believe that, in any case, if you forget what drew you into your field, if you forget the political interest that spurred you, the religious interest, the emancipatory interest in general, you end up

---

121 Vattimo, *The Responsibility of the Philosopher*, 113.

reproducing 'the crisis of the European sciences,'" Vattimo writes. That is, "once again theory can't (in the best of cases) be anything more than a simple literary exercise, or artistic-philosophical experimentation, or (more commonly), an exercise in individualism for its own sake, serving private interests and power."[122]

The Experience of Beauty

Consequentially, the thinking of the intellectual is *philosophical*. That is why she takes political responsibility—because she thinks holistically, not the other way round. Moreover, this responsibility, that is, the responsibility of the *intellectual*, is what the philosopher exhibits when he not only fulfills his function as a professor but also thinks philosophically. Philosophical thinking, whose orientation toward wholeness and political responsibility the philosopher and the intellectual thus share, may be understood as a *dialogue*— and as a conversation not only between two, but among several participants. Thinking is a conversation with the daemon in the individual, which Christians may find meaningful to perceive as God's voice, also called 'the conscience.' However, thinking is also a conversation with the collective of other people that, in the written expression of the individual's thoughts, is manifested as the imagined reader who cowrites the text. Moreover, in addition to these two dialogues, there is also a third dialogue of significance to thought, namely, 'the dialogue of experience.' I am not referring only to the conversation *about* experience that philosophy is to hermeneutic philosophers, but to a conversation *in* the experience: a dialogue between different aspects of the experience, without which both the conversation with the daemon and the conversation with other people would be unthinkable.

In order to describe the dialogue in the experience, I will now introduce my concept of 'basic experience' and its threefold structure. This concept is from my book *Den skønne tænkning* (Beautiful Thinking): it comes from the book's religio-philosophical imple-

---

122   Vattimo, *The Responsibility of the Philosopher*, 108.

mentation of philosophical aesthetics, hermeneutic phenomenology, and the connections between aesthetics, phenomenology, and hermeneutics.[123] In order to introduce the concept of basic experience, I must also explain what I mean by words such as 'aesthetics' and 'aesthetic.' This is necessary because of a widespread tendency to confuse philosophical aesthetics with the philosophy of art. In brief, the central topic of philosophical aesthetics is not art but the aesthetic experience, and the aesthetic experience is not identical to the experience of art. Instead, it is the experience of beauty that is the epitome of aesthetic experience, but not understood as an experience of something nice and neat, and not understood as an experience that only art can occasion. On the contrary, beauty is everything that has value in itself, and philosophical aesthetics is about our experience of this 'having-value-in-itself.'

Philosophical aesthetics was introduced by Alexander Gottlieb Baumgarten, and conceived within the framework of a philosophy of faculties. Therefore, I have updated aesthetics based on a way of thinking inspired by phenomenology and hermeneutics, among other approaches. So I do not think of the experience of beauty as something that we ourselves accomplish, but as something that happens to us, the source of which is not to be found in ourselves, in specific dispositions or abilities, but in the encounter between us and the occasion (not the object) of the experience. In Baumgarten's work, the so-called lower cognitive faculties are the subjective source of the experience of beauty. In *Den skønne*

---

[123] For an English summary of the book, see *Den skønne tænkning*, 947–965. The overall aim of *Den skønne tænkning* is to develop, with a point of departure in philosophical aesthetics and hermeneutic phenomenology, a philosophy of experience for all kinds of experience of transcendence (aesthetic, religious, and metaphysical experiences). At the same time, its ambition is also to provide a basis for theological aesthetics with a proper philosophical grounding, that is, theological aesthetics that is well rooted in philosophical aesthetics and not just in art theory, for instance. *Den skønne tænkning* thus provides detailed interpretations of both older and newer theorists, especially Alexander Gottlieb Baumgarten, Immanuel Kant, Walter Benjamin, and Martin Heidegger, but also, for example, Hermann Schmitz, Gernot Böhme, Wolfgang Welsch, Martin Seel, Christoph Menke, Hans Ulrich Gumbrecht, and Richard Shusterman. Furthermore, the book contains a comprehensive religio-philosophical implementation of aesthetics discussing other theorists, including Jean-Louis Chrétien, Eugenio Trías, K.E. Løgstrup, Hans Urs von Balthasar, Eberhard Jüngel, Klaas Huizing, Mark C. Taylor, Hannah Arendt, Hans Joas, and Dieter Henrich.

tænkning I translate Baumgarten's terminology into 'feeling, sensation, and presentiment,' and I also give a new interpretation of the topic, according to which it is no longer about a subject's sensitive faculties, but subjectivity in the sense of sensitivity. The experience of beauty happens in this sensitivity, that is, at a level at which subject and object are not yet constituted. Therefore, the experience of beauty may be categorized as neither purely subjective nor purely objective; on the contrary, it transcends such distinctions. For the same reason, I do not understand the experience of beauty as one in which *specific* things are felt to be valuable in themselves, let alone as an experience of what value those things are supposed to have. On the contrary, I interpret the experience of beauty as an experience of the very fact *that* something may be valuable in itself.

The Basic Experience

Intellectually, we necessarily approach the sensitivity in which the experience of beauty occurs from the level of the understanding's subject/object-structured way of thinking. Therefore, to us this sensitivity appears as an *intermediate world*, and in *Den skønne tænkning* I thus give it this name. It is at the sensitive and therefore aesthetic level of experience constituted by the intermediate world that things start to appear. This aesthetic-sensitive level of experience is the precondition for phenomena to appear, as well as permitting the understanding generated by their appearance. Thus, in *Den skønne tænkning* I conclude that what was understood as 'phenomenological' or 'hermeneutic' experience in the twentieth century had already been discussed earlier in history, but as 'aesthetic' experience. Furthermore, this kinship not only indicates what hermeneutic and phenomenological thinkers such as Heidegger and Gadamer could not see, namely that their philosophies were not critical alternatives but creative updates of philosophical aesthetics. It is also an argument in favor of considering what I refer to as 'basic experience' as something that is aesthetic in the sense of being sensitive rather than merely sensuous.

When I use the expression 'basic experience,' I am referring to a level of experience, not to any specific experience. It does not concern any particular single experience, but the attentive beginning of all perception without which we would have no experience, nor would we have any knowledge. The concept 'basic experience' thus denotes the sensitively sentient 'being-there-in-the-universe-together-with-whatever-else-there-is,' without which there would be no consciousness. As mentioned previously, this existence called 'basic experience' is *sensitive*—in it we sense the existent: ourselves in our being present, and that with which we are together in this presence. Early philosophical aesthetics already explained that sensitive experiences provide knowledge, but of a different kind than rational knowledge; therefore I would rather refer to it as 'insight.' In *Den skønne tænkning*, I add that the insight associated with sensitive experience is not only due to its *sensitivity* but also to the *faith*, in the sense of *trust*, with which we respond to the sensitively provided *insight*. Therefore, the basic experience includes not only the duality of sensitivity and insight of which philosophical aesthetics was already aware. Rather, the basic experience is characterized by a threefold structure, for besides sensitivity and insight, it also includes trust. In *Den skønne tænkning*, I refer to this as the trinity of *sensation, faith*, and *comprehension*, and it is among these three aspects of the experience that an immanent dialogue unfolds.

Thanks to *sensation*, we sensitively comprehend ourselves, one another, and the world around us, and we spontaneously have *faith* in what we *comprehend*: we trust the insight we receive through our sensitive experience. We sense, comprehend, and have faith in what we comprehend when our experience is something that *happens* to us, instead of being something we, ourselves, *accomplish*. This exchange, in which sensation includes comprehension that gives insight, which produces meaning because we rely on the insight provided by the sensation—this 'dialogue' in the experience—may be described using the ancient aesthetic concept of 'unity in diversity.' However, such a use of this concept presupposes that we reinterpret it so it does not represent a reduction of the different to the same, but an association of something that is and will remain different. Our use of the concept of unity in diversity to describe the dialogue in experience requires that we do not understand unity as a synthesis that eliminates the uniqueness of the individual elements connected by it—instead, we must see unity as a joining of something that retains its uniqueness in the association. For the three aspects of basic experience, that is, sensation, faith, and comprehension, are not in a hierarchical relationship with one another, as are the religious, the aesthetic, and the philosophical in Georg Wilhelm Friedrich Hegel's phenomenology. Sensation, faith, and comprehension are rather equiprimordial, as are attunement and understanding in Heidegger's ontology.

World Poetry

According to Walter Benjamin, philosophical thinking is qualified, unlike scientific knowledge, through its presentation of ideas and interpretation of phenomena.[124] Slightly akin to the idea referenced by Vattimo, that philosophical thinking is characterized by an orientation toward the whole, Benjamin thought that philosophy strives to present ideas, but without aiming directly at its goal. Instead, philosophy digresses to the phenomena; this is the way it tries to present ideas. The orientation toward ideas, which is thus a contributing factor in philosophy's contemplation of phenomena, means that philosophy is not just descriptive, but interpretive: its effort to present ideas gives perspective to its handling of phenomena. Consequentially, philosophical thinking is oriented toward a different level than those of phenomena and concepts, namely, the level of ideas. However, we should not look for this level somewhere else, in a distant transcendence, but in the phenomenal world, that is, in immanence. The ideas 'inhabit' the phenomena, in which they do not act as fixed entities, however, but as potential for experience and knowledge that must be actualized by philosophy, whose medi-

---

124 I am alluding to Benjamin's distinction between *Philosophie* and *Erkenntnis*, see Walter Benjamin, *The Origin of German Tragic Drama*, trans. J. Osborne (London and New York: Verso, 2009), 27ff. See also the chapter "Philosophy at a Crossroads," footnote 47.

um is the concept. This is precisely why philosophy's presentation of ideas is both necessary and infinite, and it is also the reason why the presentation elevates philosophy's handling of phenomena from mere description to interpretation that gives insight.[125]

Or to put this slightly differently: "Reality is ambiguous: it has several layers," I wrote in the preface to a book titled *Verdenspoesi* (World Poetry).[126] "This does not concern the ancient idea that there is another world to be found somewhere else. On the contrary, this concerns the world here being multidimensional. The sensuous world is sprinkled with suprasensuous meaning. There is a surplus of meaning for those who seize the moment when the sun splits the clouds or the door is left ajar."[127] I also wrote that the experience just described is an experience of a surplus of meaning, and that it is universal to human beings. "It is the experience that something may have value in itself, formerly called beauty," the preface says. "Art and philosophy are both able to intercept and shape this experience emerging from the poetic perception of the world. A perception that is important to the individual as well as to community: it induces us to live—in harmony."[128]

The ontologies articulated in Benjamin's theory of ideas and in the preface of *World Poetry*, respectively, are interrelated as follows: The kind of experience that is depicted in the preface is not

---

125 See also the chapter "Philosophy at a Crossroads" in the present volume, and the chapter "Experience, Metaphysics, and Immanent Transcendence" in Dorthe Jørgensen, *Imaginative Moods: Aesthetics, Religion, Philosophy* (Aarhus: Aarhus University Press, 2021).

126 Dorthe Jørgensen, "Preface," in *Verdenspoesi: Malerier og tankebilleder* (World Poetry: Paintings and Thought-Images) (Aarhus: Women's Museum, 2011), 73. This book, whose text is in both English and Danish, was published parallel to an exhibition that carried the same title. The book and the exhibition were the results of my collaboration with visual artist Bettina Winkelmann and a joint research stay in Damascus in spring 2010. Both book and exhibition consisted of oil paintings and thought-images (in the exhibition written on white banners that hung alongside the paintings). The texts did not comment on the paintings, and the paintings did not illustrate the texts. Both the texts and the paintings were works in their own right, but they communicated with each other thanks to their common starting point in the aforementioned stay in Damascus and the understanding of reality reflected in the book's preface, which also served as the introduction to the exhibition.

127 Jørgensen, "Preface," 73. Translation modified.

128 Jørgensen, "Preface," 73. Translation modified.

just subjective, nor is it simply objective. Instead, it is a subjective actualization of objectively given potential for experience—a potential that constitutes a 'more' in the world, and is perceived as a poetic surplus in it. This is precisely why reality is ambiguous. It is both material and immaterial; the material is 'inhabited' by immateriality; the world is packed with potential to experience a surplus, also called beauty. Or rather, the *intermediate* world contains this potential for experience, and it is also where it is actualized, namely, when those experiences happen that the potential makes possible. Hence, in the intermediate world we are presented with something we ourselves did not create, but to whose appearance and activity we do contribute. We contribute without being subjects of what is happening, for in our receptivity we not only perceive potential not created by us; this reception is itself productive, as it *actualizes the potential as experience.*

World-Engaged Philosophy

I will gather together the inspiration from Benjamin and the idea of world poetry in an argument for 'world-engaged philosophy,' which is applicable, I think, to Vattimo's lifelong work as an intellectually responsible philosopher. Today, one often gets the impression that there are only two options: 'scholastic philosophy' and 'applied philosophy.' Scholastic philosophy clings in a reactionary way to the ivory tower, whereas applied philosophy relates opportunistically to current trends and demands, which it sees as an opportunity to escape the tower. But there is a third option as well: 'world-engaged philosophy,' which is philosophy that honors its own name by unfolding as free, open, and questioning thought, and which practices this *philosophia* in a contemporary way by being attentive to our experiences. World-engaged philosophy comprises an exploration of the experiences of oneself and others in a freely reflecting and thus openly questioning way. It tries to find and articulate the universal in the specific experience without losing sight of the uniqueness of what is individual, which requires both responsive reflection on the experience, and the courage to interpret. In this way, world-engaged philosophy contributes the most important thing philosophy can deliver, which is the understanding-seeking actualization of not-yet-actualized potential for interpretation, and the critical perspectivization of the existent—a truism-subversive reflection—constituted by this actualization.

The concept of basic experience contributes to the practice of world-engaged philosophy, however theoretical the concept itself is. The idea of a dialogue between sensation, faith, and comprehension at the level of basic experience implies that *art, religion*, and *thought* are ontologically linked, despite their historical divorce caused by the modernization process. Art, religion, and thought are products of different aspects of a common experiential spring, that is, *sensation, faith*, and *comprehension*, which explains why many concrete experiences of a surplus of meaning are often categorized as both religious and aesthetic. It also explains the ease with which not only the beautiful but also the true and the good were previously referred to using the same terminology, that is, the terminology of the philosophy of beauty. Indeed, God was not only true and good but also beautiful; he was the unity of the true, the good, and the beautiful manifested in his beauty, which was thus *not* allegorical. Furthermore, the concept of 'basic experience' and the philosophy of experience, within which it is conceived, make it possible to contribute to various disciplines and professions, for example, the study of art, theology, and the philosophy of science, and both practical and philosophical pedagogy, in ways that facilitate dialogue across borders that are otherwise apparently insurmountable. Over time, much effort has been wasted on arguing in a hierarchy-producing way for the prevailing status of belief or understanding, compared to feeling and sensation, thus fortifying the borders drawn by modernity. In contrast, the philosophy of experience from which I have now lifted the veil a little appeals to an exploration of the dialogue between art, religion, and thought, which human existence invites thanks to the equiprimordial relationship between sensation, faith, and comprehension, and the dialogue unfolding in experience.

Theory and Praxis

After the publication of *The Responsibility of the Philosopher*, Vattimo and Santiago Zabala committed themselves to what they call 'hermeneutic communism.' This commitment not only shows that Vattimo's work as a philosopher remains world-engaged. It also reveals how closely connected theory and praxis are to him, and it agrees with my own view that theory in the sense of thought is a practice in itself. In *Hermeneutic Communism*, Vattimo and Zabala differentiate between the weak and those in power, not between the weak and the strong, for the weak are strong thanks to the "weak thought" they share with their hermeneutic communist allies.[129] Those in power encompass the owners of capital as well as ruling politicians and 'professionals'; in *Hermeneutic Communism*, the latter are identical to the majority of university philosophers. Those in power lean on the metaphysics they reproduce and refer to in order to legitimize their exercise of power. This metaphysics is the notion that reality is identical to the given, which epistemologically means that reality is limited to what can be known scientifically. In the perspective of the philosophy of history, it also means that the past could not have been any different and that the future is predictable, as per the 'policy of necessity' and the current absence of alternative future scenarios. According to Vattimo and Zabala, this "metaphysical realism" is an expression of the fact that the people in power are not *thinking*, as well as being the reason why they are not thinking, for to think is not to act or to describe, but to interpret.[130] However, interpretations change the interpreted, and thought thus has a practical effect—not only as theory put into practice but also precisely as *thought*. Thought changes the world by interpreting it; according to Vattimo and Zabala, it is therefore pointless to criticize hermeneutics for being conservative. Hermeneutics is rather anarchic thanks to the 'recovery' of metaphysical realism that it provides by being interpretive—a recovery con-

---

129   See Gianni Vattimo and Santiago Zabala, *Hermeneutic Communism: From Heidegger to Marx* (New York: Columbia University Press, 2011), 2.

130   Vattimo and Zabala, *Hermeneutic Communism*, 7–8.

stituting the 'strong weakening' that hermeneutics shares with the weak, to whom the given is never a matter of course but a constant challenge.[131]

In accordance with this understanding of the relationship between theory and praxis, Vattimo and Zabala have not formulated a political program for subsequent translation into political action. Their preparation of *Hermeneutic Communism* is a political act in itself, insofar as the book manifests the hermeneutics it deals with: an interpretive rather than descriptive and thus not conservative but recovering way of thinking. Furthermore, their book is also political in the sense that, being a manifestation of such interpretive and, therefore, critical thought, it tries to awaken and release the potential for something similar *outside* the book itself—in its readers and in society. According to *Hermeneutic Communism*, it is also generally the case that the task of thought is *not* to provide programs and action instructions available for a praxis that is thus exhibited as thoughtless and 'theoriebedürftig.' On the contrary, the task is to mobilize the political power that thought itself constitutes—to mobilize it in favor of releasing the potential for thinking that the practical world offers, incarnated in the weak (understood both as the oppressed groups of society and as that which is overlooked because it is marginalized by the prevailing view). Such a reflectively provided release of the reflective potential of society is the way to recover metaphysical realism, and this recovery is a prerequisite for the ability to articulate alternative future scenarios, and thus also to encourage something else than what is promoted by the policy of necessity. Hence, there is no need for new theory

---

131 Heidegger distinguished between *überkommen* (getting over in the sense of leaving something behind) and *verwinden* (getting over in the sense of coming to terms with it). The latter is translated 'recovering.' According to Heidegger, metaphysics (the predominant ontological structures) will not disappear, but perhaps recover (that is, recover from itself, from the oblivion of its own essence as metaphysics). See Martin Heidegger, "On the Question of Being," trans. W. McNeill, in *Pathmarks*, ed. W. McNeill (Cambridge, UK: Cambridge University Press, 1998), 313ff. The 'recovering' introduced by Heidegger is what Vattimo and Zabala describe as a 'weakening': "Only once we recognize how metaphysics cannot be overcome in the sense of *überwunden*, defeating and leaving at large, but only in the sense of *verwindung*, that is, incorporating, twisting, or weakening, does it become possible to change the world." (*Hermeneutic Communism*, 1.)

seen as a basis for another practice, but there is a need to think differently—then practice will also change, because thought itself is practical. Thought is even the crucial practice. It determines the future, because the way in which we think defines the limits of what we can imagine, and thus also of what we do.

'Samtale' or 'Konversation'

If the attempt of hermeneutic communism to free the political power of thought is to be truly world-engaged, it is not enough, however, that the hermeneutic thinker conceptualizes this option. He must also listen to the thought expressed in the thinking articulated by the weak. So in order to be world-engaged, hermeneutic communism must be *dialogical*, but that is also the precondition for it being *hermeneutical*. Or as Vattimo writes in *The Responsibility of the Philosopher*: "The only emancipation I can conceive is an eternal life in charity, a life of heeding others and responding to others in dialogue."[132]

Nevertheless, Vattimo has also opposed dialogue, supposedly fearing that it dominates all conflict thanks to an inherent will to consensus.[133] However, it is wrong to link dialogue with harmonism. Literary history informs us that dialogue is related to the philosophical essay, and that they are both distinguished by being polyphonic media for the searching reflection called 'aesthetic' by Kant and Baumgarten. Both the dialogue and the essay are thus open forms that do not merely explain what they treat but want to understand it. They not only describe and determine it but also explore and interpret it, and as explained previously, interpretation is a critical practice. Interpretation is critical both in the sense of the word articulated by Kant—its quest for understanding implies a study of the limits of understanding—and in the sense highlight-

132 Vattimo, *The Responsibility of the Philosopher*, 97.

133 An opinion of this kind was expressed by Vattimo in the discussion following my presentation "The Dialogue of Experience" at the conference "Effetti d'interpretazione" (Effects of Interpretation) at the University of Turin, March 16–17, 2016.

ed in *Hermeneutic Communism*: interpretation is 'metaphysics-recovering,' which means that it sides with the weak by definition. When someone sides against those in power, there is *not* just peace and harmony. Understood as a medium of the interpretive practice represented by the common thinking practiced through dialogue, the dialogue challenges the powerful, and it does not only allow for the critical element missed by Vattimo. The dialogue is itself a source of criticism.

The dialogue is the aforementioned source; it is also a framework for and a manifestation of critical thought, and it is a critical counterimage: a listening—offering time, ear, and understanding—that does *not* distinguish the current procedural democracy, but without which democracies are not democratic. It is not in dialogue but in conversation and in conversational democracy that the will to consensus threatens to dominate everything conflictual and to blur power relations. In Danish, the English word 'conversation' can be translated both as 'samtale' and as 'konversation,' and these two words have different connotations. This duality is revealing; it points out both the gift and the risk associated with conversation. The term 'samtale' is used for serious exchanges between people: schools invite parents to parents' evenings known as 'school–home samtaler,' psychiatrists have developed 'samtaler' for the relatives of their patients, and pastors offer 'pastoral care samtaler.' These 'samtaler' fail if they are not dialogical, but the same cannot be said of 'konversationer.' On the contrary, 'konversationer' tend to be monological, regardless of the number of participants, and they become something else, namely 'samtaler,' if they become dialogical. As an example of a 'konversation,' one might think of the small talk taking place around a dinner table at which people who are strangers to each other are seated. At such a table there is not only the risk of monological self-promotion, but also of monologue that in addition to being empty and noncommittal is conflict-avoiding. That is precisely the danger of democracy: that it descends into 'konversation.' This risk is not hypothetical but real—it is known from the 'aestheticization' of politics that has blurred the difference between talk show and political debate by staging the debate as a show. In the show the participants yell and use big gestures, they swear, insinuate, and offer lewd comments, but none of them take any of it seriously, and they all cloud the real conflicts. The show is harmless and does not change the world because it is devoid of dialogue and thus of thinking.

Democracy as Event

When philosophers are intellectual rather than professional, they practice world-engaged philosophy, not scholastic philosophy or applied philosophy. Intellectual philosophers do not just describe the world but interpret it, and according to *The Responsibility of the Philosopher* dialogue is the way to achieve the kind of emancipation that is driven by interpretation, because interpretation recovers the metaphysical realism discussed in *Hermeneutic Communism*. Dialogues are open and polyphonic thanks to the searching reflection by which they are constituted; so dialogue is the medium of interpretive thinking. But in the words of Kant and Baumgarten, this means that the reflection unfolding in dialogue is 'aesthetic' rather than 'determining.' Intellectual philosophers think *aesthetically*, whereas the professionals' descriptive monologues simply identify observed phenomena without reflecting upon them.

The foregoing confirms the interpretation of hermeneutics previously alluded to. I am referring to my interpretation presented in *Den skønne tænkning*, according to which hermeneutics is *not* the alternative to aesthetics that hermeneutic philosophers present it to be. Like hermeneutic phenomenology (Heidegger), philosophical hermeneutics (Gadamer) is a 'reinvention' of philosophical aesthetics. This statement does not reflect a diminution of phenomenology and hermeneutics; in *Den skønne tænkning*, the word 'reinvention' is not used in a pejorative way. Instead, the point is that the hermeneutic phenomenology and philosophical hermeneutics of the twentieth century neither simply dismissed eighteenth-century philosophical aesthetics nor merely repeated it. Phenomenology and hermeneutics actualized aesthetics on the historical conditions with which twentieth-century thought was presented. According to *Den skønne tænkning*, there is thus greater kinship among aesthetics, phenomenology, and hermeneutics than phenomenology and hermeneutics have recognized and acknowledged; but the book also shows that aesthetics was changed by its reinvention. The latter means, inter alia, that it was in a desubjectivized form that aesthetic thinking had a 'comeback.' Unlike in the eighteenth century, aesthetic thinking was no longer something done by a subject, but rather something happening to existence: it was actualized as *experience*, and the experience as *event*.

The responsiveness of the world-engaged philosopher must precisely serve the possibility that the event can happen—that genuine experience can occur, not only for the individual philosopher but also among people. World-engaged philosophers engage in dialogue with the outside world, but not to agree on what is right and wrong. Instead, they seek to hear the thought expressed in that which is articulated by the oppressed and the marginalized. They lend voice to the weak, but in recognition of their strength. Being responsive, the world-engaged philosopher creates space for the event—the happening kind of experience—that thought is if it is beautiful, that is, if it is free, open, and questioning. That is the task of the intellectual of our day: to create such spaces in a society that despite its formal democracy renders beautiful thinking, and thus genuine democracy, impossible because of metaphysical realism. Formal democracy is *not* a guarantee of genuine democracy. But democracy of the genuine and true kind occurs locally and momentarily as people listen in the aesthetic-sensitive way that allows them to hear the idea of what is said, and thus to apprehend the universal (as opposed to the general) that can be shared (because it both exceeds and retains what is individual). World-engaged philosophers who understand thought as the praxis it is, and who therefore listen and interpret rather than applying theories given in advance, draw magic circles around themselves and the participants of the dialogues they engage in. Together they and their interlocutors embody the democracy that is otherwise nonexistent, except as a caricature in contemporary media, parliaments, schools, and universities.

History as a Work

Aristotle is considered the first *literary* theorist, but his reflections in *Poetics* on the difference between poetry and history implies that he may also be considered the first theorist of *history*.[134] Aristotle's thoughts can even inspire a way of understanding and relating to history that challenges modern 'scientific' historiography. That is the reason this chapter has a point of departure in his *Poetics*. Through a creative interpretation of Aristotle's reflections on poetry and history, I will contribute a revision of what it means to be a historian.[135] It will appear that the modern philosophy of history, including Immanuel Kant's, can be interpreted as an expression of a *poetized* understanding of history. I will also show that Friedrich Nietzsche's critique of the philosophy of history was philosophico-historical itself, as well as demonstrating the poetic element in his different philosophical approach to history. With Nietzsche, we will draw closer to Walter Benjamin, who urged historians to remember the possibilities suppressed by 'historical progress,' and who practiced such a historiography himself. His works give a hint

---

134   Aristotle, *Poetics*, trans. I. Bywater, in *The Complete Works of Aristotle: The Revised Oxford Translation, Volume 2*, ed. J. Barnes (Princeton: Princeton University Press, 1984).

135   This interpretation is based partly on the chapters "Historien som værk" (History as a Work) and "Historieværket i dag" (The Contemporary Work of History) in Dorthe Jørgensen, *Historien som værk: Værkets historie* (History as a Work: The Work's History) (Aarhus: Aarhus University Press, 2006), but it is also based on Dorthe Jørgensen, *Den skønne tænkning: Veje til erfaringsmetafysik. Religionsfilosofisk udmøntet* (Beautiful Thinking: Pathways to the Metaphysics of Experience. Religio-Philosophically Implemented) (Aarhus: Aarhus University Press, 2014), for example, the chapter "Poetisk sprog" (Poetic Language).

of what it may mean for us to take the aesthetic dimension of history seriously.

A Creative Idea

Homer was 'marvelously superior,' according to Aristotle's *Poetics*, for he not only recounted history; he gave it a poetic form.[136] However, Aristotle did not have the same understanding of poetry as his predecessors. Plato and other Greeks regarded poetry as divinely inspired, and to them poetry was thus not 'art,' that is, 'a product of craftsmanship.' It is true that Plato's *Symposium* teaches that "everything that is responsible for creating something out of nothing is a kind of poetry; and so all the creations of every craft and profession are themselves a kind of poetry, and everyone who practices a craft is a poet."[137] However, this does not mean that art and poetry were the same to Plato. On the contrary, it is a reflection of the fact that the Greek word *poiesis* denoted not only poetry but also *generation*. According to Plato, all art was of a generating nature in the sense that all art was "responsible for creating something out of nothing." Nevertheless, only poetry was *defined* by being generative and was thus called 'poiesis,' whereas art was craft by definition; likewise, poetry had a muse, but art did not.

Aristotle also used the word 'poiesis' as a designation for generation, but in *Poetics* he treated poetry as a *genre*. Moreover, unlike Plato, Aristotle did not consider poetry divinely inspired; he thought of it as a human creation, that is, 'art.' Nevertheless, Aristotle described Homer's poetry as marvelous, but that was not because Homer was *inspired*; it was because he was *knowledgeable*, that is, because of his skills. Furthermore, Homer's superiority was not caused by the fact that he wrote poetry rather than prose, but was due to what distinguished poetry compared to historiography.

---

136   Aristotle, *Poetics*, 23, 1459a 30–32.

137   Plato, *Symposium*, trans. A. Nehamas and P. Woodruff, in *Plato: Complete Works*, eds. J.M. Cooper and D.S. Hutchinson (Indianapolis and Cambridge, MA: Hackett Publishing Company, 1997), 205b–c.

According to Aristotle, the historian describes "the thing that has happened," whereas the poet describes "a kind of thing that might happen."[138] The historian makes use of a simple form of imitation by which he tries to copy empirical history, whereas the poet does not describe "the thing that has happened, but a kind of thing that might happen, that is, what is possible as being probable or necessary."[139] This is the reason why Aristotle thought of poetry as "something more philosophic and of graver import than history, since its statements are of the nature rather of universals, whereas those of history are singulars."[140]

In empirical history, many things happen without having a common goal, both simultaneously and one after another in time. As the historian imitates empirical history, he thus deals "not with one action, but with one period and all that happened in that to one or more persons, however disconnected the several events might have been."[141] The historian reproduces the events as they appear, and therefore his own report, too, is without internal consistency. Hence, in Aristotle's view the historical records did not qualify as organic units and could not arouse catharsis; therefore they could not be a model for narrative poetry, which instead should look to tragedy. Like tragedy, the epos should be based on "a single action, one that is a complete whole in itself," so that it could have a purifying effect.[142] That is what Homer achieved, and therefore he was distinguished by marvelous superiority compared both to other poets and to historians.[143]

For Aristotle, the advantages of poetry did not mean that historiography should cease, or that historians should write in a dif-

---

138 Aristotle, *Poetics*, 9, 1451a 37.

139 Aristotle, *Poetics*, 9, 1451a 36–38.

140 Aristotle, *Poetics*, 9, 1451b 5–7.

141 Aristotle, *Poetics*, 23, 1459a 21–24.

142 Aristotle, *Poetics*, 23, 1459a 20.

143 Aristotle, *Poetics*, 23, 1459a 30–32.

ferent way. The consequence was rather that historiography could not be regarded as a *science*; it was not sufficiently philosophical for that, which meant not sufficiently universal. The reason for this was that Aristotle thought of theoretical science, that is philosophy, as the very definition of science. Philosophy strove for 'wisdom,' which meant broad and universal knowledge, whereas the knowledge contained in historical accounts was of a specific and circumscribed character: it was 'empirical.' If we ourselves relate creatively to Aristotle's reflections on poetry and history, it can, however, inspire something other than a discussion about how little or how much insight can be gained through history writing. His thoughts can spur an idea that is contrary to his own understanding, but is a possible consequence, namely the idea that the historian must follow the poet's example and poetize historiography.

If the historian actually learns from the poet, she does not strive to describe everything minutely, and nor does she boil it all down to a short summary. On the contrary, she highlights individual parts of history like Homer did in his poems. Furthermore, the historian presents the individual episodes so that they hang together organically, and she applies the same principle in her structuring of her overall report. In this way empirical history is subject to *interpretation*, just as tragedy interpreted myth through its dramatic organization of mythical material. The historian's interpretation appears in the form of the inner consistency achieved by history when it is given a poetic form, and the result is *wisdom*: empirical history appears in a transfigured light, just like life did in tragedy's interpretation of myth.

The Necessary Guiding Thread

If historiography is poetized in the manner described, it will be more philosophical, because poetry is philosophically disposed by nature, as Aristotle said. Such a poetizing of historiography leads into the philosophy of history, if we let this notion mean 'to regard history in a thinking way.' Hence, we may interpret Kant's philosophy of history, for example, as an expression of what I have proposed, namely that the historian follows the poet's example. Thanks to an element of 'poetic' construction in the historiography recommended by Kant, he articulated a way of considering history that transcends the immediate chaos of events. His philosophy of history can thus be said to draw the alternative (that is, Aristotle-transgressive) consequence of Aristotle's reflections on the relationship between poetry and history I have suggested. This is my message in what follows.

Both Kant's aesthetics and his philosophy of history were generated by a problem that resulted from his criticism of metaphysics: that the world previously hanging together in one metaphysical system fell apart into several different systems. Traditional metaphysics found it possible to identify a metaphysical ground of unity that bound the world together. Kant rejected all metaphysical evidence for such a ground, however, and he made God a pure idea of reason (a 'practical postulate' understood as a precondition for all morality). Kant's claim was not that there is no unity (or God), but that it cannot be recognized if it exists, and thus cannot function as a metaphysical guarantor. Furthermore, Kant split the metaphysical system into two independent and unconnected systems in terms of nature and morality, thus really letting the world of traditional metaphysics fall apart. However, thanks to this fragmentation the issue of unity forced itself even more to the front—as a question of whether there were after all some signs of unity, a question of whether humans themselves could create such unity, and a question about the necessity of unity.

In order to spot consistency in history, which now appeared not only fragmented but downright meaningless, Kant found it necessary to subject history to philosophical consideration. Regarding history in a philosophical way means, according to Kant, that one tries to discover a 'natural intention' in it; that one looks for reason understood as an order, a purpose, or a plan in history with the effect that it is not just a series of events, but develops appropriately. Only if history appears in this way does philosophy have a chance of saying anything sensible about it, Kant thought. If history is to be subjected to philosophical reflection, it must therefore appear to follow some kind of natural law: that historical events happen thanks to the providence of nature. However, history can only appear like this if philosophy tries to find a *guiding thread* in it, understood as a leading idea, an intention of reason, or a higher purpose. Philosophy must thus subject history to construction in order to be able to relate to it. Philosophy only has access to history as it appears to philosophy, not as it is in itself, and to philosophy, history is always already a product of the presentation of the universal that characterizes philosophy itself. Or, as Kant himself wrote: the guiding thread that is indispensable in a philosophical view of history serves for "exhibiting an otherwise planless *aggregate* of human actions, at least in the large, as a *system*."[144]

Aristotle did not demand a poetizing of historiography, though he put poetry higher than history. Likewise, Kant did not wish to change the métier of the historian, though he wanted people to consider history philosophically. "That with this idea of a world history, which in a certain way has a guiding thread *a priori*, I would want to displace the treatment of history proper, that is written merely *empirically*—this would be a misinterpretation of my aim."[145] Kant's philosophy of history was thus "only a thought of that which a philosophical mind (which besides this would have to be very well versed in history) could attempt from another standpoint."[146] The actualization of the idea of the historian as poet, which Kant's notion of the thread-seeking philosopher may be interpreted as, did not result in a defense of speculative-poetic excesses in historiography. On the contrary, directed polemically against Johann Gottfried Herder, Kant wrote that "yet to let a history *arise* simply and solely from conjectures does not seem much better than to make the draft for a novel. Indeed, it would not be

---

144   Immanuel Kant, "Idea for a Universal History with a Cosmopolitan Aim," trans. A.W. Wood, in *Anthropology, History, and Education*, eds. G. Zöller and R.B. Louden (New York: Cambridge University Press, 2007), 118 (8: 29).

145   Kant, "Idea for a Universal History with a Cosmopolitan Aim," 119 (8: 30).

146   Kant, "Idea for a Universal History with a Cosmopolitan Aim," 119–120 (8: 30).

able to support the name of a 'conjectural history,' but rather that of a mere *fiction*."¹⁴⁷

According to Kant, one must not only expect that it is impossible to execute empirical 'scientific' historiography on the flimsy basis that poetry forms. Poetry is also an insufficient basis for a sound philosophy of history. However, Kant had difficulties getting away from the fact that there *is* something poetic about the philosophico-historical type of account he suggested. On the edge of self-discovery, he thus wrote that "it is, to be sure, a strange and apparently an absurd stroke, to want to write a *history* in accordance with an idea of how the course of the world would have to go if it were to conform to certain rational ends; it appears that with such an aim only a *novel* could be brought about."¹⁴⁸ Similarly, he argued that the philosophical view of history is allowed to add and subtract as it best benefits the necessary guiding thread. "In the *progression* of a history it is indeed allowed to *insert* conjectures in order to fill up gaps in the records, because what precedes as a remote cause and what follows as an effect can provide a quite secure guidance for the discovery of the intermediate causes, so as to make the transition comprehensible."¹⁴⁹

Compared to empirical historiography the philosophico-historical approach thus implies *interpretation*, but interpretation is always also *poetry*.¹⁵⁰ An interpretive view of history relates to it in a composing way; it is creative, as it recreates history while retelling it. In this way, in the form of *philosophy of history* historiography became *poetry*. The idea of the thread-seeking philosopher of history brought historiography closer to narration and hence

---

147   Immanuel Kant, "Conjectural Beginning of Human History," trans. A.W. Wood, in *Anthropology, History, and Education*, eds. G. Zöller and R.B. Louden (New York: Cambridge University Press, 2007), 163 (8: 109).

148   Kant, "Idea for a Universal History with a Cosmopolitan Aim," 118 (8: 29).

149   Kant, "Conjectural Beginning of Human History," 163 (8: 109).

150   The meaning of this is not that there is no interpretation involved in empirical historiography. But here we enter another discussion concerning whether a so-called scientific approach is possible at all, and in what form it might be possible.

actualized the idea of the historian as poet. Kant's philosophy of history may thus be said to represent a 'poetizing' of historiography that was not intentional but was an integral part of his philosophico-historical answers to the problems generated by his critique of metaphysics.

The Aesthetic Roots of the Guiding Thread

The poetic quality of the thread-seeking philosopher of history can be profiled by an inclusion of Alexander Gottlieb Baumgarten's *Reflections on Poetry*.[151] In this work, poetry is presented as a type of recognition that is different from what is generally understood by cognition. According to Baumgarten, poetry is a source of 'sensitive cognition' different from 'intellectual cognition.'[152] More specifically, it is a source of *perfect* sensitive cognition, not least because of poetry's quality as "extensively clear," because of its "theme," and because of its "lucid method" (thanks to which the theme is manifested in the poem).[153]

Baumgarten found that poetry is rooted in sensitive discourse, which is characterized by a multiplicity of sensitive representations that themselves contain a variety of characteristic traits. All this diversity makes poetic language lively, and this vivacity is conducive to our knowledge of sensitive representations. The wealth of detail in poetic language gives an idea about something to which the abstract language of science does not provide access, namely the concrete. But these details are also the reason why Baumgarten's contemporaries called poetic language 'confused' and did not attribute any independent cognitive value to it. Howev-

---

[151] Alexander Gottlieb Baumgarten, *Reflections on Poetry: Meditationes philosophicae de nonnullis ad poema pertinentibus*, trans. K. Aschenbrenner and W.B. Holther (Berkeley and Los Angeles: University of California Press, 1954).

[152] In *Aesthetica* (Aesthetics) Baumgarten systematically developed his notion of 'sensitive cognition.' See Alexander Gottlieb Baumgarten, *Ästhetik, Volume 1–2*, trans. D. Mirbach (Hamburg: Felix Meiner Verlag, 2007).

[153] Baumgarten, *Reflections on Poetry*, §§ XVI, LXVI, and LXX. From *Ästhetik*, § 14, it appears that the perfection of sensitive cognition is the purpose of aesthetics.

er, Baumgarten did not regard this so-called confusion as a defect or a shortcoming. According to him, intellectual cognition is characterized by an *intense* clarity that is due to its distinctness; similarly, sensitive cognition is distinguished by its own *extensive* clarity, which is due to its wealth of details.[154] This extensive clarity and related vivacity is the prerequisite for our recognition through the poem of something to which intensively clear science does not give access. For the sake of distinctness, science makes it a virtue to include only a few distinct characteristic traits. In science, it is problematic to connect much without clear distinction, but in poetry, it is vice versa.[155] Poetry tries to evoke a density of various interconnected characteristic traits by portraying the singular in specific circumstances instead of expressing itself in general terms.[156]

However, according to Baumgarten, poems are characterized not only by a wealth of details, but also by unity or more precisely by *unity in diversity*. This duality of unity and diversity is the reason why poems are not just sensitive discourse, but perfected versions of that discourse. For the same reason, Baumgarten not only thought that it is poetic to determine things represented in a poem as much as possible, that is: to be concrete.[157] It is also poetic to gather many representations, and this sampling is actually what is poetic.[158] According to Baumgarten, this connection of representations is established through the poem's theme, which is the unity of the poem or what creates unity in it.[159] The theme links the many sensitive representations, the interrelationships, and the signifying words, and it thus also distinguishes between what must and what must not be included in the poem. Without the theme there

---

154 Baumgarten, *Reflections on Poetry*, § XVI.

155 Baumgarten, *Reflections on Poetry*, §§ XVI–XVIII.

156 Baumgarten, *Reflections on Poetry*, § XIX.

157 Baumgarten, *Reflections on Poetry*, § XVIII.

158 Baumgarten, *Reflections on Poetry*, § XVIII.

159 Baumgarten, *Reflections on Poetry*, §§ LXVIII and LXVI.

would only be diversity and thus only confusion, not unity in diversity. The elements of the poem must be related to the theme in order to be part of it, and in this way the poem acquires the organic structure that is a prerequisite for it to be a poem, not just sensitive discourse. The structure that is accomplished by the theme—the theme's organization of the poetic material—was named the 'lucid method' by Baumgarten, and the goal of this method is to let the theme appear with an increasing degree of extensive clarity.[160]

What is poetic in poetry thus depends not only on concretion, but also on the element of abstraction resulting from the theme and its selection between and bonding of the poem's many elements. It is this duality of unity and diversity—or abstraction and concreteness, reflection and sensuousness—that is the reason a poem not only titillates and touches, but may also constitute a path to knowledge. In his argument for the cognitive value of poetry, Baumgarten thus approached Aristotle's eye for the element of universality in poetry, in Aristotle's case compared to historiography. Thanks to poetry's production of unity in diversity, poetry is both more philosophical than sensitive discourse, which is not perfected and therefore just piles up characteristic traits, and more philosophical than scientific discourse, which just generalizes. We have learned something similar about the thread-seeking philosophy of history described by Kant: that its 'poetic' grip on reality does not obscure, but rather sharpens vision.

Monumental Historiography

Much has happened since the days of Kant and Baumgarten. For example, Friedrich Nietzsche gave the philosophy of history and historicism a serious shot across the bows.[161] *"Only from the highest power of the present can you interpret the past*; only with the greatest

---

160   Baumgarten, *Reflections on Poetry*, §§ LXX–LXXI.

161   In English, the word 'historicism' basically denotes the idea that everything is historically determined, which means that all phenomena should be understood with reference to their historical context. In Nietzsche's time, historicism had become scientific in the sense that it would only deal with 'facts,' and it was this kind of historicism he criticized.

exertion of your noblest qualities will you divine what in the past is great and worth knowing and preserving," he wrote.[162] Nietzsche's approach to history meant that *aesthetic judgment* came into the focus of the philosophy of history, for according to Nietzsche the evaluation of history requires that one constructs a perspective on it, and this design is imaginative work. In his interpretation the very existence of perspectives is thus a sign that among all the 'noble qualities' of the human being it is aesthetic judgment that characterizes the human gaze—including on history. The 'powerful person' must take this condition up and cultivate it, for aesthetic judgment is also a prerequisite for what according to Nietzsche is the key, namely to *commit* oneself. It was because he demanded a committed historiography that he began his reflections on history with the following quote from Johann Wolfgang von Goethe: "Moreover, I hate everything that only instructs me without increasing or immediately stimulating my own activity."[163]

"We only wish to serve history to the extent that it serves life," wrote Nietzsche as well, and this can be done in three ways, namely in the form of "antiquarian," "critical," or "monumental" history.[164] The *antiquarian* account of history preserves and admires the past, thus serving life in so far as it represents a faithful and pietistic handling of tradition, by which one gives thanks for one's existence by conserving and passing on what one is strongly influenced by. However, this account of history degenerates if it is not animated and excited by today's fresh life, thereby revealing that it is subjective, arbitrary, and restricted. In that case piety withers and the handling of history becomes a "repugnant spectacle of a blind mania to collect, of a restless gathering together of everything that once existed."[165] Furthermore, the antiquarian account of history is

---

162 Friedrich Nietzsche, *On the Utility and Liability of History for Life*, trans. R.T. Gray, in *The Complete Works of Friedrich Nietzsche, Volume 2: Unfashionable Observations*, ed. E. Behler (Stanford: Stanford University Press, 1995), 129.

163 Nietzsche, *On the Utility and Liability of History for Life*, 85.

164 Nietzsche, *On the Utility and Liability of History for Life*, 85, 96.

165 Nietzsche, *On the Utility and Liability of History for Life*, 105.

dangerous if it stifles the other two kinds of historical account, for it "understands only how to *preserve* life, not how to create it; therefore, it always underestimates those things that are in the process of becoming because it has no divining instinct."[166]

The *critical* account of history, in turn, is exercised by suffering people in need of liberation. It serves life by breaking and dissolving a past, which the critic manages by "bringing this past before a tribunal, painstakingly interrogating it, and finally condemning it."[167] Such an approach is needed but it may also degenerate, in which case one loses sight of what is worth preserving. However, such a sight is not lacking in the *monumental* account of history exercised by active and aspiring human beings. This account of history is creative and as such interpretive, which however also means that it risks becoming myth. If the monumental account of history dominates the antiquarian and the critical accounts, the image of the past can become distorted, and if exercised by persons who are not able to create anything significant, its highlighting of the great in the past may hamper the new. But as far as people who truly know how to create something great are in need of the past, it is monumental history through which they seize it. Such persons, whom Nietzsche also refers to as "strong artistic spirits," are the only ones who are really able to learn from monumental history, and their way of seeing history is the most important because it serves life the most.[168]

According to Aristotle, the organic unity generated by the poet's poetic formation of the material is what distinguishes the form of tragedy. This form is the product of a construction that is based on the presence of a theme, as shown by Baumgarten. In an Aristotelian view, the poetic formation of the material implies that the result is more universal and thus also more philosophical than that which is not poetically formed and therefore not shaped as

---

166   Nietzsche, *On the Utility and Liability of History for Life*, 106.

167   Nietzsche, *On the Utility and Liability of History for Life*, 106.

168   Nietzsche, *On the Utility and Liability of History for Life*, 100–101.

a work—which was also confirmed by the poetics of Baumgarten. However, while Kant considered the guiding thread he referred to as something the philosopher must discover in history, Nietzsche perceived the perspective created by the powerful person, with which she forms history, as something she herself must invent. Nevertheless, both the word 'thread' and the word 'perspective' signified something that, in analogy to the theme mentioned by Baumgarten, structures and thus interprets the empirical historical facts. Like the thread-seeking philosophy of history discussed by Kant, the monumental historiography discussed by Nietzsche was thus an expression of a *poetizing* of the understanding of history and thus also of a *philosophical* understanding of it. Despite Nietzsche's reluctance regarding the philosophy of history, his own understanding of history—his tribute to the powerful person's aesthetic formation of history—was an expression of this philosophy's recognition of itself as construction, instead of being an end to all philosophy of history. However, this 'rescue' of the philosophy of history was not intentional. According to Nietzsche, previous historiography merely accumulated knowledge and had a paralyzing effect. Consequently, this kind of history should be exposed to antidotes in the form of the *ahistorical* and the *suprahistorical*.[169] The ahistorical was the art and power to forget and to enclose oneself in a limited horizon, whereas the suprahistorical was the powers that lead the attention from becoming to being. However, these powers directing attention to what lends existence the character of something eternal and stable in meaning were, according to Nietzsche, art and religion, and thus again we return to fantasy, imagination, and aesthetic judgment.[170]

The Angel of History

Following Nietzsche, Walter Benjamin rejected the Enlightenment's idea of progress and historicism's 'the way it really was,' but

169   Nietzsche, *On the Utility and Liability of History for Life*, 163.

170   Nietzsche, *On the Utility and Liability of History for Life*, 163.

continued the philosophico-historical tradition of subjecting history to thought. Benjamin also shared the view that there is a need for history in a form that serves life, but to him this meant that the past should only be maintained as the possibility of true knowledge represented by the volatile memory image. In his "On the Concept of History" it thus appears that he regarded history as an image marked by "Jetztzeit" and "dialectics at a standstill," in which past and present enter into a relation that does not develop, but leaps forth.[171] "The true image of the past flits by. The past can be seized only as an image that flashes up at the moment of its recognizability, and is never seen again."[172] This image is a testimony that "the past carries with it a secret index by which it is referred to redemption."[173] In accordance with this, we are "endowed with a *weak* messianic power, a power on which the past has a claim" and which obliges us to catch the image on the fly.[174]

Benjamin's idea of a secret index tells us that he did not regard history as one-dimensional, but as characterized by rupture and continuity. It consists of the big History that is continuous, as well as the ruptures of this History represented by the many not-yet-actualized possibilities. The secret index, which the past carries with it, is a register of these possibilities and thus a reminder that history could have turned out differently. Our innate messianic power, in turn, is our ability to remember, including not least our ability to interpret history's secret index, and the claim of the past

---

171 Walter Benjamin, "On the Concept of History," trans. H. Zohn, in *Selected Writings, Volume 4: 1938–1940*, eds. H. Eiland and M.W. Jennings (Cambridge, MA and London: The Belknap Press of Harvard University Press, 2003), 395. Harry Zohn translates 'Jetztzeit' as 'now-time.' Concerning Benjamin's notion of the 'dialectics at a standstill,' see Walter Benjamin, "[N3,1]," in *The Arcades Project*, trans. H. Eiland and K. McLaughlin (Cambridge, MA and London: The Belknap Press of Harvard University Press, 2002), 462–463.

172 Walter Benjamin, "On the Concept of History," 390. Perhaps Benjamin is elaborating on a remark by Hegel in his *The Philosophy of History*: "Historiographers bind together the fleeting elements of story, and treasure them up for immortality in the Temple of Mnemosyne." See Georg Wilhelm Friedrich Hegel, *The Philosophy of History*, trans. J. Sibree (Mineola: Dover Publications, 2004), 1–2.

173 Benjamin, "On the Concept of History," 390.

174 Benjamin, "On the Concept of History," 390.

to this power means that we not only can but also should use our ability to remember and actualize the not-yet-actualized possibilities. According to Benjamin, history is thus not static nor in its final shape, but can be rewritten. The past can be 'rescued' by actualizing what is recorded in the secret index.[175] However, we must perform this rescue not for the sake of the past, but for the sake of the future, for as pointed out previously, there is only a need for history of a kind that serves life, and therefore not for the antiquarian type of historiography, which simply preserves the past.

This understanding of history is the background to Benjamin's famous depiction of "the angel of history" in his thesis IX.[176] The angel's gaze is marked by progress, the "storm ... blowing from Paradise," which against the will of the angel throws it forward in history, but the angel wishes to return in order to stay, awaken the dead, and make whole what has been smashed.[177] For where "a chain of events appears before *us, he* sees one single catastrophe, which keeps piling wreckage upon wreckage and hurls it at his feet."[178] If the angel defies the storm and pursues its hermeneutical aspiration—if it returns to stay, awaken the dead, and make whole what was smashed—it will be a historian of another kind than the Enlightenment philosophers and the historicists. For it is not the idea of progress that is the angel's guiding thread, and the angel's sense of the barbarism of history prevents it from relying on empathy. As a historian, the angel does not want to render history as we know it, but to interpret it innovatively, thus creating a new history. It wants to actualize the not-yet-actualized possibilities that hide in the pile of debris at its feet, giving shape to a new narrative about what could have happened instead of what historically did happen. The angel will dust off *hope* as it throws critical light on the

---

175   The idea of rescuing refers to the method of the treatise (that is, of philosophy) described in Walter Benjamin, *The Origin of German Tragic Drama*, trans. J. Osborne (London and New York: Verso, 2009), 27–29.

176   Benjamin, "On the Concept of History," 392.

177   Benjamin, "On the Concept of History," 392.

178   Benjamin, "On the Concept of History," 392.

established narrative and shows that much could have been different. This 'rescuing hermeneutics' is Benjamin's recipe for an adequate historiography. The historian must decipher and interpret the pile of debris lying at her feet. Rather than filing historical data, she must read and interpret "an irretrievable image of the past which threatens to disappear in any present that does not recognize itself as intended in that image."[179] This hermeneutic practice forms a work, but it does not result in a work of the *classical* kind. When not-yet-actualized possibilities are actualized, consistency is created and meaning is established in an otherwise meaningless history; but rather than idealizing the past, the idea of this 'rescue' is to atone for the sins of men by actualizing the possibilities they missed.

It was the barbarism of history that made Benjamin reject the "empathetic historiography" of historicism and instead require that history be "brushed against the grain."[180] The historian must renounce the introverted form of observation so characteristic of historicism.[181] Simply retelling history is neither meaningful nor morally just, because history has not adjusted itself in accordance with "the idea of happiness."[182] According to Benjamin, the epic element of history is the contemplative way of relating to it; historiography therefore needs to abandon traditional narration. While historicism delivered the everlasting image of the past, the point is now rather to give an immediate experience of the potential future represented by not-yet-actualized possibilities. The task is to liberate the energies bound up in historicism's idea of "the way it really was," which requires that one bursts historicism's continuum of "empty time," and the method consists of replacing the epic

---

179 Benjamin, "On the Concept of History," 391.

180 Benjamin, "On the Concept of History," 391, 392.

181 Benjamin, "Eduard Fuchs, Collector and Historian," trans. H. Eiland and M.W. Jennings, on the basis of a prior translation by K. Tarnowski, in *Selected Writings, Volume 3: 1935–1938*, eds. H. Eiland and M.W. Jennings (Cambridge, MA and London: The Belknap Press of Harvard University Press, 2002), 262–263.

182 Benjamin, "On the Concept of History," 389.

aspect of historiography with construction.[183] This is necessary both in order to wrest the not-yet-actualized possibilities free of the pile of debris, and because modern people are in danger of losing their ability to exchange experiences. Today, most of us relate to the world in an 'impressionistic' way and therefore do not understand the epic discourse of experience. We are trained to administer shock-inducing stimuli, but not to reflect.[184] If the historical presentation is to have an effect, it must therefore take advantage of the *alienating effect* that is expected from construction. It must cause a shock, but of a kind that we have not learned to parry. The presentation must force us to think by turning conventional notions upside down. According to Benjamin, this can be done by focusing on the particular, which does *not* imply that all notions of consistency are abandoned. Benjamin did not focus on the particular in order to worship it, but rather to locate the universal in it. The historian must study concrete works wrested free of singular lives taken from specific eras that are blasted out of the homogeneous course of history. However, the goal of this approach is to show that "the lifework is both preserved and sublated *in* the work, the era *in* the lifework, and the entire course of history *in* the era."[185] Disseminated through the epoch and the lifework, the larger historical course can be studied in the small concrete work; that is what Benjamin intended.

History and Obstinacy

If one follows Benjamin's request, the historical work may assume a form shown by some of his own books, for example, *Berlin Child-*

---

183   Benjamin, "On the Concept of History," 391, 395–396.

184   In "Experience and Poverty" Benjamin discusses a historical loss of experience caused by an increasingly weaker ability to reflect on one's impressions. See Walter Benjamin, "Experience and Poverty," trans. R. Livingstone, in *Selected Writings, Volume 2: 1927–1934*, eds. M.W. Jennings, H. Eiland, and G. Smith (Cambridge, MA and London: The Belknap Press of Harvard University Press, 2001).

185   Benjamin, "On the Concept of History," 396.

hood around 1900 or *The Arcades Project*.[186] The result is not large epic narratives, but collections of small fragments or thought-images. This splintering of the classic form of the work and the related expectation of alienation reveals Benjamin's kinship with the artists of his time. However, unlike many of those artists Benjamin reinterpreted the form of the work rather than abandoning the work as such. His willingness to give history shape as a work meant that he did not sacrifice all notions of consistency, though he replaced epic with construction and thus with montage. With this came meaningfulness, because the approach used by Benjamin was not just about studying the universal in the particular. It was also a way to make sense of the senseless by locating an idea in the world of phenomena or something transcendent in the immanent.

Oskar Negt's and Alexander Kluge's *History and Obstinacy* may be mentioned as another example of an alternative kind of historiography.[187] In this impressive work, Negt and Kluge trace the history that is stamped in the body, thought, labor, all behavior, and all ways of relating. They show how the abilities developed by human beings at an early stage as well as those acquired at a later date have arisen historically and come into conflict with one another, because the current organization of man is contrary to human nature's oldest senses. However, Negt and Kluge also show that these senses are not just subject to oppression but are also a source of hope, because in them the attentive historian may decipher a possible organization of a better future. Since the rise of capitalism, the social organization of human labor skills has occurred through separation, but skills are 'wayward.' They resist separation; this obstinacy is their critical response to their social organization. So although the separation of skills is ubiquitous, they themselves constitute a type of vaccine against it. However, the historian learns none of this if she relates to history in a positivistic or pure-

---

[186] Walter Benjamin, *Berlin Childhood around 1900*, trans. H. Eiland, in *Selected Writings, Volume 3: 1935–1938*, eds. H. Eiland and M.W. Jennings (Cambridge, MA and London: The Belknap Press of Harvard University Press, 2002).

[187] Oskar Negt and Alexander Kluge, *History and Obstinacy*, ed. D. Fore, trans. R. Langston (New York: Zone Books, 2014).

ly economic-theoretical way. It requires a phenomenological approach that allows for various descriptions of the separation of various skills, as well as of how these skills are reconfigured following this separation. In *History and Obstinacy*, Negt and Kluge therefore present a phenomenologically anchored theory of man understood as a historically situated concrete living creature—a theory of this creature's various capabilities, as well as the social organization of these capabilities, and their historical manifestation in different kinds of labor.

Like Benjamin, Negt and Kluge did not deselect the possibility of creating a work, but the result was unconventional. *History and Obstinacy* in its German version takes the form of a 1,283-page montage of texts and images. It is the result of a historiography that requires interdisciplinary research, but not necessarily in the sense of cooperation between many people from different disciplines. The necessary interdisciplinary quality might as well consist of the multidisciplinary knowledge that a single person—for example, a so-called Renaissance man—represents. Even on a general level, the possibility of creating interdisciplinary historical works does not depend on how many disciplines or which disciplines are involved. The decisive aspect is *which way of thinking* is practiced: that it is of a transverse nature. We do not create anything truly interdisciplinary simply by mixing and involving people from different disciplines. However, if an individual's way of thinking is of the transverse kind, she may create something highly interdisciplinary, even though she is completely alone and has expertise in something specific.

The broad view and the width of thought that contemporary historians must show, thanks to the demand for transverse thinking demonstrated by the work of Negt and Kluge, has a connection back to my initial reference to Plato and Aristotle. As pointed out previously, Plato regarded poets as inspired and artists as craftsmen, while Aristotle saw them all as craftsmen, but Aristotle also saw poetry as more truthful than historiography because it was more philosophical. From the latter arose the idea I have pursued, namely that of letting the historian learn from the poet.

I have shown that both the modern philosophy of history and its criticism may be interpreted as actualizations of the idea of a 'poetizing' of historiography—for example, thanks to their ideas of the thread-seeking, perspective-spouting, or montage-constructing historian. However, in the works of Nietzsche and Benjamin this criticism of the philosophy of history was associated with a critique of modern scientism and its penchant for knowledge rather than wisdom. The poet they let the historian become was thus *not* identical to Aristotle's artistic poet, who as a craftsman (not an inspired individual) was more knowledgeable than wise. But their kind of historian was also different from the inspired poets of the archaic period, for these poets were media for divine wisdom received in ecstasy, whereas Nietzsche's perspective-spouting historian or Benjamin's montage-constructing historian were active creators of their own narratives.

Within the framework of critical philosophy of history like that of Nietzsche and Benjamin, the historian is herself the author of her narrative, and she is an artist *as well as* a poet. The historian is an artist to the extent that she herself makes the narrative she tells; but as an artist, she is a poet because she builds her narrative not only on knowledge but also on wisdom. Like the artist, the historian is the generator of a work, and in analogy to the artist, she has a craft to learn and to teach. It is as a poet, however, that she produces her work, and her narrative therefore offers the element of poetry that in the interpretations of Nietzsche and Benjamin reveals its roots in inspiration, spirit, or enthusiasm. The historian is a writer of historical works that she herself is the author of, but she draws on a greater source. Today, we no longer know what to think of this source, originally represented by the muse, and are no longer certain what to call it, but we often refer to it—as *imagination*.

Felix Aestheticus and the Good Life

The Idea of the Good Life

What does it mean to live a good life? Many people would say that there is no common answer to this question: what is good for one person might not be good for others. In our day, we turn the question of the good life into a question of what we like as individuals, whereas people once discussed it as a question of what is good for all. This is the case, for example, in Aristotle's *Nicomachean Ethics*, one of our most important sources of knowledge about notions of the good life as they existed in classical antiquity and the medieval period.[188] According to Aristotle, good living requires that we actualize the potential characteristic of our species. Certainly, people are different—some may be disposed toward music and others toward drawing—and we must be active with regard to the things that each of us cares about, but everybody is equipped with reason, which is what separates us from animals. According to Aristotle, the good life for us as human beings is therefore that form of existence in which we let reason unfold, which is what philosophical thinking in particular makes possible. Philosophy allows human beings to actualize themselves as 'rational animals,' creatures of reason, and the best life for humans is therefore the contemplative life of the philosopher.

---

188 Aristotle, *Nicomachean Ethics,* trans. W.D. Ross, rev. J.O. Urmson, in *The Complete Works of Aristotle: The Revised Oxford Translation, Volume 2*, ed. J. Barnes (Princeton: Princeton University Press, 1984).

In modern times, however, at least two objections have been raised against Aristotle's idea of the good life. The first of these relates to the fact that humans are historical beings, which complicates the question of the good life. Since human ideas and actions change all the time, there is nothing transhistorical about the human way of life. It is therefore impossible to define the good life *as such*; what is good for us as human beings must be the constant *search* for the good life. This objection can be rejected, however, since it is *not* self-evident that there is nothing transhistorical about the human way of life. On the contrary, the tenacity with which humans have asked the same questions at different points in history, often giving interrelated answers, is remarkable. Moreover, one cannot both regard the good life as a constant search and claim to disagree with Aristotle, since searching is itself an essential ingredient of philosophical thinking, which, for Aristotle, defined the good life. The other objection to Aristotle's idea of the good life relies on the notion that, although we differ from animals by virtue of our reason, we have bodies and senses like them. Apart from being rational, humans are also natural, and we do not actualize ourselves as humans if we only use our reason. Therefore, philosophical thinking is not what defines the good life. This objection can also be problematized, however, since Aristotle did *not* reduce the human being to its reason; he only said that reason is what separates humans from animals.

In this chapter, I will discuss the ideas of the good life that Alexander Gottlieb Baumgarten, Immanuel Kant, and Friedrich Schiller formulated at the dawn of our time. More specifically, I will explore their philosophies of the *felix aestheticus*, the *cosmopolite*, and *aesthetic education*. Today, we still experience many of the contradictions that dominated the age of Baumgarten, Kant, and Schiller, but mostly without any knowledge of the solutions they proposed. Like the rationalists and empiricists of that era, we regard sensibility and understanding (sense and intellect) as opposites but have little knowledge of the attempts of the period's aesthetic theorists to transcend this opposition (such as Baumgarten's notion of sensitive cognition). Moreover, we regard individual and society as opposites, assuming that taking responsibility for something common will limit the freedom of the individual. Yet the attempts of eighteenth-century thinkers to dissolve this opposition (such as Kant's pedagogy and Schiller's aesthetics) are less well known. In our time, we still find traces of both *enlightened modernity* and *aesthetic modernity*, which are rooted in Enlightenment philosophy and in Romanticism, respectively. Nonetheless, we have forgotten that modernity was ambiguous from the outset; and when encountering ambiguity in our own time, we misinterpret it as a historical novelty.

Baumgarten's *Felix Aestheticus*

From classical antiquity until the eighteenth century, philosophers generally regarded human cognition as intellectual. Cognizing was the same as determining—that is, identifying by means of concepts—and all knowledge was a product of intellect and reason: it was rational. Hence the epistemologies of antiquity, the Middle Ages, the Renaissance, and early modernity focused on the *noeta* of intellectual cognition (that is, clear and distinct thoughts), and *aestheta* (that is, bodily sensations and emotional experiences) were regarded as inferior. *Aestheta* were mere precursors of *noeta* and could provide no cognition themselves: cognition required the transformation of *aestheta* into *noeta*. However, with his introduction of philosophical aesthetics in the middle of the eighteenth century, Baumgarten presented a new philosophy of human cognition, which involved an emotional kind of cognition, which he dubbed "sensitive cognition" (*cognitio sensitiva*), and which relied exclusively on *aestheta*.[189] Baumgarten regarded this sensitive cognition as an independent form of true cognition that—in contrast to intellectual cognition—does not determine objects but provides insight into the totality of which all objects are part, and which does so without abstracting from the uniqueness of the particular. Consid-

---

189 Alexander Gottlieb Baumgarten, *Ästhetik, Volume 1–2*, trans. D. Mirbach (Hamburg: Felix Meiner Verlag, 2007), § 1.

ering the centrality of *aestheta* to the sensitive cognition discussed by Baumgarten, we might also describe this cognition as *aesthetic* cognition, or—to adopt a slightly more contemporary term—as aesthetic *experience*. Hence, philosophical aesthetics is the philosophy of aesthetic experience, specifically understood as *sensitive experience*.

In antiquity, the true, the good, and the beautiful were connected; but with the modern scientification of philosophy arose today's distinctions between cognition, action, and taste, or between epistemology, ethics, and aesthetics. Nevertheless, although philosophical aesthetics was introduced as an epistemology, it has ethical implications and may even be regarded as an alternative way of formulating ethics. There are three reasons for this. Firstly, the epistemology constituted by philosophical aesthetics is really a *philosophy of experience*. Secondly, the experience with which it is concerned is essentially the *experience of beauty*. Thirdly, the experience of beauty is the experience of something having *value in itself*, alongside the related experience of *totality*, *cohesion*, and *meaningfulness*. The ethical implications of philosophical aesthetics and its status as an alternative form of ethics are thus rooted in the fact that the cognition focused on by aesthetics is characterized by being *sensitive* and hence *emotional* (rather than sensory and irrational) and by not resulting in the determining of particulars but in *insight into something universal*.

In Baumgarten's *Aesthetica*, the ethical implications of aesthetics appear, for example, from his description of the *felix aestheticus* (the lucky aesthete).[190] The *felix aestheticus* is distinguished by his mastery of the *art of beautiful thinking*, that is, thinking based on sensitive cognition—or specifically, on the experience of beauty—and resulting in a nonreductive production of meaningfulness. In order to think beautifully, one must be equipped with a natural disposition for this kind of thinking; a disposition described by Baumgarten as "innate natural aesthetics," which again

---

190 See, Baumgarten, *Ästhetik*, §§ 27ff. The Latin *felix aestheticus* means the 'lucky aesthete' in the sense of the skilled and successful aesthete.

requires the possession of an "innate graceful and tasteful spirit."[191] Having such a spirit means being disposed to allowing one's sensitive cognitive faculties to be encouraged, work together in appropriate distribution, and thus contribute to tastefulness in the cognition. The aesthetic spirit of the *felix aestheticus* thus relies on the aesthete possessing not only a certain measure of rational faculties in the form of intellect and reason but also all the sensitive faculties, which, in *Aesthetica*, are described as: 1) "increased sensitivity"; 2) "the natural disposition for imagining something"; 3) "the natural disposition for penetrating insight"; 4) "the natural disposition for recognizing something and memory"; 5) "the poetic disposition"; 6) "the disposition for having a taste that is not ordinary, but refined"; 7) "the disposition for anticipating and expecting something"; and 8) "the disposition for characterizing one's perceptions."[192] As well as an "innate aesthetic temperament," the natural aesthetics Baumgarten describes as the condition for being a *felix aestheticus* also involves having a certain will, which is the will to cultivate one's innate sensitivity.[193] One must be prepared to nurture and develop one's disposition for beautiful thinking, which means that one must be willing to undergo aesthetic exercises and instruction.

According to Baumgarten, the philosophical discipline known as logic involves not only intellectual cognition but also the perfecting of this cognition, which is the *cognition of truth* and *true cognition*. Likewise, philosophical aesthetics not only involves sensitive cognition but also the perfecting of this cognition, which is the *cognition of beauty* and *beautiful cognition*. When the *felix aestheticus* allows his sensitive faculties to be encouraged, to work together in appropriate distribution, and to contribute to tasteful-

---

191 Baumgarten, *Ästhetik*, §§ 28, 29.

192 Baumgarten, *Ästhetik*, §§ 30–37. Baumgarten's Latin terms are: 1) *acute sentiendi*; 2) *dispositio naturalis ad imaginandum*; 3) *dispositio naturalis ad perspicaciam*; 4) *dispositio naturalis ad recognoscendum et memoria*; 5) *dispositio poetica*; 6) *dispositio ad saporem non publicum, immo delicatum*; 7) *dispositio ad praevidendum et praesagiendum*; and 8) *dispositio ad significandas perceptiones suas*.

193 Baumgarten, *Ästhetik*, §§ 44, 47.

ness in his cognition, he practices the art of thinking sensitively to perfection, which is the art of beautiful thinking. The perfection of sensitive cognition consists in performing the *aesthetic* versions of what is the perfection of all types of cognition, which is "richness," "greatness," "truth," "clarity," "certainty," and "life."[194] Sensitive cognitions are characterized by their wealth of details, however, since they contain many 'marks' in the form of impressions of what is being observed; and perfect sensitive cognitions are distinguished by the high degree of harmony among these elements, which generates unity in the mental content. *Unity in diversity* is thus what defines the perfection that characterizes perfect sensitive cognition. Allowing one's sensitive cognitive faculties to be encouraged, to work together in appropriate distribution, and to contribute to tastefulness in the cognition is to accomplish a thinking that contains many impressions yet is still able to concentrate on the essential. The secret is to think in a way that is both concrete and universal; which neither abstracts from the observed phenomena nor loses itself thoughtlessly in their materiality.

Philosophical aesthetics thus represents an ethos calling for *beautiful* and not just *sensitive* thinking; thinking that not only has an eye for the particular but also has a sense for the universal, or, more specifically, a sense for the universal in the particular. We have seen that, in order to be a *felix aestheticus*, one must not only have a disposition for sensitive cognition but also be willing to develop one's disposition through exercise and instruction. One must be prepared to perfect one's ability for sensitive cognition and thus develop the art of beautiful thinking. The cognitive disposition with which the aesthete is equipped thus implies a moral obligation to perfect this ability; it constitutes an educational task. If one is equipped with the ability to cognize sensitively, one is obliged to take on the educational task of cultivating it; and indeed everyone—not only a select few—is invested with sensitivity in the form

---

194 Baumgarten, *Ästhetik*, § 22. Baumgarten's Latin terms are *ubertas, magnitudo, veritas, claritas, certitudo*, and *vita*.

of feeling, sensation, and presentiment.[195] Beautiful thinking is thus a common human potential; and thus all of us—not simply a special group of presumed aesthetes—face the task of actualizing this potential. Hence, the designation *felix aestheticus* is not synonymous with 'genius,' if by this word we mean a person belonging to an exclusive category. On the contrary, the *felix aestheticus* is synonymous with the 'ideal human being' understood as something that everyone can become, at least in principle, if only he or she takes on the educational task faced by humans as sensitive creatures.

Our ability to feel, sense, and apprehend, and thereby cognize sensitively, involves a moral obligation. This ability obliges us because it was *granted* to us (we did not produce it ourselves), and because it was granted to us as a *disposition* (not as something already formed). The gift is therefore a task; it obliges us to develop the disposition for beautiful thinking that it constitutes. This gift is also a task because people who really accept it and learn to think beautifully perceive more of the world and think more deeply about what they perceive than people who only think logically; and because achieving a more comprehensive understanding of the world makes us better equipped to act in accordance with the idea of the good. According to Baumgarten, we get furthest by letting sensitive and intellectual cognition act in concert, which constitutes *aestheticological cognition*.[196] This is how we get closest to the insight into the metaphysical wealth of everything, that is, the truth of all that is, which otherwise is only accessible to God. However, it is the element of sensitive cognition in aestheticological cognition that makes the latter so strong and lets it exceed intellectual cognition. Hence, it is primarily *aesthetic sensitivity* that is needed to achieve the greatest imaginable insight, including insight into the ideas of

195 'Feeling, sensation, and presentiment' is the phrase used in my book *Den skønne tænkning* to translate the battery of sensitive faculties described by Baumgarten within a rationalistic framework into a contemporary terminology associated with a more phenomenological way of thinking. See Dorthe Jørgensen, *Den skønne tænkning: Veje til erfaringsmetafysik. Religionsfilosofisk udmøntet* (Beautiful Thinking: Pathways to the Metaphysics of Experience. Religio-Philosophically Implemented) (Aarhus: Aarhus University Press, 2014).

196 The idea of 'aestheticological cognition' refers to Baumgarten's concept of 'aestheticological truth' (*veritas aestheticologica*); see Baumgarten, *Ästhetik*, § 427.

the true, the good, and the beautiful. When the *felix aestheticus* immerses himself sensitively in the phenomena without abstracting from their concrete manifestations, but also without losing himself sensuously in their materiality, he apprehends the universal in the particular and holds both together in his thought in a nonreductive way. What is individual and what is mutual then also cease to be alien to each other. The individual is rather the pathway to the mutual, because the mutual is contained within the individual, and the individual itself partakes in the mutual.

From the philosophy of experience that aesthetics essentially is, we can therefore derive both an anthropology and an educational program. Whilst the human had been regarded since antiquity as the rational being, Baumgarten's aesthetic anthropology tells us instead that it is the sensitively feeling, sensing, and apprehending being. The related aesthetic educational program aims to perfect sensitive cognition and thus serves to develop the human potential for beautiful thinking. Hence aesthetics tells us, first, that we must understand that feeling, sensation, and presentiment are more characteristic of us than logical thinking, and that this sensitivity involves something emotional (as opposed to irrational) which, precisely because of its emotionality, may result in aesthetic experience that itself has cognitive value. Secondly, aesthetics tells us that we must make space for feeling, sensation, and presentiment to act in concert in the way that results in aesthetic experience, or specifically in the experience of beauty, and that we must nurture the source of beautiful thinking that this type of experience constitutes. Aesthetics obliges us to cherish the possibility of experiencing beauty in order to become better at cognizing and thinking in a way that concentrates on the essential without giving up the concrete observation; the results of such cognition and thought are both concrete and universal. We can indeed get better at thinking beautifully, which is not merely a question of excelling as individuals. Education (in the sense of formation, *Bildung*) is never just about unfolding one's own talents but about unfolding them in a way that integrates the individual into something bigger. When we perfect our ability to cognize sensitively and think beautifully, we are integrated into the world we are part of, because it is through this type of cognition—or specifically, when we think beautifully—that the world really presents itself to us: not as a sum of single objects but as a totality of interrelated phenomena.

The theoretical thinking of the understanding observes; and the practical thinking of reason is directed toward given possibilities of action; but the aesthetic thinking of feeling, sensation, and presentiment adds something new to the world. It creates nonreductive unity in diversity, since it is both receptive and productive; it is open to impressions and to the possibility of unity but itself produces the concrete unity in which this possibility manifests itself and through which it becomes accessible to experience. Due to this duality of receptivity and productivity, the *felix aestheticus* is able, as mentioned, to connect the concrete and the abstract, the particular and the universal, or the individual and the communal in a nonreductive way instead of contrasting them. Although this aesthetic thinking differs from both theoretical thinking and practical thinking, it contains and assembles both of them, since it is directed toward perfection understood as cohesion. Hence, the one who thinks beautifully brings the most comprehensive array of subjective faculties into play and accomplishes the most wide-ranging thinking. For beautiful thinking emanates from the beautiful spirit—described earlier as the disposition of the *felix aestheticus* to allow his sensitive cognitive faculties to act in concert in the best way—which is the real human spirit understood as the only spirit comprehensive enough to contain and express the complete human being. This confirms that Baumgarten's description of the *felix aestheticus* is not a portrayal of exceptionally gifted individuals but the characterization of a disposition that is *natural* to human beings and therefore also of humans' *determination* as humans. The *felix aestheticus* is the essence of the human being understood as the sensitive and hence creative being. Rather than separating sheep from goats among actual people, Baumgarten's description of the *felix aestheticus* indicates what we should all aspire to in our attempt to actualize ourselves as human beings. We must nurture our ability to cognize sensitively; in doing so, we not only educate ourselves—we also create works that together constitute a culture of beautiful thinking, in which we meet each other as creative beings and share our sensitivity and experience with each other through our works.

Schiller's Aesthetic Education

In 1790—forty years after the publication of Baumgarten's *Aesthetica*—Kant's *Critique of Judgment* appeared.[197] Although Kant's aesthetics must be regarded as an example of philosophical aesthetics rather than philosophy of art, he distanced himself from what he saw as Baumgarten's ambition with this kind of philosophy. In the *Critique of Judgment*, Kant analyzed taste from the perspective of transcendental philosophy in order to prove the universality of pure judgments of taste. In contrast—according to Kant's reading of Baumgarten—Baumgarten hoped to make aesthetics into a 'science' by proving the cognitive validity of sense perception, thus bringing aesthetic judgment under rational principles.[198] Kant mistook the sensitive cognition described by Baumgarten for mere sense perception, and he therefore misunderstood Baumgarten. In reality, they dealt with the same thing, that is, the experience of beauty (which Kant described as the 'pure judgment of taste,' and Baumgarten as 'perfect sensitive cognition'), and they both had an eye for the centrality of the experience of beauty to morality. Although Kant tried to keep the true, the good, and the beautiful apart to a higher extent than Baumgarten did, the connection between the beautiful and the good, as well as the potential function of aesthetics as an alternative way of formulating ethics, became clearer with Kant's aesthetics, also due to his designation of the beautiful as the symbol of the morally good.[199] However, it is the letters on

---

197   Immanuel Kant, *Critique of the Power of Judgment*, eds. and trans. P. Guyer and E. Matthews (New York: Cambridge University Press, 2000).

198   Immanuel Kant, *Critique of Pure Reason*, eds. and trans. P. Guyer and A.W. Wood (Cambridge, UK: Cambridge University Press, 1998), A 21–22, B 35–36.

199   Kant, *Critique of the Power of Judgment*, 227 (5: 353).

aesthetic education that Schiller wrote a few years after Kant's *Critique of Judgment* that make clear what all of this meant in practice and how a moral-philosophical development of the ethical dimension of aesthetics might answer questions related not only to aesthetic theory but also to pedagogy and social philosophy.[200] In *On the Aesthetic Education of Man in a Series of Letters*, Schiller gave voice to an aesthetic utopianism that would later exert major influence on the aesthetics of liberation—such as that of Theodor W. Adorno and Herbert Marcuse—and which would form a continued source of inspiration for political aesthetic theorists like Jacques Rancière.[201]

Until the emergence of the modern 'scientific' theories of art, that is, until the nineteenth century, it was widely held that art must be useful. For example, the value of art was thought to depend on whether it improved morality, and the beautiful was regarded as something that fell under the good: praising the good in a sensuous way was regarded as the essence of the beautiful. In antiquity and the Middle Ages, the philosophies of beauty thus dealt with the place of the beautiful in the order of the good, while the art theories dealt with art's place in the moral order.[202] When Baumgarten introduced philosophical aesthetics, however, he asked what the experience of beauty really is (it is the sensitive cognition of perfection), instead of merely asking what beautiful art is good for (with its perfect form, it represents the metaphysical order of the world).

---

200   Friedrich Schiller, *On the Aesthetic Education of Man in a Series of Letters*, eds. and trans. E.M. Wilkinson and L.A. Willoughby (Oxford: Clarendon Press, 1967). Schiller's letters were first published in 1795.

201   See, for example, Theodor W. Adorno, *Aesthetic Theory*, eds. G. Adorno and R. Tiedemann, trans. R. Hullot-Kentor (London: The Athlone Press, 1997), and *Notes to Literature: Combined Edition*, ed. R. Tiedemann, trans. S.W. Nicholsen (New York: Columbia University Press, 2019); Herbert Marcuse, *The Aesthetic Dimension: Toward a Critique of Marxist Aesthetics*, trans E. Sherover (Boston: Beacon Press, 1978), and *Art and Liberation*, in *Collected Papers of Herbert Marcuse, Volume 4*, ed. D. Kellner (London and New York: Routledge, 2007); Jacques Rancière, *The Politics of Aesthetics: The Distribution of the Sensible*, ed. and trans. G. Rockhill (London: Bloomsbury, 2013), and *Aesthetics and Its Discontents*, trans. S. Corcoran (Cambridge, UK: Polity Press, 2009).

202   See "The Metamorphosis of Beauty" in Dorthe Jørgensen, *Imaginative Moods: Aesthetics, Religion, Philosophy* (Aarhus: Aarhus University Press, 2021).

In other words, he moved the focus from art's purpose to the nature and form of aesthetic experience. In line with this development, Schiller regarded art as something that can effect something else without any exterior assistance, rather than something that must serve the purpose of something else. He went further than Kant or Baumgarten in this direction, since he wanted to derive a moral gain from the very autonomy that art had obtained with the modernization of society and the related separation of the true, the good, and the beautiful. According to Schiller, there is no opposition between art and morality. On the contrary, he regarded art and morality as so compatible that, in *On the Aesthetic Education of Man,* he explicitly made aesthetics the foundation of ethics. Inspired by Kant's idea that the beautiful is the symbol of the morally good, Schiller awarded the experience of beauty the greatest task imaginable: to contribute to the *liberation of the human being.*

In line with the tradition of Aristotelian physics and metaphysics, the word 'liberation' here describes the complete actualization of the potentials of the individual and the realization of what one truly is. Since Schiller expected the experience of beauty to contribute to the liberation of humanity, he regarded the experience of beauty as something that allows us to actualize ourselves as human beings.[203] The notion of the liberating effect of beauty, which this expectation implies, reveals a close kinship between ethics and epistemology in his thinking. Schiller was less interested in the nature and form of taste or aesthetic experience than Kant and Baumgarten were; but he was very interested in the double nature of feeling and thinking that characterizes humans and in the question of the moral norm for action.[204] Indeed, Schiller's philosophy of aesthetic education builds on the notion of the duality of human nature and the questions that this duality evokes. He established a number of dichotomies. One of these was the dichotomy of the 'sense-drive' (*sinnlicher Trieb*) and the 'form-drive' (*Formtrieb*),

---

203 Schiller, *On the Aesthetic Education of Man*, II.5.

204 Schiller, *On the Aesthetic Education of Man*, XXI.2. In German, the two components of human nature are *Empfindung* and *Denken*.

which corresponds to the dichotomy of feeling and thinking, and he explained how to dissolve it.[205] The sense-drive appertains to humans as sensuous beings, while the form-drive appertains to humans as rational beings; but, if humanity is to be liberated, these opposing forces must be reconciled, which is what the 'play-drive' (*Spieltrieb*) makes possible.[206] The sense-drive and the form-drive are united and transcended in the play-drive, which appertains to humans as aesthetic beings. It is in Schiller's idea of art that we find the basis of this notion of the dichotomy-dissolving quality of play and its connection to humans as aesthetic beings.[207] In his view, art is characterized by a will and an ability to unite; it creates balance in its own internal dichotomy between matter and form. For him, it was therefore *art* that could serve as a model for the healing of torn modern humans and their fragmented world; and the education needed for this healing had to be *aesthetic*. Thanks to the ability to unite and appease that Schiller attributed to art, the aesthetic would be able to reconcile the human being as sensuous with the human being as rational while at the same time helping to heal society.

As we have seen, Schiller's notion of an aesthetic impulse, known as the play-drive, which is central to his philosophy of aesthetic education, originates from his idea of art as something that is both material and spiritual. Many other phenomena also have these two sides, but art is characterized by its peculiar ability to *unite*, which occurs when it gives form to its content. In fact, art is the more ideal the more it gives form to its content; the aim of art is the complete union of form and content, and the more it lets its content dissolve in form the better it is.[208] It is the complete

---

205 Schiller introduces these drives in *On the Aesthetic Education of Man*, XII.1, XII.4. Elizabeth M. Wilkinson and Leonard A. Willoughby mostly translate 'sinnlicher Trieb' and 'Formtrieb' as 'sense-drive' and 'form-drive,' but in XII they write 'sensuous drive' and 'formal drive.'

206 Schiller, *On the Aesthetic Education of Man*, XIV.3. See also XX.4.

207 Schiller, *On the Aesthetic Education of Man*, IX.2. See also XXII.

208 Schiller, *On the Aesthetic Education of Man*, XXII.5.

union of form and content, therefore, that constitutes the beauty of a work of art; when this union exists, the artistic endeavor is successful. Ultimately, it is not simply art but its *beauty* that makes reconciliation possible, and beauty contains this potential because *play* is what rules in beauty (just as beauty rules in play).[209] However, in modern society, all other areas than art are characterized by disharmony, because all unity and cohesion have been lost. In the course of the historical development from antiquity to modernity, man has been divided into sense and reason and into his various societal roles, and the relations between people have been broken. Both man and society are torn and therefore unfree; this was not the case in ancient Greece.[210] The ancient Greeks and their society were characterized by harmony, and, at some point in the future, we will (at least in principle) be able to experience even more cohesion and freedom than they did. However, this presupposes that beauty is allowed to exert its liberating effect, which did not happen in Schiller's time and is not happening now.

Since obtaining interior and exterior harmony requires that beauty can exert its effect, the liberation of the human being through aesthetic education, which Schiller desired, will not take place in the near future. The problem of the modern human being and its world is not limited to the fact that we are unfree and that the society we live in is fragmented. According to Schiller, freedom *was* already on the agenda in his lifetime, and the material conditions for liberating the human being *were* already created; but the society that had created the possibility of liberation itself prevented this freedom from becoming real.[211] The problem was—and still is—that nothing in society supported the *spiritual* aspect of the liberation, which meant that liberation *in general* was hindered. Nothing in society encouraged the development of the interior harmony and balance that is the precondition for gaining exterior free-

---

209   Schiller, *On the Aesthetic Education of Man*, XV.8: "With beauty man shall *only play*, and it is *with beauty only* that he shall play."

210   Schiller, *On the Aesthetic Education of Man*, VI.

211   Schiller, *On the Aesthetic Education of Man*, V.

dom. Only the aesthetic offered inspiration; only the experience of beauty and beauty's nature as play could possibly nourish human self-development and liberation. But, according to Schiller, nothing in his own time fostered any experience of beauty, though experiencing beauty is what is needed to develop individual autonomy, since such experience is the only way one can acquire a sense of cohesion, internally and externally. Modern society rather creates a divide within each of us (thinking versus feeling), between fellow humans (the struggle for the resources), and between humans and their environment (the abuses of nature by the rationally thinking human being).[212]

In Schiller's aesthetics, the theoretical aspect of aesthetics is clearly overshadowed by its practical aspect. Although the advantage of beauty is its ability to unite the fragmented, it is the liberating effect of this union that is important. Schiller presented an aesthetic reformulation of Kant's moral question concerning freedom, which thereby became a question concerning liberation. According to Schiller's diagnosis of modern society, the issue of liberation he identified can only be solved by defying that same society and initiating an aesthetic education of its citizens. Schiller wished to actualize the ideal State in which the human being is free, but he recognized that the materialization of this State of freedom requires free human beings.[213] The actualization of the ideal State and the self-actualization of the human being are indissolubly linked, and the problem of whether the State or the human being comes first in practice must be solved through aesthetic education. The aim of aesthetic education is to initiate an emotional development of the members of society so that their minds may undergo the development that is a prerequisite for bringing about the ideal State. Hence, the materialization of this State of freedom demands an aesthetic education of man in which the sensuous and rational sides of the human being are reconciled. To bring about the ideal

---

212 Schiller, *On the Aesthetic Education of Man*, V–VI.

213 For the notion of a 'State of freedom' (*Staat der Freiheit*), contrary to a 'State of compulsion' (*Staat der Not*), see Schiller, *On the Aesthetic Education of Man*, IV.7.

State, it is necessary to build an aesthetic State; and it will then become apparent that these two States—the ideal and the aesthetic—are identical, just as the actualization of the ideal State will turn out to be identical with the actualization of the human being as human being.[214] In other words, the liberation of the human being and the healing of society coincide. Both demand that human beings learn to control their nature without suppressing their sensitivity. It is this ability to interact gently with nature without being controlled by it that can and must be developed through aesthetic education. But this also means that the aim of the education that Schiller calls into use is less about the enlightenment of the mind and more about the cultivation of the character; it is an education more focused on morality than on knowledge.[215] For the same reason, beautiful art is more relevant than rational thinking as a means of education. Unlike reason, art can bridge gaps—including between reason and what conflicts with reason—and it is such bridges that the individual human being and modern society require.

Schiller's demand for an aesthetic education thus gives expression to the idea that the human being must move through the *realm of beauty* in order to access the *realm of freedom*.[216] Beauty is the path to freedom because beauty is the way in which freedom appears to us; beauty is freedom in appearance.[217] Only in the realm of beauty may we experience ourselves as complete human beings, our mutual relations as kindly tuned, and society as a cohesive organism. In the realm of beauty, we move in a world that—like art, which consists of both form and matter—itself consists of both spirit and sensuousness. In the realm of beauty, we move in an "aesthetic mode" *(ästhetische Stimmung)*, in which we are both physical and moral creatures, without being in conflict with ourselves, and in which we experience the possibility of being complete human

---

214 Schiller, *On the Aesthetic Education of Man*, XXVII.9–12.

215 Schiller, *On the Aesthetic Education of Man*, IV.

216 Schiller, *On the Aesthetic Education of Man*, II.5.

217 Schiller, *On the Aesthetic Education of Man*, XXIII.7, footnote 1.

beings.[218] This experience of completeness is only possible in the aesthetic mode, however, and even then the completeness is not experienced as real; we only experience it as a possibility. Schiller's philosophy of the guiding of the human being into the aesthetic mode through aesthetic education, whereby the actualization of the ideal State is made possible, is anchored in a clear awareness of the division and fragmentation that constitute actual reality. Therefore, art and the aesthetic (only) have a utopian function in his philosophy.

Kant's Cosmopolite

In the context of the *history of ideas*, Schiller's philosophy of aesthetic education can be regarded as a development of Baumgarten's concept of the *felix aestheticus* and the necessity of cultivating one's disposition for becoming what we really are as human beings: sensitive beings who potentially think beautifully. In the context of the *history of philosophy*, however, Schiller built on Kant's—and not Baumgarten's—aesthetics, and it is therefore Kant's terminology and thinking we recognize in *On the Aesthetic Education of Man*. It is consequently legitimate to regard Schiller's reflections on aesthetic education as an attempt to go beyond Kant's aesthetics by translating his theoretical analysis of taste into a practical philosophy of the development of taste. While Kant examined the true nature and the universality of the experience of beauty (which he called 'pure taste'), Schiller explained why the experience of beauty (which he called 'playful') should be central to the education of the young. However, Schiller's philosophy of aesthetic education can also be regarded as a response to Kant's reflections on pedagogy—developed in lecture form in the 1770s—and to the questions that these reflections raised. Yet Schiller does not refer to Kant's lectures on pedagogy in *On the Aesthetic Education of Man*, and nor could he have read them at the time of writing, since they were not

---

218 Schiller introduces the term 'aesthetic mode' in *On the Aesthetic Education of Man*, XXI.5. It reappears in XXII.1 and XXVI.1—and in XXIII.4 and XXIII.5, too, but here phrased as the "aesthetic modulation of the psyche."

published until 1803.[219] Hence, as with the relation between the aesthetics of Baumgarten and of Schiller, the historian of philosophy can demonstrate no direct continuity in the relation between Schiller's aesthetics and Kant's pedagogy; the historian of ideas, however, may recognize an overarching historical line, though this can only be experienced through interpretation.

Kant saw the newborn child as an incomplete being who possesses a disposition for the good that needs to be developed. The task of improving and cultivating oneself is thus imposed on the human being from birth: at the outset, we are closer to the animals than to the idea of the human that it is our task to actualize. As human beings, nature provides us with physical and emotional needs from birth, but, at this stage, we lack the self-control that is the precondition for developing our disposition for the good. This means that human existence has a purpose—a purpose known as *humanity*—which the individual cannot fulfill by his or her own power. The fulfillment of this purpose requires education (*Erziehung*) and the participation of other people who have been educated themselves. "The human being can only become human through education. He is nothing except what education makes out of him," Kant explained to his students.[220] But since Kant also stated that "the human being is the only creature that must be educated"—since survival and fulfilling purpose in the animal world only requires instinct—we may derive a definition of the human being as *the learning being* from his pedagogy, just as we may derive definitions of the human being as *the sensitive being* and *the playing being* from the aesthetics of Baumgarten and Schiller, respectively.[221] We encounter the notion of the human being as the learning being again in Rancière's *The*

---

219 Immanuel Kant, "Lectures on Pedagogy," trans. R.B. Louden, in *Anthropology, History, and Education*, eds. G. Zöller and R.B. Louden (New York: Cambridge University Press, 2007).

220 Kant, "Lectures on Pedagogy," 439 (9: 443).

221 Kant, "Lectures on Pedagogy," 437 (9: 441).

Ignorant Schoolmaster, but in an updated form cleansed of the discipline that is part of the education described by Kant.[222]

According to Kant, the education that is necessary for human beings involves "care (maintenance, support), discipline (training) and instruction, together with formation."[223] Care prevents the child from getting hurt through blind actions, and discipline raises it above the merely animalistic by imposing restrictions; but it is only through formation that the child becomes human. Kant uses the word 'formation' (*Bildung*) in different senses; but here he refers to what he describes later in his lectures as *moral* formation. He makes a distinction between physical education and practical education, describing the latter as moral education as well. The purpose of practical-moral education is to form the human being and allow it to live as a freely acting moral being. It is "education towards personality, the education of a freely acting being who can support itself and be a member of society, but who can have an inner value for itself."[224] The practical-moral education involves "*scholastic-mechanical* formation," "*pragmatic* formation," and "*moral* formation."[225] The purpose of scholastic-mechanical formation is the development of skillfulness (*Geschicklichkeit*); the purpose of pragmatic formation is the development of prudence (*Klugheit*); and the purpose of moral formation is the development of ethics (*Sittlichkeit*). This third purpose explains why it is moral formation Kant refers to when stating that education is a question of providing not only care, discipline, and instruction, but also formation; for the development of ethics is the highest aim of education, since it essentially serves to turn the child into a human being.

It is not only the aforementioned forms of formation (scholastic-mechanical, pragmatic, and moral) that Kant describes

---

222 Jacques Rancière, *The Ignorant Schoolmaster: Five Lessons in Intellectual Emancipation*, trans. K. Ross (Stanford: Stanford University Press, 1991).

223 Kant, "Lectures on Pedagogy," 437 (9: 441).

224 Kant, "Lectures on Pedagogy," 448 (9: 455).

225 Kant, "Lectures on Pedagogy," 448 (9: 455).

as formation. He also describes the sum of these forms—that is, practical-moral education as a whole—as formation when he says that "the human being needs care and formation. Formation includes training and instruction."[226] Here Kant uses the word 'formation' in a very broad sense, whereas he uses it in a more specific sense when speaking of moral formation, which is the essence of what he understands as formation in his lectures on pedagogy—just as pure taste (the experience of beauty) is the essence of what he understands as taste (aesthetic experience) in his aesthetics. Moral formation is the true definition of formation, since the real purpose of education is *ethics*. Along with care, discipline, and instruction, scholastic and pragmatic formation are important elements in human education, but they are only steps on the way to moral formation; for moral formation is what develops ethics and ensures the ability of the individual not only to take care of him- or herself but also to take the common good into account. Or as Kant himself puts it: "The human being needs *scholastic* formation or instruction in order to become skillful for the attainment of all of his ends. It gives him value in relation to himself as an individual. But by means of formation towards prudence he is formed into a citizen, thus receiving public value. There he learns not only how to direct civil society for his purposes, but also how to fit in with civil society. Finally, through *moral* formation he receives value in view of the entire human race."[227]

In Kant's lectures on pedagogy, his understanding of moral formation as the development of ethics, in which individual and humanity become related, is connected to his concept of *cosmopolitanism*, which has come to resonate with our time. This concept relies on the anthropology that Kant expressed in his lectures and which is connected to his call for moral formation. As mentioned, the task of the human being is to actualize the idea of what it means to be human; and since it is unable to do so from the outset, it is bound to be the learning being. According to Kant, the human be-

---

226   Kant, "Lectures on Pedagogy," 438 (9: 443).

227   Kant, "Lectures on Pedagogy," 448 (9: 455).

ing must manifest the humanity that is its purpose: it must rise to become the freely acting moral being that it has the potential to become. It is precisely for this reason that the human being must not only learn to reach its goals and commit itself to society; it must also develop the ethics the manifestation of which Kant describes as "philanthropy towards others" and "cosmopolitan dispositions."[228] As human beings, we are equipped with a natural self-preserving impulse, that is, the selfishness necessary for our survival; but we are also equipped with the ability to relate to others, that is, the potential for sociability necessary for our practical-moral education. Furthermore, with our innate disposition for the good and the related potential for education, we are equipped with the potential to morally embrace not only ourselves and our kin but also other people. We hold the potential to develop into cosmopolites, which is what the education of the young should aspire to; for, as Kant himself remarks: "In our soul there is something that makes us take an interest 1) in our own self, 2) in others with whom we have grown up, and then also 3) an interest in the best for the world must come to pass. One must make children familiar with this interest so that they may warm their souls with it. They must rejoice at the best for the world even if it is not to the advantage of their fatherland or to their own gain."[229]

The crucial pedagogical question, however, is how to realize in practice the moral formation that is the precondition for ethics, and thus also for philanthropy toward others and cosmopolitan dispositions. It is easy enough to understand how to care for, to discipline, and to instruct a child; but how does one develop a child's disposition for the good, ultimately understood as its ability to take the common good into account? This is the fundamental question within the general pedagogical question about how we can integrate the individual into the community, or into society: how does a human being become a citizen without losing his or her individual freedom, and despite originally being controlled by nature

---

228 Kant, "Lectures on Pedagogy," 485 (9: 499).

229 Kant, "Lectures on Pedagogy," 485 (9: 499).

rather than reason, and hence by his or her own needs rather than the common goal? This is the question Schiller addresses in *On the Aesthetic Education of Man*—though without reference to Kant's pedagogy—when he describes the human being as determined not only by a *sense-drive* (nature) and a *form-drive* (reason) but also by a *play-drive*. According to Schiller, with this play-drive, the human being possesses something that—if allowed to work—will dissolve the opposition between nature and reason and between private needs and common goals. In the *aesthetic mode* associated with the play-drive, we go beyond ourselves in the direction of something mutual but without losing ourselves. When playing, we interact with something else, or with others, in such a way that both we and that, or they, unfold freely; and this produces what Schiller calls *the aesthetic State*: a society of individuals who are free, and whose freedom is not a cost to society but is common freedom. We can use this to answer the question raised by Kant's educational theory, that is, of how to achieve the moral formation we need in order to generate philanthropy toward others and cosmopolitan dispositions. The answer is thus that such a formation presupposes the *experience of beauty*. It is by giving the young the opportunity to experience beauty that we give them the chance to experience the dissolving of the opposition between the sense-drive and the form-drive in the play-drive, or the dissolving of the opposition between nature and reason in freedom, since, as described previously, beauty is freedom in appearance. The young must experience the aesthetic mode described by Schiller in order to develop a moral mindset. By becoming citizens in the aesthetic State, they will constitute the society of freely acting moral beings, also known as cosmopolites, that Kant described as the aim of education.

As mentioned in the previous paragraph, Schiller does not refer to Kant's educational theory. In his lectures, furthermore, Kant himself expresses an opinion that seems to preclude any connection between his *educational theory*, Baumgarten's *philosophy of the felix aestheticus*, and Schiller's *philosophy of aesthetic education*: he does not attribute any independent significance to the moral formation of what I described as sensitivity in my section on Baumgarten, which includes the imagination. On the contrary, for Kant, the development of ethics depends far more on what I described as intellectuality and, in particular, the component of reason. However, if we take Kant's aesthetics into account, and in a different way than Schiller did in *On the Aesthetic Education of Man,* both Kant's own aesthetics and Schiller's reflections on his aesthetics may serve as a modification of Kant's educational theory and may also establish a connection between this theory and Baumgarten's philosophy of the *felix aestheticus*. If we consider an element in Kant's aesthetics that seems to have escaped Schiller's attention, we can reveal further connections between Schiller's idea of a characteristically human ability for play and Kant's ideas of ethics, philanthropy toward others, and cosmopolitan dispositions; and we may also be able to connect this moral-philosophical idea with Baumgarten's aesthetic idea of the *felix aestheticus*. This element is Kant's reflections in the *Critique of Judgment* on what he describes as the *expanded way of thinking,* and the centrality of such thinking to *reason*'s way of thinking.[230]

Schiller's concept of the play-drive can be regarded as a rethinking of Kant's concept of aesthetic judgment understood as the ability to let imagination and understanding play freely with each other. In the *Critique of Judgment*, this interplay, in which the understanding does not control the imagination—as it does in logical judgments—but allows it to work freely, turns out to have moral significance, even though it is classified by Kant as something aesthetic. This is because the interplay results in what Kant calls pure aesthetic judgment, the object of which is the beautiful; in other words, the result is what we today would call the experience of beauty; and, as mentioned earlier, Kant concludes in the same work that the beautiful is the symbol of the morally good. The beautiful and the good are not identical, but they are deeply related: the experience of beauty is not only pleasurable but also morally sig-

---

[230] See, Kant, *Critique of Judgment*, § 40 (5: 293–296). Kant's German term is *die erweiterte Denkungsart*. Paul Guyer and Eric Matthews translate the word *erweitert* as 'broad-minded,' but for reasons stated in the chapter "Philosophy at a Crossroads," footnote 74, I prefer 'expanded.'

nificant. This is due to the aesthetic way of thinking, which is the source of the reflexivity that takes place in aesthetic judgments—as opposed to logical judgments—and where understanding and imagination interact freely. Kant describes this way of thinking as the expanded way of thinking, and he considers it appertained to judgment—as opposed to reason's and understanding's ways of thinking, which are characterized by consistency and an absence of prejudice, respectively.[231] The expanded way of thinking is not only distinguished by the free interaction between understanding and imagination but also by *empathy* and *transcendence*: empathy with what one sees, or with whom one encounters; and transcendence of one's own or the other's position, involving the direction toward a common third position. If we follow Kant's reflections in the *Critique of Judgment*, the expanded way of thinking—which is aesthetic in the sense of being sensitive rather than intellectual—is the actual precondition for practicing the ethics that he describes in his lectures on pedagogy. One must be able to think aesthetically in order to demonstrate philanthropy toward others and cosmopolitan dispositions, or, in other words: thinking in the expanded way and demonstrating philanthropy toward others and cosmopolitan dispositions are simply different terms for the same activity. When it is necessary to experience the aesthetic mode in order to develop a moral mindset—that is, to pass through the aesthetic State in order to access the moral society—it is therefore not only because one needs to experience beauty in order to know what true freedom is. It is also because it is as aesthetically thinking beings that we learn what it means to think in a cosmopolitan way: that is, with a sense for the common good—not only with a sense for oneself and one's kin. One must be a *felix aestheticus* in order to become a *cosmopolite*; one must think *beautifully* in order to bring the *good* life to fruition.

---

231   Kant, *Critique of Judgment*, 174–175 (5: 294–295).

Toward an Aesthetics of Well-Being

Aesthetics of Existence and Competence Development

Many people talk about seeing themselves and their lives as a work of art. This thought builds on the postmodern idea that 'the grand narratives' about, for example, God, reason, and truth have collapsed. All the values that were seen to be absolute in the past have lost their credibility, and 'the subject,' which used to be the seat of moral knowledge and action, has dissolved. The identity of postmodern man is thus unclear and his existence uncertain. According to thinkers like Michel Foucault these problems can be solved by developing what he calls an *aesthetics of existence*, and this 'aesthetics' is precisely about regarding oneself and one's life as a work of art.[232] Foucault links the aesthetics of existence and the problems to which it is a response to the ancient Greeks. He believes that Greek ethics were focused on the "problem of personal choice," and that these ethics were a reaction to problems similar to those we are experiencing today with our loss of faith in religion-based ethics and our distaste for our private lives being controlled by law.[233] Foucault is manipulating history, however, for actually Greek ethics were closely linked to mythology, in other words the religiosity of the time. These ethics found their cohesion, their effect, and their credibility in references to the sphere of absolute values that

---

232 Michel Foucault, "On the Genealogy of Ethics: An Overview of Work in Progress," in *The Foucault Reader*, ed. P. Rabinow (London: Penguin Books, 1991), 350–351.

233 Foucault, "On the Genealogy of Ethics," 341.

the Greek gods still represented in mythological form at the time of Plato and Aristotle. In fact, the preference of Foucault and other postmodern theoreticians for reflecting ethical questions in aesthetics does not derive from antiquity but from the eighteenth century. More specifically, it is related to a phenomenon known at the time as 'the beautiful soul.' Admittedly, the beautiful soul does refer back to antiquity, to the Greek ideal of a beautiful-and-good person, but when old ideas are taken up again, they generally result in something new. This also happened to the beautiful-and-good person, when it became the beautiful soul, and the same is happening now when the beautiful soul has become 'me as a work of art.'

Early in antiquity, beauty-and-goodness consisted of external attributes, such as a well-proportioned body, expensive clothes, and a high-class name, all of which were regarded as evidence of qualities of an intellectual and moral nature. Gradually beauty-and-goodness came to be seen as something more internal that needed to be *trained* into being, and the Greeks began to consider what they themselves could *do* to become beautiful-and-good. Nonetheless, this internalization was nothing compared to the sentimentality later linked to the beautiful soul of the eighteenth century. Furthermore, it is the self-encirclement of this sentimentality that has now been massively superseded by the individualism in the postmodern aesthetics of existence. In the eighteenth century, people still felt duty bound to a common morality that had general validity, whereas today this would be incompatible with postmodern thinking. The present-day idea of seeing oneself and one's life as a work of art is merely the individual's personal project, nursed for one's own benefit. It is an expression of an individualistic idea of self-actualization that chimes in with the current interest in competence development. Many workplaces now expect 'personal competences,' and many employees view courses on competence development as an opportunity to actualize themselves. In reality, however, the desired competences are often something as impersonal as 'being flexible and ready for change,' while 'action competence'—so highly regarded by 'competence educators and educationalists'—amounts to no more than the ability to make use of one's knowledge and skills in areas different from those in which they were acquired. Where qualifications have value in themselves and retain that value over time, competences are opportunistic: they are an answer to something else, ultimately the prevailing trend of society, to which they have to adapt in order not to depreciate. That is why there is always a need for yet another course, and the effort of actualizing oneself is not only never-ending, but also futile.

The present preference for competences rather than qualifications shows how the focus has moved from the *content* of knowledge to its *usefulness*. This is in line with the instrumental way of thinking in our knowledge society, in which knowledge is no longer a goal in itself, but only a means for growth and control. Thus knowledge plays a different role today than in the past, and simultaneously the concept of knowledge has shrunk considerably. The interest today is solely in the *particularized* knowledge produced by highly *specialized* fields of science or appertained to specific competences. Formerly there were a number of different concepts of knowledge, and wisdom, the Greek *sophia,* was seen as its highest form. To be more precise, wisdom was not seen as the opposite of knowledge but embraced all the other forms of knowledge. If there is still a focus today on anything from those days, it is not on *sophia* but on *phronesis*, that is, the practical knowledge of how to act in a given situation and how to act 'wisely' in life. Wisdom has been left to the new religious movements; modern research and society in general are only concerned with scientific understanding and general life knowledge. The result is a neopositivism in the human and social sciences, and a competence development of an increasingly aggressive psychological kind. Souls are formed on an assembly line, not for the benefit of the individual, but in order to increase efficiency and maximize profit. This is the purpose of competence development, for in the knowledge society nothing is more profitable than people who can get on in the world, who can see the possibilities and exploit them for personal gain; this does not demand qualifications, but competences. The competent person is a wily person—different from the thinking person. The wily person moves around and helps to run the engine room in a society allegedly giving priority to 'creativity and innovation.' He stages himself and is 'his own work,' whereas the thinking person questions and perhaps ponders over what a 'work' actually is.

Reason and Wisdom

Can modern people do no more than acquire knowledge and meet the demands of their surroundings? Is there no potential for reason, or is it simply taboo because postmodern theoreticians have made reason suspect? The Enlightenment philosopher Immanuel Kant was not afraid of reason, but he also distinguished between reason and understanding. Although according to him enlightenment is about using one's own understanding, he was fully aware that understanding is not enough.[234] Understanding operates with cause and effect, it calculates and finds explanations, and it is oriented toward usefulness. Without understanding we would not survive; but it is not the understanding and its way of thinking that graces us as human beings. On the contrary, the peculiar quality of the human being is its ability to ponder on its impressions, put a perspective on its knowledge, and reflect on its thoughts and behavior, for which it needs reason, not understanding. Reason differs from understanding in that it does not simply subordinate empirical data to general concepts in order to state something—for instance, that this is a flower, and this flower is called a 'violet.' Instead, reason forms and finds its orientation in ideas of that which cannot be observed empirically, and which we therefore know nothing exact about, such as God, the soul, and the world as a whole. Human reason can therefore only flourish where there is room to refer to more than just pragmatic facts, not least to something larger and more comprehensive than the human itself. The good life has as a prem-

---

[234] In his call for enlightenment, Kant does not distinguish literally between 'reason' (*Vernunft*) and 'understanding' (*Verstand*), but he makes use of this distinction in other important works, including his aesthetics. See Immanuel Kant, "An Answer to the Question: What Is Enlightenment?," in *Practical Philosophy*, ed. and trans. M.J. Gregor (Cambridge, UK: Cambridge University Press, 1996), and *Critique of the Power of Judgment*, eds. and trans. P. Guyer and E. Matthews (New York: Cambridge University Press, 2000).

ise that we can give reality to our striving for such a reference, traditionally known as metaphysical truth, and the higher insight that this striving facilitates, and which was previously called wisdom. If we are to live optimally, we must add to the way of thinking controlled by understanding a further way of thinking based on reason. There must be room for the 'holistic' way of thinking, which is characteristic of reason and is the precondition for us pursuing not just knowledge, but also wisdom.

This line of thought may seem strange today, but it was a matter of course from antiquity until recently. It is not the thought that wisdom as well as knowledge, both reason and understanding, are necessary that is strange. It is we who are strange if we believe that as the single exception in world history we can ignore this thought. As late as the eighteenth and nineteenth centuries one could become a professor of 'world-wisdom' (*Weltweisheit*). With Plato in mind this may seem rather ambitious, since he himself warned that only gods can be wise, whereas humans must be satisfied with simply *striving* for wisdom. Nevertheless, Plato did not want to stop the human desire for wisdom, but to encourage further thinking, even after one believes that one has found the truth. The point was not that one should be interested only in knowledge, but that in one's search for wisdom one must be aware that one cannot possess it, only long for it. This was also the task for those people who were given professorships in world-wisdom in the time of Kant, and Kant himself even differentiated between philosophy according to its "scholastic concept" (*Schulbegriff*) and philosophy according to its "cosmopolitan concept" (*Weltbegriff, conceptus cosmicus*), that is, world-wisdom.[235] Scholastic philosophy is philosophy carried out as a technical discipline concerned only with those questions of an analytical kind that interest experts in this discipline; questions to which they are each likely to believe they have solid answers. Cosmopolitan philosophy, on the other hand, is philosophical thinking that is concerned with what in principle is of interest to us all, such

---

235   Immanuel Kant, *Critique of Pure Reason*, trans. P. Guyer and A.W. Wood (Cambridge, UK: Cambridge University Press, 1998), A 838–840, B 866–868.

as existential and ethical questions, and deals with its subject in the free, open, and questioning way that was originally characteristic of philosophical thinking. In many cases the professors of world-wisdom in the real world have probably not handled this task particularly well, but it is worth holding on to the principle. The message is to reflect on questions of general interest—being attentive to people's experiences and to the universal in the personal—and to do so in such a way that we not only gain knowledge, but also strive for insight of a more comprehensive kind.

Linked to the narrative of the knowledge society is also the story of globalization. In analogy to the narrowness of the concept of knowledge in the knowledge society, the truth about globalization is probably ambiguous. Even so, it is a fact that many problems of, for example, a social, economic, political, or environmental nature must be seen in a global context to be understood properly. Globalization may not be total, but in many areas it is a reality, and what can be more relevant in the age of globalization than world-wisdom? The relevance is already given in the expression itself, *world*-wisdom, and it is supported by the semantic meaning of the word: to have comprehensive insight into issues that concern the particular, but are simultaneously of general interest. Furthermore, many people will probably think that we grow in knowledge day by day, since the level of education is increasing all the time, and our educational courses are becoming more and more academic. Today we 'study' to become whatever, a hairdresser for example, and the number of university-style colleges has exploded. However, in reality the consequence is *not* more wisdom, not even 'practical wisdom' (life knowledge), because there is far more theorizing than philosophizing, even at the institutes of philosophy. This does not mean that we need more academic philosophy, for as Kant said of scholastic philosophy, it is just a technical speciality for experts, that is: theorizing. There is rather a need for more of the free, open, and questioning reflection that philosophy was originally defined to be—thinking that is not determined from without but has its purpose in itself, and thinking that reflects on what that means. This philosophical thinking is a prerequisite to avoid narrow-mindedness and to comprehend the complexity of, for example, political and ecological issues of a global scale. Such world-wisdom has never been more necessary than in the knowledge society, with its highly specialized expert cultures and growing demand for global interaction.

Intermezzo

The postmodern way of thinking contrasts unity and diversity only to give priority to *diversity*. In contrast, when we think philosophically, we try to recognize *unity* in diversity. From the postmodernist side philosophical thinking is therefore accused of *reducing* diversity; it is blamed for 'essentialism.' However, when philosophy is of the free, open, and questioning kind, as it was originally expected to be, that is, when it is seeking *wisdom*, it does not erase all empirical differences in order to replace them with a single common denominator. Philosophical thinking does not aspire to simplification, but rather to finding something that unites. It aims to find harmony between what is different—not between what is similar. Since philosophy seeks not only knowledge but also wisdom, it allows for both understanding and reason to blossom. In so doing it manages to create a link between unity and diversity, moreover in such a way that diversity is not made subordinate to unity or vice versa. Today, however, the words 'reason' and 'understanding' are used as if they mean the same, because most of us have forgotten all about the ability to think 'holistically,' which was the original meaning of the word 'reason.' Our time is controlled by the approach managed by understanding that is known from modern research, which focuses on aspects of cause and effect, and from modern politics, which give priority to the utility value of things. We think not only *with* the understanding but also *without* support from reason, and we therefore think theoretically and altogether unphilosophically. We are inclined to contrast things, we often end up with either/or instead of both/and, and this bad habit is legitimized by the postmodern ideology that it is inadvisable to seek anything that unites because then diversity is violated. It is therefore necessary to put *thinking* on the agenda, more precisely the thinking based on reason, and this will in fact mean *aesthetic thinking*. For what is it about thinking that potentially lets it find a form so that it strives for both knowledge and wisdom? What creates the display of reason that makes it possible to reflect on something from various perspectives? Kant already asked these questions, though with other words, and his answer was: the aesthetic power of judgment's expanded way of thinking.[236] When we judge aesthetically we not only decide whether something is nice or not, and our aesthetic judgment is not solely concerned with art. The expanded way of thinking appertained to the aesthetic power of judgment is the very precondition for all the cognitive faculties of the human being to combine—from sense to reason—so that the highest of them, reason, can come into play. This so-called aesthetic way of thinking is required for reason to carry out its characteristic transcending of the empirical, without losing its ground connection: to form and to orientate itself toward ideas about what we can neither register with our senses nor grasp with the understanding, yet that concerns us as human beings.

Aesthetic Thinking

The word 'aesthetics' has long been on the lips of many people, including many postmodernists, but a change of paradigm is necessary to understand it correctly. Today the word 'aesthetics' evokes associations of art theory or theories about the aestheticization of everything from politics to consumerism, but when it was introduced in the mid-eighteenth century by Alexander Gottlieb Baumgarten, it was used to define a new discipline in philosophy.[237] This discipline had the aesthetic experience as its crucial

---

236   See Kant, *Critique of Judgment*, § 40 (5: 293–296). Kant's German term is *die erweiterte Denkungsart*. Paul Guyer and Eric Matthews translate the word *erweitert* as 'broad-minded,' but for reasons stated in the chapter "Philosophy at a Crossroads," footnote 74, I prefer 'expanded.'

237   Alexander Gottlieb Baumgarten, *Reflections on Poetry: Meditationes philosophicae de nonnullis ad poema pertinentibus*, eds. and trans. K. Aschenbrenner and W.B. Holther (Berkeley: University of California Press, 1954), § 116, and *Ästhetik, Volume 1–2*, trans. D. Mirbach (Hamburg: Felix Meiner Verlag, 2007), § 1.

issue, and it did not see such experience as anything particularly sensuous, but as a kind of cognition. The latter is important for our understanding of how we can operate with a concept such as aesthetic thinking. It is precisely as a way to *cognition* that the aesthetic experience has an importance for philosophy, understood as thinking of the free, open, and questioning kind. Furthermore, in the eighteenth century people were aware that there are various kinds of aesthetic experiences, for example, both the satisfaction in what tastes good and the sublime pleasure in the incomprehensible. However, they were also aware that it is the experience of beauty that is the epitome of aesthetic experience and that it is not just a question of whether something is nice or not. The experience of beauty is far more comprehensive, and this, too, is of vital importance to an understanding of how aesthetics and thinking are linked, for it says something about what kind of cognition it really is that we achieve through aesthetic experience. Rather than being about whether something is nice or not, the experience of beauty is the experience that something has value in itself, and that one is part of something bigger.[238] It facilitates a feeling of belonging to this world, and it is thus an existentially important experience of cohesion and meaningfulness. The experience of beauty throws an unaccustomed light over what is a given, it is hard to understand, and it is thought-provoking. Nevertheless, it is communicable, and even though it is always individually manifested, it is not private, but on the contrary is available for all.

According to Kant, the source of the experience of beauty is our aesthetic power of judgment, whereas it is understanding that produces conceptual cognition, while reason expresses itself in moral action. The difference between conceptual cognition, moral action, and the experience of beauty stems from the fact that they are products of three different ways of thinking.[239] Understand-

---

[238] See Dorthe Jørgensen, *Skønhed—En engel gik forbi* (Beauty—An Angel Passed By) (Aarhus: Aarhus University Press, 2006), and "Sensuousness and Transcendence," in *Imaginative Moods: Aesthetics, Religion, Philosophy* (Aarhus: Aarhus University Press, 2021).

[239] Immanuel Kant, *Critique of Judgment*, § 40 (5: 293–296).

ing's way of thinking, which results in conceptual cognition, is distinguished by an absence of prejudice. This is what is expressed in Kant's dictum that enlightenment comes from following one's own understanding. In contrast, reason's way of thinking, known from the moral imperative about never wanting to do anything that one does not wish to see elevated into a universal law, is characterized by consistency. Whereas judgment's way of thinking is qualified by being expanded, because it follows the principle of placing oneself at the standpoint of everyone else and thus considering many views without submitting to any one of them. In other words, the expanded way of thinking is characterized by sympathetic insight, and precisely for this reason judgment is not merely about deciding whether something is nice or not. As mentioned, Kant believed that the expanded way of thinking is of fundamental importance for the activity of reason—both for its practical execution of moral actions and for its theoretical creation of, and orientation toward, ideas such as that of 'the common good,' which is a prerequisite for moral action. With the expanded way of thinking, individual interests are left behind in order to benefit the common good, and it is therefore the crucial precondition for making the moral imperative of reason real. If we were devoid of aesthetic judgment, we would not be able to act morally, and thus ethics rests on aesthetics. However, this thought presupposes of course that the word 'aesthetics' is understood correctly and not as it often is today, when aesthetics is simply reduced to art theory or to theories concerning the aestheticization of everything from politics to consumerism.

While Kant is explicit about the ethical implications of the expanded way of thinking, he is more unclear concerning the cognitive ones. He did indeed have an eye for the experience of beauty as that which leads to comprehensive insight. However, he would not call this cognition, because cognition for him was per definition conceptual, and the experience of beauty is by nature without concept.[240] Nonetheless, it is the absence of concept that allows

---

240 The word 'concept' here and in what follows refers only to understanding's kind of concepts. The experience of beauty is not without an idea, by Kant also called a concept of reason.

this type of experience to transmit important insight, and it is thus precisely what brings together aesthetic experience and thinking, and thus also wisdom. When experiences are aesthetic, that is, concerned with beauty, a free and harmonious interplay is felt in one's mind between understanding and imagination. The freedom and harmony stem from the fact that in the aesthetic experience there is no preexisting concept about *what* is experienced, but there is a *search* for a concept, and thus there is reflection, albeit of a searching kind. In the aesthetic experience the link to the concrete and to the sensuous is intact, because thanks to the absence of concept the particular (the object) is not subordinated to anything general (a concept). Yet a kind of reflexivity is practiced whereby 'thinking' is carried out as well, because a search process is happening—namely for a concept, which nevertheless is not found. Thus the thinking that is taking place when there is an aesthetic experience is itself aesthetic, in the sense of being expanded, namely due to the expanded way of thinking appertained to judgment. This also means that when we are thinking in the aesthetic way we are doing exactly what many philosophers used to expect from reason: we are reflecting in a free, open, and questioning way and are striving not just for knowledge but for wisdom as well. Such genuinely philosophical thought is hard to expect from reason at a time where it has been reduced to understanding, but if we nevertheless want both knowledge and wisdom, we can encourage one another to do more aesthetic thinking.

The Creative Person

Aesthetics is first and foremost about the experience that there is something that has value in itself and that one is part of something bigger: it is about beauty. The postmodern aesthetics of existence has nothing to do with aesthetics, but is an expression of aestheticism. It is not aesthetic, but aestheticistic to look upon oneself and one's life as a work of art, as this project is empty of all ideas of morality and truth that are of a common and binding quality. Yet this individualism does not mean that as a countermeasure we are forced to forget all about the idea so popular today of being 'creative.' We just have to understand it properly, that is, to interpret creativity more broadly and see the individual as part of something bigger. In the knowledge society creativity is regarded as a question of innovation: to have new ideas that can increase both efficiency and profit. However, if we take the word 'creativity' seriously, it is not a question of novelty value or profit; it is about *creating*. Furthermore, this creation is not only about what was once the focus, namely the concrete shaping of a material, which is what an artist does, for instance. Nor is it just about generating new ideas, a process that is rated so highly today, not least when the ideas are of a so-called useful nature. On the contrary, human creativity is essentially the ability to transcend that characterizes humans: to be able to imagine something that is not there—that does not exist in a tangible state. This ability not only plays a role for the religious person's belief in a god who cannot be seen, or the novelist's production of literary characters that are also difficult to measure and weigh; it is also the premise for a historian's work if she wishes to contribute to the interpretation of history and not just file historical data. Similarly, natural scientists must be able to transcend the empirical to formulate hypotheses, while politicians without imagination will be criticized for lacking vision and thus the ability to act.

Human beings are by nature creative, but that does not mean that what graces them is controlling nature (recreating it in their own image) or producing useful ideas (being a frictionless pawn in the machinery of the knowledge society). That humans are by nature creative means that they are aesthetic, which implies that they can undertake expanded thinking. It is precisely thanks to this ability that we can transcend what is given, and imagine what is not there. The expanded way of thinking is as mentioned characterized by sympathetic insight, and the implied empathy is employed not only when putting oneself in the position of the other. Something similar is the case when one imagines a god, a character in a novel, a past event, a possible result of an experiment, another state of society, and all the other things that come into our minds, and without which we would be cultureless—and thus would not be humans.

The knowledge society and the postmodern way of thinking jeopardize what is human about the human being and put at risk what is cultural in culture. For despite all the talk about creativity and innovation, the knowledge society's narrow concept of knowledge and its 'utilitarianism' reveal a thinking controlled by understanding, which throws suspicion on imagination and is the cause of the neopositivism we find in the present-day humanities, for instance.[241] Similarly, postmodern antimetaphysics throws suspicion on the ability to transcend, and this is precisely why postmodernism is stuck in a dualistic pattern of reflection that forces it to contrast unity and diversity in an unphilosophical way. Both the aesthetics of existence and competence development must therefore be replaced by the process of formation that the ambition to acquire a beautiful soul could be, provided this is not just interpreted sentimentally as a question of increasing one's affectability and enjoying one's aesthetic experiences. Rather, it should be considered a question of holding the ethical and cognitive implications of beauty in respect: the message of the experience of beauty that there is something of value in itself and the coherence between what would otherwise be kept separate, established by the expanded way of thinking.

The point is to be able, in thought, to be present in more than one place at a time and to reflect on things at different levels without contrasting the thoughts thus produced. This is necessary for making a link between, for example, the historical and the suprahistorical, tradition and the new, or the local and the global. It is thanks to this way of thinking that we can lift ourselves up above our private needs and desires to consider the common good, so necessary in a time marked by individualism. It is also this way of thinking that makes it possible to gather without reducing what is different to what is the same: to think of the universal without losing a sense of what is unique about the particular. This is what is needed in a society marked by fragmentation and globalization.

---

241 See "The Philosophy of Imagination" in *Imaginative Moods* for the history and meaning of the notion of 'imagination,' including the importance of imagination for aesthetic thinking.

Furthermore, aesthetic thinking is necessary in order to recognize the kinship between human and natural science. They both presuppose creativity, are both dependent on imagination, are both at a loss without expanded thinking, and both relate to the world in an aesthetic way—that is, sympathize with their object instead of holding it at arm's length—when they have substantial cognitive realizations. Similarly, it is also aesthetic thinking that is needed for the formation of character as a world citizen, because this demands that one acknowledges oneself as the holder of not just one, but two 'citizenships,' namely the national as well as a global, without feeling split and at odds with oneself. To actualize oneself as a beautiful soul of a nonsentimental and nonaestheticistic, but truly of the *beautiful* kind—that is, one who can think in an expanded way—is therefore not just an issue for aesthetes or specialists. On the contrary, it is something we should all be involved in and concerned about, not only in theory but also as a practical skill. Or it will be if we want a society where we don't just chase knowledge but also show the will to wisdom, and where we thus demonstrate that in spite of everything we still lay claim to reason.

Immanent Transcendence

Miraculous Origins

Philosophers have often emphasized the truth-value of philosophy compared to poetry, but many poets have challenged philosophical thought by reflecting poetically on issues resembling the questions of the philosophers. A philosopher can marvel at how cognition takes place and how to know that it is true; likewise, many poets have wondered what poems and stories essentially are and what they mean to humans. "Everything comes from somewhere," the boy Haroun reasons in Salman Rushdie's novel *Haroun and the Sea of Stories*; therefore he believes that stories cannot simply come out of thin air.[242] Haroun is the son and only child of the storyteller Rashid Khalifa, who to his admirers is Rashid the Ocean of Notions but to his jealous rivals is the Shah of Blah. In spite of his legendary storytelling, Rashid struggles to answer when his son asks him about the origin of his stories. They come from the great Sea of Stories, he cryptically declares whilst making strange and distracting physical gestures. "I drink the warm Story Waters and then I feel full of steam," he continues in the same style. Rashid's answer does not satisfy Haroun, for where does his father keep all this hot water? "In hot-water bottles, I suppose," the son says and irritatingly adds that he has never seen any. "It comes out of an invisible Tap installed by one of the Water Genies," replies Rashid. "You have to

---

242 Salman Rushdie, *Haroun and the Sea of Stories* (London: Granta Books, 1990), 17. The other quotations in this paragraph are also from page 17, except the last, which is from pages 17–18.

be a subscriber." However, the answer does not satisfy Haroun, who now wants to know how to become a subscriber, but the Shah of Blah replies, "Oh, that's much Too Complicated to Explain." "Anyhow," says Haroun grumpily, "I've never seen a Water Genie, either." His father shrugs. "You're never up in time to see the milkman, ... but you don't mind drinking the milk. So now kindly desist from this Iffing and Butting and be happy with the stories you enjoy."

New knowledge might be compared to the milk Rashid refers to. Some people lap up knowledge like milk and swill without questioning the milk's origin, while others search for the milkman to find a reason for the effect observed in the form of new milk bottles. Yet a third way of acting is also possible. Instead of lapping up or seeking rational explanations, one can wonder about and reflect on the very possibility of cognition. One can marvel at the miracle that ignorance is replaced by knowledge. All of a sudden, there is something where before there was nothing—or at least not what is now present. Similar to the stories enjoyed by Haroun, cognitions appear to be coming out of thin air, but perhaps they, like the tales told by the storyteller, have a different origin. Cognitions seem to have objects external to themselves; they apparently exceed themselves in the direction of something other, which is thus transcendent, at least to cognition. But how is that possible, and does the production of knowledge in fact qualify as a miracle?

Traditionally, miracles are considered expressions of a god or another supernatural being intervening in the universe and violating the laws of nature. In the Old Testament, God continually acts this way; he causes supernatural events. As God, in Genesis, calls the heavens and the earth, the plants and the animals, he creates matter out of nothing, and he brings the human into the world by giving breath to lifeless material. In the New Testament, Jesus also performs miracles when he turns water into wine, transforms one loaf of bread into several, or shows that he can revive people from the dead. Today, however, the word 'miracle' also has a more secular meaning that simply refers to statistically unlikely but happy events, such as being cured from serious illness or surviving a serious accident. In addition, it is used to denote something that is not unlikely but still overwhelmingly pleasing, for example, a child's birth or love that is returned. Whether the word 'miracle' is used with a religious or a secular meaning, it denotes something that is perceived as a wonderful event. This accords with the etymological meaning of the word. However, instead of perceiving miracles as events that either break with laws of nature or that follow laws of nature but bring an exceptional amount of joy, one can also understand miracles as sudden experiences of a dimension of the world we rarely notice. The word 'miracle' can also denote an unexpected experience of something 'more,' a *transcendence in immanence*, that deviates radically from both everyday experience and scientific knowledge. It can mean the kind of experience that caught the attention of modern writers and thinkers like James Joyce and Walter Benjamin, or contemporary artists such as Peter Greenaway.

Irony and Mythology

According to legend, the Greek Icarus drowned because of hubris: he flew too high and fell deep down. Greek poets often alluded to Icarus' flight in passing, and, in the literature of ancient Rome, the myth was of interest to Augustan writers. Ovid narrates the myth of Icarus at some length in the *Metamorphoses*, which was much imitated during late antiquity and the Middle Ages and has decisively influenced European art and literature.[243] The myth of Icarus describes how the Athenian craftsman Daedalus and his son Icarus tried to escape King Minos' tyranny in Crete by flying off the island. Daedalus fashioned two pairs of wings out of wax and feathers, which he fastened to the bodies of his son and himself. Before their departure from the island, Daedalus warned Icarus against flying too low or too high because the sea's dampness would clog his wings and the sun would melt the wax, but Icarus ignored his father's cautions. Overcome by the giddiness that flying lent him, Icarus soared into the sky, but, in the process, came too close to the

---

243 Ovid, *The Metamorphoses of Ovid: Books VIII–XV*, trans. H.T. Riley (London: George Bell and Sons, 1893), VIII.183–235. https://www.gutenberg.org, accessed October 26, 2017.

sun, which melted the wax. Icarus' wings fell apart, and he drowned as he splashed into the sea that still bears his name, the Icarian Sea.

Icarus is dead, according to the myth, but, in 2000, Malmö Konsthall (Malmö Exhibition Hall) contemplated his possible return. In front of the museum was a ramp for Icarus to land on and a bench for his potential audience. Perhaps the Greek myth was wrong or perhaps it has been misinterpreted by posterity. Where is the evidence of Icarus' fate? Where is the body? Can anyone testify that he actually fell into the sea, or will he return and save us from our inability to fly or walk on water? The ramp outside Malmö Konsthall was the final part of an installation entitled "Flying over Water," created by British multimedia artist and film director Peter Greenaway.[244] Baroque tableaus, a sensual aesthetics, and a wealth of historical references and allusions are well-known elements in works created by Greenaway, who, for this reason, is often considered a postmodernist. Nevertheless, entering the installation in Malmö was *not* like arriving in a universe dominated by postmodern irony, but rather like entering a world created by a Benjaminian imagination. In the early twentieth century, Benjamin reinterpreted the Romantic irony of Novalis and Friedrich Schlegel, which was rejected in the previous century because it was confused with the irresponsible attitude known from the aesthete described by Søren Kierkegaard in his *Either/Or*.[245] Romantic irony was regarded as a matter of morality and was thus subject to ethical criticism, though, as shown by Benjamin, it was actually a matter of language and knowledge. Irony in this sense of the word reflected the Romantics' appreciation of the language-inherent formation and deformation of meaning, and the constitutive inconsistency between what is sensitively experienced and what is conceived in thought.

244 This installation was staged in continuation of a Greenaway exhibition bearing the same title that was shown in Barcelona at the Foundacio Juan Miro in 1997.

245 Søren Kierkegaard, *Either/Or: Part I–II*, in *Kierkegaard's Writings, Volume 3–4*, eds. and trans. H.V. Hong and E.H. Hong (Princeton: Princeton University Press, 1988). Walter Benjamin, *The Concept of Criticism in German Romanticism*, trans. D. Lachterman, H. Eiland, and Ian Balfour, in *Selected Writings, Volume 1: 1913–1926*, eds. M. Bullock and M.W. Jennings (Cambridge, MA and London: The Belknap Press of Harvard University Press, 2002); see, in particular, the section "II. The Work of Art."

If there was anything ironic about the installation "Flying over Water," this irony was of the sort discussed by Benjamin: it was Romantic. Although Greenaway's installation was fun and democratic in its accessibility, it lacked neither existential depth nor metaphysical perspective. Greenaway did not simply use the myth of Icarus as an exchangeable starting point for a free fable. In his installation, the ancient myth was rather subject to an actualization characterized by analytical accuracy and serious care. Through his interpretation, the myth of Icarus underwent an extensive de- and reconstruction in which Greenaway, as an artist, utilized his encyclopedic knowledge and his passion for gathering, numbering, and systematizing. The result was a huge multimedia artifact that included references to countless historical artworks and cultural history: a total work of art, which activated the imagination of the museum visitor. Translated into a philosophical idiom, Greenaway's intention with "Flying over Water" appeared to be the creation of a new mythology for contemporary men and women; and the idea of such a mythology was expressed as early as the "Oldest System-Programme of German Idealism" and is thus not a postmodern invention.[246]

The desire for a new mythology originates in the belief that abstract ideas need to be aesthetically processed and that mythology's metaphoric language is the medium for such processing. In addition, the idea that a new mythology is necessary originates in a critical recognition of the weakening effectuated by modern secularization processes of strong values, such as Truth, God, and Reason. Before the time of the Romantics, art could make use of classical mythology without reservation, but secularization has made it impossible to maintain this procedure. Nevertheless, there is still a need to process and illustrate human experience and thought metaphorically, but this must now occur with the help of a *new*

---

246 The "Oldest System-Programme of German Idealism," written in 1796/97 and found almost a hundred years later in the notebooks that G.W.F. Hegel kept, is accessible in an English translation by Taylor Carman in *European Journal of Philosophy* Vol. 3, No. 2 (August 1995), 199–200. It is unknown and much debated whether the authorship of the program's content belongs to Hegel, F.W.J. von Schelling, or Friedrich Hölderlin.

mythology created by contemporary artists. In this matter, with its demand of imaginative thinking, only art can help us out. Art is mimetic, but, as Friedrich Wilhelm Joseph von Schelling stated, it mimes not only concrete natural phenomena but also the creative principle of nature, and it thus recognizes the truth about both nature and art itself. Art recognizes that nature is not just breathless matter but also visible spirit: it is the appearance of the creative force. Similarly, art also recognizes that art itself is not only spirit but also nature, because it contains something unconscious. According to Schelling, the absolute manifests itself in nature as an immanent element of spirituality, that is, nature is a revelation of divinity. However, the absolute is not recognizable in the same way as worldly things are, but only thanks to a kind of mysterious experience, and this experience is expressible only through images and symbols. This is what delimits philosophy but distinguishes art, for art is concrete and sensuous by nature, and when it converts its aesthetic form, as modern art does, it fulfills the aforementioned wish: it contributes to the development of a new mythology.

The Dream of Flying

The "Flying over Water" installation in Malmö Konsthall was an extraordinary spectacle. Investigating the icons of manmade flight, Greenaway explored the human dream of flying, not only in its physical but also in its metaphysical sense. A recreation of the Greek myth of Icarus, "the first pilot, the first flyer, the first air disaster," was the starting point for a set of thirty sections that mapped Icarus' aerial journey from its first conception to the fall.[247] This mapping served to explore the fate of the protagonist of the myth, but it also served to explore our dreams, a common human wish "to go beyond ourselves, to challenge everything existing and thus reach for the impossible."[248] The result was an overwhelming

---

247 Peter Greenaway, *Flyga över Vatten / Flying over Water*, ed. B. Nordal (Malmö: Malmö Konsthall, 2000), 26.

248 Bera Nordal, "Introduction," in *Flyga över Vatten / Flying over Water*, 3.

lesson in the *art of seeing*, achieved by the displaying of objects and events in unexpected and provocative ways that sharpened the observer's eye and awakened her attention, thus leading to recognition of what was essential. Furthermore, the result was also an impressive lesson in the *art of thinking*, achieved by the aforementioned awakening of attention and by asking questions concerning countless subjects related to the myth, including the quality of the feathers, the wind conditions, the physical attributes of Icarus, and the splash when he fell from the sky into the sea. Which bird gave its life so that Icarus could fly? Is it better to be a marathon endurance runner or a muscular sprinter if one wants to fly? Did Icarus really die or is his presumed death rather the product of posterior prejudices?

We have seen Icarus referred to as the first pilot, but he was neither the first nor the last in history to dream of flying. Admittedly, humans do not fly in the Old Testament unless tested by God. Such a test appears in Job 30:22: "You lift me up on the wind; / you make me ride on it, / and you toss me about in the roar of the storm." However, the flying creatures described in the Bible include not only birds, insects, and other animals with wings but also angels, cherubs, the seraphim, and the Lord himself. Flying treated as a dream of escape from fear and trembling is also present, as it appears in Psalms 55:4–6. "My heart is in anguish within me; / the terrors of death have fallen upon me. / Fear and trembling come upon me, / and horror overwhelms me. / And I say, 'Oh, that I had wings like a dove! / I would fly away and be at rest.'" Countless contemporary films, paintings, and literary works show that the dream of being able to fly has not disappeared. It still plays a major role in human imagination despite the fact that modern technology has enabled us to ignore the law of gravity for a century and airline tickets are now so cheap that many of us fly on a regular basis. The 2016 exhibition "The Dream of Flying" staged at Brandts in Odense, Denmark, is a recent testimony of the continued actuality and comprehensive nature of the wish to fly—a wish that encompasses the idea of both physical and metaphysical elevation; the latter being the source of its timeliness.

In *Phaedrus*, Plato recalls a myth told by Socrates about the soul, thus describing metaphysical elevation. In this myth, the soul is compared to a team of winged horses and their charioteer. One of the horses is "upright in frame and well jointed, with a high neck and a regal nose; his coat is white, his eyes are black, and he is a lover of honor with modesty and self-control; companion to true glory, he needs no whip, and is guided by verbal commands alone."[249] The other horse is "a crooked great jumble of limbs with a short bull-neck, a pug nose, black skin, and bloodshot white eyes; companion to wild boasts and indecency, he is shaggy around the ears—deaf as a post—and just barely yields to horsewhip and goad combined."[250] What the first horse desires the other will deny, and what the first horse obediently follows the other will reject in anger. If the soul is to reach its goal, the recognition of pure ideas residing in the sky, the coachman must control the pair of horses, which requires a taming of the wild horse. Nothing is more beneficial than contemplating the ideal, and Socrates' myth thus teaches us that self-control is the way to happiness, but it also tells us that beauty and reason are not contradictory, for the experience of beauty is the presupposition of the desired for contemplation. This is explained with reference to the belief that the soul was originally winged and could approach the ideas, but, long ago, it fell to the ground and lost its feathers. Ever since, it has resided in the human body. Thanks to its heaviness, the wild horse holds the soul firmly in the earthly realm, but, if someone experiences beauty, a stream pours into his body through his eyes, warming him up and making him sweat. The hard places where the wings once grew melt, and, as nourishment flows in from beauty, the feathers begin to regrow and the soul regains its wings.

---

249 Plato, *Phaedrus*, trans. A. Nehamas and P. Woodruff, in *Plato: Complete Works*, eds. J.M. Cooper and D.S. Hutchinson (Indianapolis and Cambridge, MA: Hackett Publishing Company, 1997), 253d.

250 Plato, *Phaedrus*, 253e.

Thread and Pearls

The movement hitherto referred to as flying is of a transcending nature, regardless of its source and end. Although Icarus fell into the sea, he momentarily exceeded the earthly human condition by briefly transcending the human inability to fly. Likewise, the soul that regains its wings transcends the phenomenal world when it approaches ideas by flying high in thought. Historically, transcending movements of this sort were often interpreted religiously. Icarus is not the only creature in Greek mythology who flies (albeit momentarily), but such creatures are not usually human. They are usually gods, demigods, or of divine ancestry, or they are mythological heroes or animals; they include, for example, Perseus, Pegasus, the Sphinx, Cupid, Hermes, and Phaethon. As mentioned in the previous section, the Bible also regards flying as a particularly divine phenomenon; angels are winged, but humans are not. For the same reason, Jesus is the human figure that European art and literature most often describe as transcending the earthly by way of flying. Jesus is distinguished by his two natures, both divine and human, and is therefore able to fly as he does in Luke 4, "led by the Spirit in the wilderness" and returning "in the power of the Spirit to Galilee."

In spite of modern secularization, it is still meaningful to regard flying in the metaphysical sense of the word as an experience of divinity. However, this interpretation evidently presupposes that we desist from applying the traditional religious meaning of the word 'divinity.' It presupposes that we abstain from using this word to denote the one God, the many gods, or the divine perceived as a religious entity, and instead use it to indicate a realm that is neither theistic nor merely human, that is, a dimension extending beyond the human affairs addressed by ethics and the divine addressed by religion and theology. Pursuant to this alternative meaning of the word 'divinity,' experiencing divinity is *not* identical to religious experience. Experiencing divinity is rather a transhistorical phenomenon, which neither philosophy nor religion has the privilege of interpreting, but which has been subject to a number of historical interpretations, including interpretations of a religious origin. Homer claimed that poetry arises when a poet is seized by 'divine madness,' also referred to as 'enthusiasm' by Plato, and suddenly begins to sing.²⁵¹ Plato interpreted such transcending as a *metaphysical* experience of the ideas of the True, the Beautiful, and the Good, and, in the Middle Ages, phenomena of a similar kind were regarded as *religious* experiences of the presence of God. Since the beginning of the modern era, we have been inclined to explain all such experience as an *aesthetic* phenomenon. This aesthetic interpretation, by which the focus moved from God and Creation to the artist and the artwork, arose in the Renaissance but was not articulated philosophically until the eighteenth century.

To better understand the relation between the experience of divinity and the various historical interpretations of such experience, I suggest comparing their interrelation to the relation between the thread and the pearls of a pearl necklace. Metaphysical, religious, and aesthetic experiences constitute some of the pearls held by the necklace, and the experience of divinity is the thread that ties the necklace together. Unlike the pearls, the thread holding the pearls together is intangible and invisible. One could also say that the experience of divinity does not have its own discourse, whereas metaphysical, religious, and aesthetic experiences have priority in philosophy, religion, and art, respectively. The point is that the experience of divinity never appears in a pure form. It will always (only) exist in the form of one or the other historical interpretation, that is, as metaphysical, religious, or aesthetic experience. Rather than being a particular single experience, the experience of divinity is the aspect common to the various historical types of experience that are of a transcending nature. It forms the 'more'—the experience of a surplus, of intensified meaning—that all such experiences include. If one tries to provide a concrete description of the experience of divinity, one will thus inevitably describe an experience that some will interpret as aesthetic and others will categorize as metaphysical or religious. To exemplify the matter, a surplus might overwhelm a person visiting an installation by Gre-

---

251 Homer, *The Odyssey*, trans. S. Butler and ed. L.R. Loomis (Cabin John: Wildside Press, 2007), 90 (Od. 8.62–65 and 8.73–74).

enaway, but a similar experience could also occur when witnessing Mount Etna erupting, when attending a service in a Portuguese village church, when marveling at Hagia Sophia in Istanbul, or when listening to Quran poetry.

Early German Romantics such as Novalis and Friedrich Schlegel even assumed that human interaction can give rise to experiences of a surplus, and they thus preferred spiritual love, which was the source of their idea of *symphilosophy* (to philosophize with one another), to the crush, the falling in love, that has priority today. "Perhaps there would be a birth of a whole new era of the sciences and arts if symphilosophy and sympoetry became so universal and heartfelt that it would no longer be anything extraordinary for several complementary minds to create communal works of art. One is often struck by the idea that two minds really belong together, like divided halves that can realize their full potential only when joined," Schlegel remarks in an "Athenaeum Fragment."[252] This Romantic idea of symphilosophy constitutes a possibility never really actualized by posterity. The members of the avant-garde of the twentieth century cooperated in their attempts to dissolve the gap between art and life, and, as a critical response to the mono-disciplinarity of contemporary academia, many universities claim to prioritize interdisciplinarity. However, interdisciplinary studies rarely qualify as *thinking* but are rather characterized by abstract theorization, and the avant-garde was too activist to replace theory with *philosophy* but instead regarded all questions as a matter of practical action. However, modern writers and philosophers such as Joyce and Benjamin have described other forms of experiencing a surplus than by way of symphilosophy and referred to these other forms as, for example, *epiphany* or *higher experience*, that is, some sort of secular revelation.[253] I consider the interpretation suggest-

---

252 Friedrich Schlegel, "Athenaeum Fragments, 125," in *Philosophical Fragments*, trans. P. Firchow (Minneapolis and London: University of Minnesota Press, 1991), 34.

253 James Joyce, *A Portrait of the Artist as a Young Man*, ed. J. Johnson (New York: Oxford University Press Inc., 2008); Walter Benjamin, "On the Program of the Coming Philosophy," trans. M. Ritter, in *Selected Writings, Volume 1: 1913–1926*, eds. M. Bullock and M.W. Jennings (Cambridge, MA and London: The Belknap Press of Harvard University Press, 2002).

ed by such notions the truly contemporary option, even though we usually still categorize our experiences of a surplus as something of an aesthetic quality. The result of this truly contemporary interpretation I categorize *not* as metaphysical, religious, or aesthetic experience, but as an experience of *immanent transcendence*.

Experiencing immanent transcendence is identical to experiencing a surplus of meaning, that is, intensified meaning, without having any idea of how to interpret the experience. The notion 'experience of immanent transcendence' describes the situation in which the person undergoing the experience cannot apply any of the traditional narratives to interpret it. Unlike metaphysical experience (in the traditional sense), the experience of immanent transcendence does not involve any application of a philosophical system. Unlike religious experience, the experience of immanent transcendence is not subject to an interpretation of, for example, Christian observance, and, unlike aesthetic experience, it is not perceived as particularly sensuous or as bound to the perception of an artwork or some other artifact. However, like metaphysical, religious, and aesthetic experiences, the experience of immanent transcendence is indeed one of a surplus and thus of divinity (in the previously described meaning of the word), though it represents a different, contemporary version thereof. Experiencing immanent transcendence implies that humans still experience in glimpses something other than plain empirical facts, but also that the meaning of such experience is immanent: it happens in immanence and neither discloses nor refers to anything transcendent. The experience of immanent transcendence infuses us with a feeling of contemplating something that is greater than and beyond us, but without carrying us out of this world.

The Phenomenon of Myrna

I originally applied the notion of experiencing divinity in *Skønhedens metamorfose* (The Metamorphosis of Beauty).[254] I chose the word 'divinity' because it contains a reminder of Homer's idea of the emergence of poetry, and because it was important for me to point to an aspect of continuity in history that is often neglected in our time. However, it follows from the previous section that I did *not* use the word 'divinity' with a religious meaning. The divinity in question exists only as a sort of ungraspable and incomprehensible 'more' within and common to the sequel of experiences usually referred to as metaphysical, religious, or aesthetic experiences. Consequentially, experiencing divinity is *not* synonymous with religious experience, as stated in the previous section. Religious experiences have an object in the sense of a god or something divine called by name; the experience of divinity does not. If a person has a religious experience, she thinks that she knows somehow what she is experiencing, namely the presence of what she believes to be her god, whereas the experience of divinity does not have any identifiable god as its 'object.' That is why 'experiencing divinity' is synonymous with 'experiencing transcendence'; it is equal to experiencing a surplus of meaning but not to experiencing some religious significance of such meaning.

In the previous section, I spoke of both the experience of transcendence, also referred to as the experience of divinity, and the experience of *immanent* transcendence as experiences of a surplus of meaning. In order to explain the relation between divinity and immanent transcendence further, I will now include the phenomenon of Myrna Nazzour, a melkite Catholic living in Damascus with her Orthodox husband and two children. When I stayed in Damascus for six weeks in 2010, Myrna's home had become a place of religious pilgrimage because she repeatedly experienced stigmata and received prophecies. Furthermore, oil ran from icons in her home, even from copies of icons. It was especially when the Cath-

---

254 Dorthe Jørgensen, *Skønhedens metamorfose: De æstetiske idéers historie* (The Metamorphosis of Beauty: History of Aesthetic Ideas) (Odense: Odense University Press, 2001).

olic and the Orthodox Easter coincided that Myrna experienced stigmata. In 2010, these two holy periods overlapped, but, this time, something different happened: oil flowed from Myrna's own hands. This incident was witnessed by a young anthropologist for whom it caused a scientific crisis. Had he lost some of his scientific distance now that he was involved in the matter? What should he do? The impression of the event provoked thinking on the anthropologist's part, thereby qualifying itself as an experience proper, but was it an experience of divinity, of immanent transcendence, or something else?[255] What did people experience when they met Myrna? I attended a church service in her home one Saturday evening after Easter, but was this service a religious or an aesthetic phenomenon for me?

Myrna, her family and their fellow believers interpreted their impressions *religiously*. When their impressions qualified as experiences—that is, when they were transformative—they were therefore religious experiences. The interpretation is what determines the matter; the impression itself is neutral. However, if a Westerner met Myrna, this person might be inclined to interpret the phenomenon *aesthetically*. The interpretation would probably be aesthetic in the narrow way in which the term is typically used today and, according to which, the aesthetic only consists of external form and sensuousness. It would thus all be about Myrna as physical body and her appearance; the pattern of her stigmata and the red color of her blood; the fragrance of the oil, her distorted facial expression; the plastic footstools in the chapel, into which her home had been transformed. This type of aesthetic view of Myrna would be attached to something sensuous and would not be transformative; it would not qualify as an aesthetic experience proper, but only as

---

255   The word 'impression,' alternatively 'mere impression,' is used as a translation of the Danish word 'oplevelse' in order to distinguish in English between what in Danish (and German) is called 'oplevelse' (Erlebnis) and 'erfaring' (Erfahrung), respectively. Furthermore, the word 'experience' refers *not* to physical sensation, sense impression, empirical experience, life experience, or rational understanding, but to something that by its transcending nature truly qualifies as *experience*. We may become affected by impressions, and they may develop into experiences, but unlike the experiences, mere impressions have no transformative power and bring no insight.

an aesthetic impression. However, another person might relate in a different aesthetic way to the phenomenon of Myrna—a way that results in an experience of *beauty*. In this case, somebody seated in Myrna's home would be gripped and think that, for a moment, he is experiencing a cohesion and meaningfulness he himself refers to as beauty. Still, it is the interpretation that is decisive, and, here, the interpretation implies that the impression gripping the person to such a degree that he becomes significantly involved, and thus changed, qualifies as an experience of beauty. It is not a religious experience, for, despite Myrna's Christian understanding of what is happening in such situations, the person in question does not interpret it religiously. He interprets it aesthetically, but in a far more genuine meaning of the term than that described above.

Whether the experience of Myrna is considered a religious experience of God's presence or an aesthetic experience of beauty, it involves experiencing divinity, in the sense of intensified meaning. It is this experiencing of divinity that the interpretations share, and, thanks to this kinship, we can communicate with each other across the boundaries of different discourses—aesthetics and theology, in this case. However, the interpretation of the surplus of meaning that qualifies the experience as intensified may also result in an experience of *immanent transcendence*. Like religious and aesthetic experiences, the experience of immanent transcendence is an interpretation of the experience of divinity, meaning that the experience of immanence also contains intensified meaning, but it does not appoint, for example, God or beauty as its object. In the case of an experience of immanent transcendence, it remains completely undetermined what is actually experienced. It is thus a prerequisite for there being any experience of immanent transcendence that someone experiences something of essential existential significance without being in the possession of a narrative with which he or she can interpret what is happening. An opening up of the world takes place; someone is changed; the person senses and feels it, but without any notion of where it comes from or what its result is.

The Invisible Tap

All experiences of divinity are experiences of transcendence, but not necessarily of something transcendent. Experiences of divinity exceed ordinary experience and knowledge and thus transcend the established paradigms of daily life and academic practice, without necessarily including ideas of a world outside the one in which we live. The latter restriction to immanence applies to experiences of immanent transcendence in particular. We have also learned that it is common to experiences of divinity, considered as experiences of transcendence, that they are experiences of a surplus. The 'more' they include was referred to as intensified meaning because of the accompanying feeling of *cohesion* (unity between the parts of the perceived object, between the object and the world, and between the person and something larger) and because this cohesion constitutes a feeling of *meaningfulness* (experiencing unity accommodates a basic existential need). That said, it is relevant to return to the questions posed in the first section of this chapter. In this section, I stated that humans can do something other than simply lap up or seek rational explanations for what they perceive: they can also wonder and reflect on the very possibility of the appearance of anything to perceive. This is a phenomenological reformulation of the issue presented at the beginning of this chapter, which in its initial epistemological formulation was about knowledge and cognition, and which, according to ordinary epistemological thought, thus implied an idea of an ego in control of the process. However, according to the alternative phenomenological approach now applied, the question rather concerns experience regarded as something that happens to us and the appearances implied in such events. We can marvel at the possibility of transcendence but also reflect on its possible source.

With Haroun and his father in mind, it is worth pondering on the relation between the Sea of Stories and the Ocean of Notions. The tales told by Rashid stem from the Sea of Stories, we learned, but the storyteller himself is an Ocean of Notions. This difference could be significant, as the Rashid described by Rushdie is experiencing a creativity crisis. His ability to narrate has disappeared, the source has dried up, which is explicable if he confuses stories with notions and the imagination with the understanding. However, the passages from Rushdie's novel quoted previously do *not* support this interpretation, for they declare that the storyteller himself, that is, his abilities, are *not* the source of his narration. The source is external to the storyteller, whose ability to narrate depends on the tap providing him with hot water from the Sea of Stories, thus turning him into the Ocean of Notions. The tap is the link between the knowledge of the storyteller and the poetic source of his knowledge. In antiquity and the Middle Ages, this invisible tap was referred to as the imagination, in Greek *phantasia* and in Latin *imaginatio*. Similar to philosophers of those times, Rushdie seems to think of the imagination as not creative in and by itself; its creativity rather stems from a higher or wider power, the Sea of Stories. Likewise, the Muse provided the Greek poet with the divine madness without which there would be no singing and thus no poetry, and the beauty of earthly phenomena warmed up the soul thus paving the way for a contemplation that would not be possible without the heat. Even Greenaway's modern Icarus appears to be dependent on a certain power, though, unlike the poet and the soul, he himself is ignorant of this and therefore fails. The technology that Icarus relies on cannot replace the creativity without which there would be no dream of flying or manmade wings.

Like the stories Haroun enjoys, human knowledge appears to come out of thin air, but it in fact does *not*. As Martin Heidegger stated in *Kant and the Problem of Metaphysics*, a profound reading of Immanuel Kant's *Critique of Pure Reason*, knowledge rather originates in imagination.[256] It is customary to think of the imagination referred to by Kant, the *Einbildungskraft*, as a subjective faculty that is independent of powers external to human consciousness. However, readers well acquainted with the philosophy of Kant will also know that there is space in his system for transcendence of the human mind. The mind transcends itself when it produces

---

[256] Martin Heidegger, *Kant and the Problem of Metaphysics*, trans. R. Taft (Bloomington: Indiana University Press, 1997). Immanuel Kant, *Critique of Pure Reason*, eds. and trans. P. Guyer and A.W. Wood (Cambridge, UK: Cambridge University Press, 1998).

ideas of what cannot be conceptualized by the understanding, that is, intellectually. Perceiving a concrete phenomenon, reason (not understanding) involuntarily produces an idea of the thing in itself, which constitutes the metaphysical reference of the thing as it is observed. Similarly, reason produces an idea of freedom as its response to the appearance of a man or woman, and this idea constitutes the metaphysical reference of humans. The productivity exhibited by reason generates from imagination, which is of a transcending quality (it exceeds the phenomenal) but does not leave immanence (it does not give access to a world of noumena). Imagination is even the root of the most basic prerequisites for knowledge, that is, sensibility and understanding, Heidegger stressed in his reading of Kant. Without imagination, there would be no link between perception and conception and thus no knowledge. However, sensibility and understanding do in fact cooperate, namely thanks to their common origin in and inclusion of imagination, which also implies that, even at this most basic epistemological level, transcendence is taking place. Therefore, it is no illusion when cognitions appear to have a transcending quality, but this quality stems from the process itself, that is, from the imaginary part of it, which, according to Kant, is common to both ordinary experience and aesthetic experience but is stronger in the latter.[257]

Immanence and Transcendence

It is customary to think of transcendence as 'the transcendent' and to identify the latter with something divine regarded as an entity (the divine, not divinity as previously defined). Furthermore, it is common to perceive the word 'immanence' as necessarily indicating that something divine is manifesting itself in the worldly. Following this line, immanence is inevitably associated with, for example, incarnation or pantheism. However, one could just as well abstain from using the word 'immanence' to denote the presence

---

[257] For more on the concept of imagination, see "The Philosophy of Imagination" in Dorthe Jørgensen, *Imaginative Moods: Aesthetics, Religion, Philosophy* (Aarhus: Aarhus University Press, 2021).

of something divine. In the terminology applied in the previous sections, the word 'immanence' was rather a neutral term for the world that immediately surrounds us and of which we ourselves are a part. We are in the immanence; the world we live in is the immanence, not only understood as materiality but also as all that is intangible in culture. This view is consistent with the literal meaning of the Latin term *in manere*, which the word 'immanence' comes from and which means 'to remain in.' Likewise, the word 'transcendence' was *not* applied as a synonym for 'the transcendent' or as a word necessarily connoting a divine power (not just divinity understood as a surplus of meaning). It was rather used to indicate an *experience*—the *experience* of transcendence—that is different from a transcendent *entity*. Rather than being the concept of a 'something,' the concept of transcendence, thus, denotes movement, and, if someone experiences *immanent* transcendence, the movement leads into nothing transcendent: it does not access any realm beyond immanence. The movement is rather a 'movement on the spot'—a movement in the immanence, a disturbance of its opacity. Furthermore, this movement has no subject in the sense of a controlling agent; there is no ego 'having' the experience. Behind the movement that the experience of immanent transcendence forms, there is not a particular god whose will penetrates into the immanence, nor is there a human ego exceeding the immanence. However, transcendence takes place and is happening in immanence, that is, in the world immediately given to us: *the intermediate world*.[258]

Furthermore, the words 'transcendence' and 'immanence' are often used to denote two conflicting versions of the divine, namely, the divine understood as absolutely distant and inaccessible to human beings, and the divine understood as present every-

---

258   See the chapter "The Dialogue of Experience," last section, for a definition of the concept of the intermediate world. In the chapter "The Intermediate World" in my book *Imaginative Moods: Aesthetics, Religion, Philosophy* (Aarhus: Aarhus University Press, 2021), I also refer to the experiential sphere described by this concept as 'sensitive subjectivity,' which reflects my use of the terms 'intermediate world' and 'sensitive subjectivity' in *Den skønne tænkning: Veje til erfaringsmetafysik. Religionsfilosofisk udmøntet* (Beautiful Thinking: Pathways to the Metaphysics of Experience. Religio-Philosophically Implemented) (Aarhus: Aarhus University Press, 2014).

where and immediately accessible to everyone. When the meaning of 'transcendence' and 'immanence' is defined this way, it appears meaningless to introduce a concept of immanent transcendence, which however changes if the words are used in the manner described in the previous paragraph. With this change, the concept of immanent transcendence becomes useful for everyone who wishes to describe what happens to humans who are enlightened by experience that is different from ordinary, empirical experience and who mistrust the existing narratives and are thus unable to interpret what they experience. Besides referring to experience that does not leave immanence behind, the applied concept of immanent transcendence therefore implies that the experience denoted by this concept refers *neither* to anything transcendent beyond immanence *nor* to any transcendent entity in immanence itself. The concept of immanent transcendence rather refers to an experience characterized by an opening up of the mind and a broadening of the person's view of things, which is gratifying but also disturbing and thus potentially frightening. Such experience is not a subjective action or achievement but an event. Therefore, experiencing immanent transcendence is what is happening when it feels as if the *world* suddenly opens up and lets 'more' come forward, and when those to whom this occurs do *not* know how to interpret it.

Flying high, Icarus experienced an expansion of his world thanks to the opening up of his and his father's minds performed by imagination, but, as Greenaway stated in "Flying over Water," he was also "the first flying disaster."[259] As a contemporary artist, Greenaway took advantage of the fact that, despite the archaic origin of the myth of Icarus, his ill-fated journey makes him a potential symbol of modern humans. In "Flying over Water," Icarus constituted the link between different opposites—air and water, sky and sea, to fly or to drown, ambition and failure—and his story was permeated by uncertainties and question marks. This all contributed to the both ironic and amusing nature of the work. In his installation, Greenaway decomposed and recomposed the myth of Icarus,

---

259   Greenaway, *Flyga över Vatten / Flying over Water*, 26.

thus producing a contemporary mythology about human longing for transcendence and modern failure, which itself revealed that the Romantic wish for a new mythology lives on. The secularization process has certainly affected everything in our modern-day world, but it is primarily the Church that has paid the price. Ever since the eighteenth century, 'God's death' was announced repeatedly, but, despite many people's lack of religious belief, most people still experience some sort of transcendence, and thus divinity. It is something other than the possibility of such experience that is now gone, namely the authority of the Church and the general confidence in its Christian interpretation of what we experience. Even the reliance on great narratives of a secular nature is widely rejected; contemporary expressions of dogmatism and fundamentalism are manifestations of frustration rather than of belief in something greater. In a situation like this, it is tempting to think that only art can save us, but it would be better to resist this temptation. Art can contribute to the development of much-needed sensitive articulations of contemporary experiences, but philosophy is necessary in order to protect and appreciate art in an age of technology.

The disrespect for poetry repeatedly expressed by philosophers must not be replaced by its opposite: a corresponding disrespect for philosophy. As mentioned initially, many poets have reflected on questions resembling those of the philosophers and challenged philosophical thought. The results were not always exemplary, but neither were the results of the philosophers. In an age dominated by calculative thinking, that is, the way of thinking performed by the understanding, which regards all perceived phenomena as effects of identifiable causes, we are in danger of crippling the human ability to marvel at what we perceive and reflect in an expanded way. Therefore, we must engage in cultivating the innate human capacity for wondering still present in children, and art is a cultivation of this sort. Art creates spaces for aesthetic thinking—reflection that originates in wonder and stays aware of its wondrous roots with the result that it is open-ended and thus free, questioning, and inclusive. Philosophy, for its part, tries to protect the spaces for aesthetic thinking created by art against the calculative thinking cultivated in society in general, and it furthers our appreciation of the effort of art by developing our understanding of the aesthetic thinking carried out in artworks. This contribution of philosophy presupposes, however, that philosophy itself actually knows how to think beautifully, not only in art but also within philosophy. Likewise, the aforementioned effort of art presupposes that art knows how to engage in conscious structuring of reflective processes, within itself and regardless of how free the performed thinking must stay in order to remain aesthetic. The Icarus installation presented by Greenaway and the story of Haroun told by Rushdie, which are both poetic in multilayered and thought-provoking ways, are products of such aesthetic thinking in *art* and *literature*. Similarly, the concept of immanent transcendence with its constellation of elements usually regarded as contradictory and its use of the thus created oxymoron to denote significant human experience lacking adequate expression is a product of *philosophical* aesthetic thinking.

Limit and Threshold

Why border studies? What is the value of studying borders? Answering such questions requires consideration of the meaning of the notion of borders. Consideration of this sort is a philosophical task, which is one of many reasons why border studies implies or ought to imply philosophical thinking. One cannot perform good humanist or social scientific research without reflecting on one's approach, the nature of one's object, the meaning of one's key concepts, and the purpose of one's work. So why border studies? Because human beings experience borders—be it in terms of concrete borders, spiritual limits, or existential, moral, or epistemological thresholds—and because humans seek to understand what they experience, which demands interpretation and thus also expression and reflection. Humans wish to learn, Aristotle said; border studies contributes to the fulfilling of this eternal wish.[260] Conducted in its broadest sense, border studies offers possibilities to develop new knowledge in all fields of human life, not only social-scientifically or epistemologically but also existentially and morally.

Border studies encompasses a variety of disciplines, including *border aesthetics*. However, border studies is part of cultural studies, and it is therefore less influenced by philosophy than by the social sciences, or the human sciences (such as literary studies). Aesthetics, on the other hand, is a philosophical discipline, originally introduced by Alexander Gottlieb Baumgarten as the

---

260 Aristotle, *Poetics*, trans. I. Bywater, in *The Complete Works of Aristotle: The Revised Oxford Translation, Volume 2*, ed. J. Barnes (Princeton: Princeton University Press, 1984), 4, 1448b 14–15.

philosophy of sensitive cognition. Contemporary representatives of the study of art (literary studies, art history, visual studies, etc.) often refer to Baumgarten's idea of sensitive cognition but mostly misinterpret it as sense perception or sensuous experience. However, according to Baumgarten, sensitive cognition includes much more than sensation, for example also imagination, memory, and presentiment, and it is a transgressive kind of experience, the object of which is ultimately the beautiful.[261] Contemporary border aesthetics reproduces the current confusion of sensitivity and sensuousness; similar to the study of art, border aesthetics is also more concerned with concrete artifacts than with experience and knowledge (as is the case in, for example, the anthology *Border Aesthetics*).[262] Furthermore, border aesthetics has not developed the hermeneutic phenomenological way of thinking already latent in early philosophical aesthetics, but has rather adopted the methodical approach of modern science. The consequence of this is a reproduction in border aesthetics of the art-theoretical way of thinking inherent to disciplines such as literary and visual studies.

In this chapter, I wish to let the metaphysics of experience described in my book *Den skønne tænkning* (Beautiful Thinking) contribute to the required development of border aesthetics.[263] This metaphysics of experience is rooted in philosophical aesthetics and hermeneutic phenomenology; letting it contribute to border aesthetics thus also means letting these forms of philoso-

---

261   Alexander Gottlieb Baumgarten, *Ästhetik, Volume 1-2*, trans. D. Mirbach (Hamburg: Felix Meiner Verlag, 2007), §§ 14–27. Dorthe Jørgensen, *Den skønne tænkning: Veje til erfaringsmetafysik. Religionsfilosofisk udmøntet* (Beautiful Thinking: Pathways to the Metaphysics of Experience. Religio-Philosophically Implemented) (Aarhus: Aarhus University Press, 2014), 83–158.

262   Mireille Rosello and Stephen F. Wolfe, "Introduction," in *Border Aesthetics: Concepts and Intersections*, eds. J. Schimanski and S.F. Wolfe (New York and Oxford: Berghahn Books, 2017), 1–4.

263   This presentation rests on Dorthe Jørgensen, "The Philosophy of Imagination," in *Handbook of Imagination and Culture*, eds. T. Zittoun and V.P. Gläveanu (New York: Oxford University Press, 2017), reprinted in Dorthe Jørgensen, *Imaginative Moods: Aesthetics, Religion, Philosophy* (Aarhus: Aarhus University Press, 2021), and the following chapters of *Den skønne tænkning*: "Poietisk transcendens" (Poietic Transcendence), 325–341, and "Det sublime ved det skønne" (The Sublime in the Beautiful), 687–705.

phy contribute. Compared to contemporary border aesthetics, the metaphysics of experience has a stronger sense of the sensitive nature of aesthetic experiences and of the fact that they provide intuitive insight rather than rational knowledge. Furthermore, the metaphysics of experience differentiates between experience and impression/perception, highlighting the transformative power of experiences and the importance of aesthetic experience for human moral action, and thus also for ethics. The widespread idea that what is aesthetic is necessarily the antithesis of what is ethical is a tragic misunderstanding. The ethical potential of beauty was obvious to ancient philosophers such as Plato, who regarded truth, beauty, and the good as ontologically interrelated, and it was also evident to modern philosophers like Immanuel Kant, who identified the beautiful as the symbol of the morally good.[264]

Pure Imagination

With the development of modern society, understanding's calculative thinking became a priority, and imagination became alien.[265] Considered as the radically other compared to the understanding, the imagination was left to romanticists and other dreamers, whereas in antiquity and the Middle Ages, sensation, imagination, and thinking were strongly interrelated.[266] According to Aristotle's *On the Soul*, thinking without sensation and imagination is not possible.[267] The intellect cannot cognize without use of the imag-

---

264   Immanuel Kant, *Critique of the Power of Judgment*, eds. and trans. P. Guyer and E. Matthews (New York: Cambridge University Press, 2000), 227 (5: 353).

265   In accord with classical German philosophy, I distinguish between 'reason' and 'understanding' (*Vernunft* and *Verstand*). The understanding is the faculty of concepts and intellectual reasoning (analysis, identification, generalization, calculation), whereas reason is the faculty of ideas and rational thinking (synthesis, perspective, universalization, moral action).

266   Jørgensen, "The Philosophy of Imagination."

267   Aristotle, *On the Soul*, trans. J.A. Smith, in *The Complete Works of Aristotle: The Revised Oxford Translation, Volume 1*, ed. J. Barnes (Princeton: Princeton University Press, 1984), III.8, 432a 9–13.

es produced by imagination, and this production requires sensory input. Neither sensation nor imagination results in cognition, but both are necessary for the intellect to produce its knowledge. This view of the soul can also be studied in many other texts from the antiquity, the Middle Ages, and the Renaissance. However, from Martin Heidegger's *Kant and the Problem of Metaphysics*, it appears that the human being became estranged from itself when the imagination—by both Kant and Heidegger referred to as *die Einbildungskraft*—became suspect due to the modern preference for the understanding (as opposed to both reason and imagination).[268] In this work, Heidegger focuses on Kant's two depictions of the mind in *Critique of Pure Reason*, according to which the mind is characterized either by *sensibility* and *understanding*, or by *sense, imagination*, and *apperception*.[269] However, in connection with the first model, Kant already mentions that sensibility and understanding "may perhaps arise from a common but to us unknown root," and this is what Heidegger pursues in his interpretation of Kant.[270]

Heidegger distinguishes between *ontic experience* and *ontological cognition*, and he mentions that the former rests on the latter.[271] Ontic experience is the experience of something as something

---

268 Martin Heidegger, *Kant and the Problem of Metaphysics*, trans. R. Taft (Bloomington: Indiana University Press, 1997).

269 Immanuel Kant, *Critique of Pure Reason*, trans. P. Guyer and A.W. Wood (Cambridge, UK: Cambridge University Press, 1998), A 51, B75; and A 94.

270 Kant, *Critique of Pure Reason*, A 15, B 29. In Kant's *Critique of Pure Reason*, the understanding referred to is the previously mentioned faculty of concepts and intellectual reasoning, which also applies to Heidegger's *Kant and the Problem of Metaphysics* as far as it represents an interpretation of Kant's work. However, as is evident from other works by Heidegger, and compatible with his preference for the imagination when interpreting Kant, Heidegger is actually more interested in *Verstehen* than *Verstand*, that is, the process of understanding rather than the faculty of understanding. In *Kant and the Problem of Metaphysics*, the word 'understanding' means both.

271 Heidegger, *Kant and the Problem of Metaphysics*, 7. Richard Taft translates 'ontologische Erkenntnis' as 'ontological knowledge,' but 'ontological cognition' is a more precise translation. It is easy to misinterpret Heidegger's terms 'ontic experience' and 'ontological cognition,' but their meaning is indisputable. The word 'experience' in 'ontic experience' refers *not* to phenomenological experience but to experience/cognition in everyday terms and in terms of what modern science relies on. Likewise, the word 'cognition' in 'ontological cognition' refers *not* to the intellectual knowledge studied by contemporary cognitive science,

specific, which presupposes an ontological cognition of the very being of that something. For example, one cannot identify an object as a cake unless one has perceived the very appearance and presence of that object. In order to identify an object, one must have perceived it as *phenomenon*: identification ('ontic experience') presupposes phenomenological experience ('ontological cognition'). Therefore, philosophy must examine not only how identification takes place but also how the appearance can occur, without which there would be nothing to identify. According to Heidegger, the most important question is what makes ontological cognition possible—that is, how it is possible to recognize the very appearance of phenomena—and pure imagination is the answer. The latter is only perceivable, however, if one interprets imagination in the light of an interpretation of the human being as *Dasein*, not as consciousness. Unlike Kant, whose approach was marked by a dualism of mind and matter, one must choose a phenomenological approach in order to be able to view imagination as a basic structure of Dasein rather than as a faculty of the mind; or one will not be able to reach an understanding of imagination as something that is ontological, rather than empirical and psychological.

According to Heidegger, pure imagination is not a faculty between sensibility and understanding, but their *common origin*. This does not mean, however, that the imagination comes first, but rather that both sensibility and understanding are rooted in imagination and thus both include imagination.[272] For the same reason, imagination is not only receptive (to perceptions), but is *spontaneous receptivity*, and thinking is not only spontaneous (creative of concepts), but is *receptive spontaneity*. Furthermore, the imagination is not only creative *and* receptive, but is receptive *as* creative.[273] This is why the imagination can form the horizon within which something can appear and be present—and can keep that horizon

---

but to a broader kind of insight, by phenomenologists usually called 'experience.'

272 Heidegger, *Kant and the Problem of Metaphysics*, 96.

273 Heidegger, *Kant and the Problem of Metaphysics*, 197.

open. It is in the form of receptive creativity that the imagination allows for ontological cognition, which itself is based on the synthesis that imagination essentially is. The imagination enables the appearance that is the prerequisite for any experience and cognition to occur. It establishes the 'space for play' that this appearance presupposes.[274]

If the human being is Dasein, as Heidegger suggests, it is essentially existence and thus being-in-the-world. Dasein is not an isolated subject, not enclosed in an inner realm from which it seeks to recognize an outer world. Dasein is already 'out' in the world, 'out' among other beings (things and humans).[275] As being-in-the-world, we are by nature open to all beings, the being as such, and ourselves as existence. Therefore, our ability to perceive something *as* something and view it in a certain perspective rests not only on the fact that the world already contains other beings. It also rests on the verity that, as Dasein, we are open to a horizon of indeterminacy, within which something can appear. This horizon is formed and kept open by the imagination, which is thus far more characteristic of humans than is understanding.[276] It is due to the imagination regarded not as a mental faculty but as a basic structure of human existence that our openness, the "transcendence of Dasein," is possible and that we distinguish ourselves from things and animals by being world-forming.[277]

Pure imagination expands existence, bringing us close to things not only in our direct perception of them but also in memory and free imagination. When we recall or imagine something, we are thus not just dealing with an inner image of that which was or which we now fantasize about; we are also close to it, directing our-

---

[274] Heidegger, *Kant and the Problem of Metaphysics*, 50.

[275] Martin Heidegger, *Being and Time*, trans. J. Stambaugh, rev. D.J. Schmidt (Albany: State University of New York Press, 2010), 58.

[276] Heidegger, *Kant and the Problem of Metaphysics*, 30.

[277] Martin Heidegger, *The Fundamental Concepts of Metaphysics: World, Finitude, Solitude*, trans. W. McNeill (Bloomington and Indianapolis: Indiana University Press, 2001), § 42.

selves to it itself rather than to an image of it. Admittedly, the past is no longer available for perception and the fantasized never was, but memory and free imagination bring us close to both the past and the imaginary without making us leave our present place of residence. As existence, Dasein expands itself to the physically absent with the result that even the absent can be present. This partially explains why we can experience what according to ordinary notions of experience is beyond the reach of experience, and think in a way that is broader than the rational way of thinking. As will become apparent in the section "Free Imagination," imagination makes aesthetic experience and expanded thinking possible, thereby challenging the epistemological borders developed by Kant himself and confirmed by most modern philosophers. Imagination is thus responsible not only for the previously mentioned and, by Heidegger, highlighted forming of a horizon, but also for the possibility of transcending the established picture of the world by crossing the limits of what is usually considered to be possible thought and experience.[278]

On the Limit

Half a century after Heidegger, Eugenio Trías formulated a philosophy of the limit in which he neither rejected the transcendent nor reproduced the traditional metaphysical idea of it. In this philosophy, Trías pays respect to the fact that we can study the transcendent only provided we can experience it, that is, we cannot study it 'in itself.' However, he also addresses the consequences of the realization that the mere idea of a border itself fosters a vision of something beyond that border. When Kant insisted that there is a limit to what we can know, it thus implicated some awareness

---

[278] Heidegger did not recognize the fundamental structures of existence (pure imagination, for instance) as aesthetic; nor did he recognize phenomenology as an expression of philosophical aesthetics. The reason for this lack of recognition is pragmatic rather than systematic; it is due to his historically determined identification of aesthetics with the philosophy of art. See Martin Heidegger, "The Origin of the Work of Art," in *Poetry, Language, Thought* (New York: Harper Perennial Thought, 2013), and the chapters on Heidegger in Jørgensen, *Den skønne tænkning*, 275–357. However, aesthetics was introduced by Alexander Gottlieb Baumgarten as a philosophy of experience, not a philosophy of art; see the chapters on Baumgarten in Jørgensen, *Den skønne tænkning*, 83–158.

about what we *cannot* know. The transcendent is beyond the limit of human cognition described by Kant, but according to Trías, the transcendent manifests itself on the limit—or we would not be able to think about it. Therefore, the limit of what we can know not only separates but also unites the transcendent and the immanent. It allows the transcendent and the immanent to encounter each other in the form of *symbolic events*. When such events take place, the transcendent is not subject to cognition in the sense ascribed to this word by Kant, and therefore philosophy should not attempt to determine the content of the transcendent. The transcendent appears as beautiful because it manifests itself symbolically. Rather than attempting to identify the transcendent, philosophy must therefore examine its symbolic manifestations and articulate the insight (not knowledge) that they convey. The task is to investigate the experiences of beauty that the symbolic events constitute and explore the transcendence associated with these experiences.

The symbol is not "a 'vicarious' substitute for whatever other thing one might think it symbolizes or represents," says Trías.[279] It is not a 'something' that 'represents' something other, but must rather be understood in verbal form as an existential event.[280] Trías also uses the word 'symbol' in its original meaning as a term for a 'throwing together' (*sym-ballein*), and he refers to the transcendent as the 'holy'; therefore, the symbol is the event that the holy and its presence are "thrown together."[281] The symbol depicts the transcendent in immanence by making the holy present and by giving its presence "form and figure."[282] Through the symbolic event, the holy, which is unrecognizable to understanding, reveals itself on the limit at which we experience it sensitively, not empirically. The holy manifests itself to the human being who can therefore testi-

---

279 Eugenio Trías, *Pensar la religión* (Barcelona: Ediciones Destino, 1997), 241.

280 Trías, *Pensar la religión*, 152, 241.

281 Trías, *Pensar la religión*, 121.

282 Trías, *Pensar la religión*, 121.

fy to its presence, although the holy as such remains unavailable.[283] Trías conceives the duality of revelation and concealment that thus characterizes the holy by distinguishing between the *holy* and the *sacred*. The holy is the dimension of the transcendent that remains unavailable, whereas the sacred is the dimension of it that appears and can be experienced and used. However, although we can distinguish analytically, they represent "two dimensions of the same *phenomenon* (the holy-and-sacred)," which, according to Trías, is also the case in Rudolf Otto's *mysterium tremendum et fascinans*.[284]

Nevertheless, such symbolic events no longer take shape as visionary experiences, but happen "in secret."[285] They are unshaped but still play an important role for us as humans. As examples of unshaped symbolic events, Trías mentions love, the painful experience of loss, the imminence of death (of both others and oneself), "all the agonizing and transformative experiences that make existence seek a change of its *ethos*, its attitude, its action."[286] Such experiences transcend rationality, break its command, and are an important quality criterion in art.[287] According to Trías, art contains traces of the holy in the form of the beauty of the artwork, and beautiful art is thus by definition sublime: the trace of the holy is its "terrifying beauty."[288] However, modern art is a product of secularization and is thus essentially critical. We therefore seldom expect modern art to contain traces of the holy, but according to Trías, such traces are in fact present, and he even believes that art ceases to be art if it loses its connection with the holy it demystifies. "Modern art must aim at being a secularized work that quenches its

283 Trías, *Pensar la religión*, 152–153.

284 Eugenio Trías, "Thinking Religion: the Symbol and the Sacred," trans. D. Webb, in *Religion*, eds. J. Derrida and G. Vattimo (Stanford: Stanford University Press, 1998), 106, endnote 7.

285 Trías, *Pensar la religión*, 227.

286 Trías, *Pensar la religión*, 228.

287 Trías, *Pensar la religión*, 227–228.

288 Eugenio Trías, *Lo bello y lo siniestro* (Barcelona: Editorial Seix Barral, 1982), 17.

thirst in the (holy) source, which it simultaneously keeps trying to drain."[289] Good contemporary art is aware of this paradox, which it shapes rather than ignores. It dances on the limit between the transcendent and the immanent and does not become hypnotized by one side, whether the holy or the worldly.

Trías's ideas of the holy and the beautiful are integral elements of the modernity criticism that his philosophy as such represents. According to him, modernity is characterized by insisting on radical immanence, which means that it rejects and suspects anything but what reason itself can account for; it especially suspects the holy. This is why he critically attempts to lead everything said and written up to the *area of the limit*. "Only here is it possible to interpret the withdrawn that the symbol presents and makes available to perception."[290] Translated into the terminology used in other sections of this chapter, it is a question of lifting oneself up and over the way of thinking controlled by understanding, which dominates modern science and modern society. The task is to expand thinking, make it more elastic, so that it can interpret phenomena in the light of not only what we can experience empirically and have exact evidence for, but also what is on the other side of the limit of cognition. Only if we, by way of expanded thinking, stay in the limit's area will we be able to see the repressed for which we usually have no eye; for example, the sublime in the beautiful, the holy in art, and the sensitive in philosophical thought. Such expanded thinking is not just rational thinking rather than intellectual reasoning, but aesthetic thinking: it presupposes free imagination, interpreted *not* as a mental faculty but rather as an ontological power that transcends what is only subjective. The aforementioned stay in the limit's area thus cannot result from personal intention. One must surrender to the imagination in order to think in the expanded way and thus think aesthetically. The encounter with the holy is not accessible at will; it is an event.

---

289 Trías, *Pensar la religión*, 118.

290 Trías, *Pensar la religión*, 133.

At the Threshold

The word 'border' usually describes a line, primarily separating two countries or states, whereas the word 'borderland' denotes the land on either side of the border, but is also used to describe an unclear state or condition between two things, for example between sleeping and waking, dream and reality, or myth and history. To the extent that the limit referred to by Trías has anything to do with a border, it is as a borderland. The limit is extensive not only in length but also in width, because it encompasses both sides, and as Trías describes the limit, it is rather associated with personal experience than with political geography. There is an aspect of spatiality to the limit, which lets it appear more akin to a threshold than a line. This is confirmed by the Latin word *limen*, which denotes a threshold rather than a boundary, and according to which liminal phenomena stand on some social or experiential threshold. Trías makes use of the meaning of the Latin *limen* when developing his understanding of the limit as a place of experience that qualifies as event and is of existential significance. Similarly, Walter Benjamin's philosophy contains a concept of the *threshold*—articulated in his *Arcades Project*, where it is evident that this concept denotes something other than a boundary.[291] "Threshold and boundary must be carefully distinguished," says Benjamin. "The *Schwelle* [threshold] is a *zone*. And indeed a zone of transition."[292] Like the limit referred to by Trías, the threshold described by Benjamin distinguishes itself by connecting rather than separating. Both limits and thresholds allow us to come from one place to another. They allow passages over them, transitions between spheres or states; they invite innovative change, whereas boundaries tend to halt movements.

However, according to Benjamin, the thresholds in human life have become difficult to see, and a person's threshold-crossing therefore seldom results in experience. "Rites de passage—this is the designation in folklore for the ceremonies that attach to death

---

291 Walter Benjamin, *The Arcades Project*, trans. H. Eiland and K. McLaughlin (Cambridge, MA and London: The Belknap Press of Harvard University Press, 2002).

292 Benjamin, *The Arcades Project*, 856; see also 494.

and birth, to marriage, puberty, and so forth. In modern life, these transitions are becoming ever more unrecognizable and impossible to experience. We have grown very poor in threshold experiences."[293] We still pass many thresholds, but it now happens in concealment. One can get married without a major ceremony, divorced with a click on the internet, and leave the world completely unnoticed.[294] Nowadays, we might pass even more thresholds than people used to do, but we do not celebrate as they did, and with the absence of ceremony, the opportunity for experience (not just impression or perception) disappears. "Falling asleep is perhaps the only such [threshold] experience that remains to us," writes Benjamin.[295] When we fall asleep, we move from one world to another, which to most of us is still associated with ritual. "But together with this, there is also waking up," adds Benjamin.[296] Awakening sheds a light over the threshold-crossing movement from wake to sleep that is similar to the light previously shed by ceremonial celebration over the essential events of life. Awakening, which itself crosses the threshold of the land of dreams but in the opposite direction, makes the move into sleep and dreaming available for *experience*.

As examples of current threshold experiences, Benjamin also mentions "the ebb and flow of conversation and the sexual permutations of love—experience that surges over thresholds like the changing figures of the dream."[297] In addition to the critical observation that we become inexperienced by emptying life of ceremony and ritual, Benjamin's reflections are thus probably about the need to become more aware of the passages that even modern life contains. We might interpret the meaning of his considerations as an appeal to develop our sensitivity toward the structuring of life con-

---

293 Benjamin, *The Arcades Project*, 494.

294 'Divorce with a click on the internet' refers to the Danish possibility of immediate divorce (*straks-skilsmisse*), which was introduced in 2013.

295 Benjamin, *The Arcades Project*, 494.

296 Benjamin, *The Arcades Project*, 494.

297 Benjamin, *The Arcades Project*, 494.

stituted by our crossings of its thresholds—the thresholds of both the life of the mind and the life of action. Human life is shaped by such crossings, which together constitute the narrative of a person's history. The shape that life thus obtains, and the life story the individual acquires, appear more clearly, the more distinctly his or her threshold-crossing is highlighted, whether through *celebration* or *reflection*. Clarity promotes experience, and experience is insightful: the single event, which any crossing of a threshold is, appears this way as an integral part of the totalities that the individual's life and life as such constitute. Experience in this sense of the word is what requires attention—that is, attention to what is happening, in this case a threshold-crossing—and demands more attention, the more it happens in concealment. Experience requires the aesthetic sensitivity that genuine attention includes; this brings us back to the imagination, the engine in the land of dreams we do best to visit every night.

Sleep is vital, but the journeys in the form of free reflection that manifest themselves in art, philosophy, and religion do not happen in the embrace of sleep. Such journeys are waking imaginations that take place at the threshold, in its space, rather than in the land of dreams on the other side of the threshold—a land whose existence we only know due to awakening. The magical threshold characters that anyone reading Benjamin encounters in his texts do not originate in the dark chamber of sleep, but in the half-lit threshold space of awakening. In accordance with this, Benjamin considered neither dreaming nor intoxication as purposes in themselves.[298] The point is not to escape from the waking life, not even from the command of rationality, but to gain momentum in the alternatives we obtain glimpses of by putting the understanding on hold and by reflecting on the memory of what that brings. In concealment, the dream is awaiting the awakening, Benjamin thought; the dream wishes not to be cultivated, but interpreted. The importance of imagination is due not to its suspension of cognition, but

---

298   Walter Benjamin, *On Hashish*, trans. H. Eiland et al. (Cambridge, MA and London: The Belknap Press of Harvard University Press, 2006).

to what it itself contributes to cognition, and which surpasses the reproduction of sensory input for which older theories of imagination only had an eye. What is important is that the imagination can transform conceptual, determinate intellectual cognition into sensitively expanded and as such aesthetic cognition that provides insight into wider contexts and thus anticipates the common good.

Free Imagination

We have seen that pure imagination is world-forming; according to Heidegger, it makes cognition possible by opening the horizon within which something can appear. Kant emphasized, however, that we can only know what is immanent: the fact that the transcendent is unavailable for cognition is precisely what defines it as transcendent. Nevertheless, we have also seen Heidegger demonstrate how pure imagination can make the absent present, which, however, did not result in knowledge but in memory and expectation. Heidegger also paid respect to the limit of cognition defined by Kant, provided 'cognition' means what it means in the philosophy of Kant, namely the identification made by understanding. If, however, we allow a different use of the word 'cognition'—which is what Baumgarten did when introducing his concept of sensitive cognition—we will experience a movement of the limit of cognition, so unsurpassable to Kant. In his aesthetics, Baumgarten describes an interplay between sensitive and intellectual cognition, in which cognition is oriented toward not logical truth but 'aestheticological' truth, and by which we know more than we do by intellectual cognition.[299] Aestheticologically, we do not get insight into everything, but into more of what is otherwise available only to God: the absolute, the essence of the world, the metaphysical fullness of it all.[300] Kant rejected the aesthetics in which Baumgarten presented this

---

[299] Baumgarten, *Ästhetik*, § 427; Jørgensen, *Den skønne tænkning*, 123.

[300] Baumgarten, *Ästhetik*, § 560; Jørgensen, *Den skønne tænkning*, 123.

thought,[301] but in his own *Critique of Judgment*, Kant himself studied one of the prerequisites for the sensitive cognition described by Baumgarten and for the associated relocation of the limit of human knowledge. He studied the *free* imagination.

As sources of sensitive cognition, Baumgarten mentions different forms of imagination, both "phantasia" and "facultas fingendi," and in the *Critique of Judgment*, Kant examines the role of free imagination in judgments of taste, and thus also in moral action.[302] Whereas in his *Critique of Pure Reason* Kant investigated the cognitive judgments produced by determining judgment, in the *Critique of Judgment* he investigates the judgments of taste produced by reflecting judgment.[303] Like cognitive judgments, judgments of taste require both understanding and imagination, but since imagination acts more freely in judgments of taste, we are now dealing with imagination that is not just pure but free. In principle, the power of judgment attempts to determine the phenomena presented to it, but if there is no concept available for this determination, and it is thus not possible to identify the phenomenon, judgment begins to reflect. The absence of concept makes judgment start searching for a concept, and if this search remains ineffective, the result is a judgment of taste, not a cognitive judgment. In this seeking reflection, imagination unfolds more freely than in the work of determining judgment because it is not constrained by any concept. The freedom that thus characterizes the work of aesthetic reflecting judg-

---

301 Kant, *Critique of Pure Reason*, A 21/B 35, footnote; Immanuel Kant, *Critique of Judgment*, § 15 (5: 226–229).

302 Alexander Gottlieb Baumgarten, *Metaphysics: A Critical Translation with Kant's Elucidations, Selected Notes, and Related Materials*, eds. and trans. C.D. Fugate and J. Hymers (London: Bloomsbury Academic, 2014), §§ 557ff., 589ff, In Baumgarten's aesthetics, *phantasia* (the imagination) is termed *dispositio naturalis ad imaginandum* (the natural disposition for imagining something), and *facultas fingendi* (the faculty of invention) is termed *dispositio poetica* (the poetic disposition); see Baumgarten, *Ästhetik*, §§ 31, 34.

303 I am referring to the first part of the *Critique of Judgment*, which is devoted to an analysis of aesthetic judgments, the pure judgment of taste in particular. Judgments of taste are thus not only reflective but also aesthetic—they are aesthetic reflective judgments. However, reflecting judgment also produces teleological judgments; this category is subject to analysis in the second part of the *Critique of Judgment*.

ment, and which manifests itself in the feeling of pure well-being that accompanies pure judgments of taste, fosters an expectation in Kant's mind that here one might find a possible connection between understanding and reason, and thus also between theory and praxis. His aesthetics derives from the hope that the interplay between imagination and understanding characterizing pure judgments of taste promotes the ability of reason to transcend the sensuous without ending in barren abstraction—that the encounter with the beautiful confirms our potential as humans to actualize ourselves as free moral beings in a natural world governed by causal necessity.[304]

In § 59 of the *Critique of Judgment*, Kant concludes that the beautiful is the symbol of the morally good.[305] This affirmation of the hypothesis described earlier takes place on the basis of an analysis in which Kant finds that judgment—in the sense of aesthetic reflecting judgment—is associated with a way of thinking that differs from both understanding's "unprejudiced" way of thinking and reason's "consistent" way of thinking.[306] Judgment's way of thinking is distinguished by being *expanded*, which makes it essential for *reason's* way of thinking to blossom; that is, for the idea of the good to be translated into morally good conduct.[307] For according to Kant, acting morally is not just a matter of ignoring oneself and giving priority to the interest of another person. Moral action is rather characterized by doing what is best for the totality of which both persons are part. In order to act morally, one must have an eye for something that exceeds both one's own needs and another person's needs, namely the idea of the *common good*. In Kant's *Critique of Practical Reason*, it already appeared that such an idea is

---

304   Kant, *Critique of Judgment*, 63 (5: 176).

305   Kant, *Critique of Judgment*, 227 (5: 353).

306   Kant, *Critique of Judgment*, 174 (5: 294).

307   Kant, *Critique of Judgment*, 173–175 (5: 293–295). Kant's German term is *die erweiterte Denkungsart*. Paul Guyer and Eric Matthews translate the word *erweitert* as 'broad-minded,' but for reasons stated in the chapter "Philosophy at a Crossroads," footnote 74, I prefer 'expanded.'

a product of reason, and in his *Critique of Judgment,* he shows that it takes aesthetic judgment to translate ideas of reason into practical action.[308] The actualization of the idea of the common good presupposes the expanded way of thinking appertained to aesthetic reflecting judgment. This is the conclusion because imagination unfolds more freely in this kind of thinking than in the identifying practice of determining judgment, and because free imagination is what opens a horizon within which not only concrete phenomena but also abstract ideas can appear, while one's sense of the concrete remains intact.

The Moral Value of Aesthetic Transgression

Trías and Benjamin explored the limit and the threshold as places where more occurs than just somebody imagining something nonexistent. At the limit or threshold, genuine experience takes place: someone obtains insight into something that is larger than the person herself and which changes her. The limit and threshold experiences described by Trías and Benjamin are thus not only productive of insight. They are also existentially transformative and are thus of both moral and cognitive significance. Such experiences therefore differ radically from what Kant and many others mean by 'experience,' namely sensory experience or empirical experience, just as the insight gained from the experiences described by Trías and Benjamin differs from what 'cognition' usually means, namely the knowledge produced by the understanding. Trías's and Benjamin's limit and threshold experiences are rather akin to what Baumgarten referred to as sensitive cognition because they are not only sensuous but also sensitive, and for this reason productive of insight (as opposed to knowledge). In addition, the experiences investigated by Trías and Benjamin are related to the judgments of

---

308 Immanuel Kant, *Critique of Practical Reason*, ed. and trans. M.J. Gregor (Cambridge, UK: Cambridge University Press, 1999). In the *Critique of Judgment*, Kant thus concludes, "that taste can be called *sensus communis* with greater justice than can the healthy understanding, and that the aesthetic power of judgment rather than the intellectual can bear the name of a communal sense" (Kant, *Critique of Judgment*, 175 [5: 295]).

taste described by Kant, since imagination unfolds more freely in such experiences than in sensory/empirical experiences and in understanding's kind of cognition. The limit and threshold experiences are *aesthetic* in as much as they stem from the power called 'free imagination' by Kant.

From Kant's aesthetics, it appeared that theory and praxis remain opposed to each other if one does not think in the aesthetic-expanded way; however, a connection is indeed possible if one thinks aesthetically. This assessment forms part of the background for Kant's statement that the beautiful is the symbol of the morally good, which, translated into a more current terminology, means that the experience of beauty gives insight into the common good. The experience of beauty opens an extra horizon within the horizon of cognition formed by pure imagination—a horizon itself forming another world in the existing world and thus exceeding the latter. Moreover, the experience of beauty makes it possible to act morally, for, as mentioned previously, this requires an eye for something that includes more than what we are usually aware of: a level of ideas, the awareness of which lifts the thinking, and which has formative influence on our moral behavior, provided the awareness is aesthetic-sensitive, not abstract-theoretical. Beauty is a promise of happiness, said Stendhal.[309] It gives a hint of how life could be if we, in the words of Kant, were thinking in the aesthetic-expanded way, and thus acting for the benefit of the common good. Beauty radiates with a demand of change, said Rainer Maria Rilke; an appeal referred to by Trías as the sublime in the beautiful, and by Benjamin called the "expressionless."[310]

Kant's aesthetics can contribute to the development of an understanding of the experiences of transcendence that limit and threshold experiences essentially are. Due to the dualist nature of his philosophy, there is, however, a need for adjustment, which was

309   Stendhal, *Love*, trans. G. Sale and S. Sale (London: Penguin, 2004), 66, footnote 33.

310   Rainer Maria Rilke, *The Poetry of Rilke*, ed. and trans. E. Snow (New York: North Point Press, 2011), 223; Walter Benjamin, "On Semblance," trans. R. Livingstone, in *Selected Writings, Volume 1: 1913–1926*, eds. M. Bullock and M.W. Jennings (Cambridge, MA and London: The Belknap Press of Harvard University Press, 2002), 224.

met in the foregoing by the inclusion of Heidegger's hermeneutic phenomenological approach. Whereas, in a Kantian view, aesthetic experiences are something that a subject produces with the help of imagination and understanding, limit and threshold experiences are, in a Heideggerian view, something that happens to someone who is not in control of the event. As in Benjamin and Heidegger, the metaphysics of experience mentioned at the beginning of this chapter aims at suspending the paradigm of the dualist philosophy of mind and surpassing its reduction of experience and cognition to mental acts performed by subjects equipped with understanding, reason, and imagination. Contrary to this, contemporary border aesthetics weighs the role of the subject in the border crossing, and the artifacts it studies therefore often include personal tales about individual border crossings. First-person experiences are of course important to any research inspired by aesthetics, phenomenology, and hermeneutics, but the current border aesthetics' highlighting of the subject (the individual ego) obstructs an exploration of the genuinely transgressive nature of experiences such as the limit and threshold experiences discussed by Trías and Benjamin. For this and for other reasons, border aesthetics can advantageously seek help in the metaphysics of experience, which, thanks to its roots in philosophical aesthetics and hermeneutic phenomenology, also contributes inspiration from these philosophical 'schools.'

The emphasis of current border aesthetics on the subject and its actions leads to an inappropriate weighting of *identity issues*. Due to its emphasis on the subject-transcending quality of limit and threshold experiences, an experience-metaphysically based border aesthetics would rather weigh *ethical issues*. The established border aesthetics focuses on what it means for the individual to cross a border or not succeed in such an attempt; it flirts with psychology rather than profits from ontology. An experience-metaphysically based border aesthetics would also not ignore the significance for the individual person of the formation of individual identity. However, it would further invite an inclusion of reflection on the common human significance of the individual's encounter with something larger, including the implied decentering of the person. Admittedly, moral action requires personal integrity, but not only viewed as having an eye for more than one aspect of oneself or for the many tales that together constitute one's life story. It is not enough to be a 'whole person' in this sense of the phrase; nor is it enough to have an eye for other people as such 'whole people.' One must also be aware of something that exceeds both, which presupposes what Kant called the expanded way of thinking. However, just as experience is something we do not provide by ourselves, thinking (unlike identification) is something we ourselves are not in command of.[311] Thinking takes place, driven by an imagination that is world-forming and world-transcending, and thus also world-destructive. The imagination both creates and dissolves forms; it brings concepts in motion and it moves borders, limits, and thresholds.

---

[311] Martin Heidegger, *What is Called Thinking?*, trans. J. Glenn Gray (New York: Perennial, 2004).

Hospitality and World Poetry

Festivity

"Who is the 'host' of that famous party described in Plato's *Symposium*?" asks Andrea Nye in "The Hidden Host." "Is the host Agathon, in whose house the Symposium takes place? Is it Socrates, in whose honor the feast is held? Is it Plato, who evokes the scene for us?"[312] Nye argues that the real host is neither Plato nor Socrates; nor is it one of the other banquet guests. It is instead the priestess Diotima, who is only present in thought. "The root meaning of 'host' is a physical body on whose flesh parasites feed. The host is the nourishment they steal and convert to prolong their own dependent existences."[313] According to Nye, Diotima feeds the thought of Plato and the guests described by him. "She is the spokesperson for ways of life and thought that Greek philosophy feeds on, ways of thought whose authority Plato neutralized and converted to his own purposes."[314] Plato, Socrates, and the other male characters presented to us in *Symposium* are parasites because they neither recognize nor acknowledge the female source of their thought but rather distort it in their use of it. At the banquet, Socrates presents the lesson about Eros (the god of love) he once learned from Diotima, but he refers to it as a speech about duality and hierarchy, when it was

---

312   Andrea Nye, "The Hidden Host: Irigaray and Diotima at Plato's Symposium," *Hypatia: A Journal of Feminist Philosophy* Vol. 3, No. 3 (Winter 1989), 45.

313   Nye, "The Hidden Host," 45.

314   Nye, "The Hidden Host," 57.

really about unity and creativity. In the *Symposium*, Plato lets the male banquet guests listen to the words of Diotima, but only in order to master her thought by changing it into its opposite. Diotima's original lesson on the benefits of balancing materiality and spirituality he turns into a Platonic lesson on the flight of reason from the material to the spiritual.

Diotima's philosophy of love differs from both the theory of Forms in Plato's *Republic* and the mystical Pythagoreanism developed in the *Phaedrus*.[315] "Far from suggesting that the body is a degraded prison, Diotima sees bodily love as the metaphor and concrete training ground for all creative and knowledge-producing activities."[316] "The beauty-in-itself that the initiate in Diotima's philosophy may experience as the culmination of her training is not a transcendent Platonic Form …, but an indwelling immortal divine beauty, an attracting center that foments fruitful creation in all areas of existence."[317] In Diotima's view, the task is thus *not* to "dwell in the world of absolute beauty as the philosopher of Plato's Republic aspires to dwell in the upper sunlit world of the Forms. To cut oneself off from the natural generative center of human life … is to be content with only abstract, unreal ideas of virtue and to fail to achieve real virtue which must be lived and generated in the visible, physical world."[318] Rather than fleeing from what immanence itself contains—the aforementioned indwelling immortal divine beauty—the task is to keep in touch with it, because this is the way to live a "new enlightened existence," avoiding false images of virtue and achieving real virtue.[319] Due to Diotima's teaching of Socrates, Platonic thought includes the fertile female divinity referred to as

---

315   Plato, *Republic*, trans. G.M.A. Grube, rev. C.D.C. Reeve, and *Phaedrus*, trans. A. Nehamas and P. Woodruff, in *Plato: Complete Works*, eds. J.M. Cooper and D.S. Hutchinson (Indianapolis and Cambridge, MA: Hackett Publishing Company, 1997).

316   Nye, "The Hidden Host," 46.

317   Nye, "The Hidden Host," 46–47.

318   Nye, "The Hidden Host," 47.

319   Nye, "The Hidden Host," 47.

absolute beauty, but it secularizes and depletes this source. What originally constituted a creative power in immanence becomes a barren transcendent form. Diotima's focus on the process is substituted by Plato's focus on the result; sensitive experience is suppressed by rational knowledge.

However, a parasite is characterized not only by consuming the nourishment it receives from its host but also by inculcating and disseminating this nourishment. Platonic thought thus includes Diotimian thought; male Western philosophy is bisexual: there is a female side to it. This is probably one of the main reasons why misogyny still dominates Western philosophy and why female philosophers are exposed to a resentment that can manifest itself in hostile work environments. In the form of his female colleague, the male philosopher is confronted with an alarming inner voice, that is, the creative source without which he would have no ideas, and he is confronted the more intensely with this demon, the better—that is, the more creatively—his female colleague happens to think. Her presence exposes him to the problem that, in order to become a good philosopher, he himself must develop his femininity. He must unfold the female part of his mind, his creativity, which is suppressed by his rationality, that is, his wish to control what is thought rather than giving birth to new thought. Plato's theory of Forms and his mystical Pythagoreanism, however, disseminated Diotima's philosophy even as they distorted it. Likewise, the idea of indwelling immortal divine beauty and its creative power are still at work in Western secularized philosophy, even though the female identity of that beauty has become invisible in its Platonic shelter. The early German Romantics' idea of poetry testifies to the presence of the Diotimian idea of beauty; their understanding of poetry as a creative power in all being may be considered a late product of this idea. Diotima's invitation to wisdom was thus passed on by the Romantics; it runs in their invitation to poetically transmitted aesthetic-sensitive cognition.

Hospitality

Where there is a host, we also expect to find hospitality. Jacques Derrida defined this as inviting and welcoming the stranger, but distinguished between *the law of hospitality* (that is, unconditional hospitality, which is absolute and unlimited) and *laws of hospitality* (that is, conditional hospitality, which is relative and limited). First, there is "the law of unlimited hospitality (to give the new arrival all of one's home and oneself, to give him or her one's own, our own, without asking a name, or compensation, or the fulfilment of even the smallest condition)."[320] Second, there are "the laws (in the plural), those rights and duties that are always conditioned and conditional, as they are defined by the Greco-Roman tradition and even the Judeo-Christian one, by all of law and all philosophy of law up to Kant and Hegel in particular, across the family, civil society, and the State."[321] Conditional hospitality is what we experience in daily life and discuss in politics, whereas unconditional hospitality—which commands a breaking of the former, that is, the laws of hospitality—is a philosophical issue. Unconditional hospitality requires an opening up toward and a giving to people who are complete strangers: the absolute, unknown, and anonymous other. It requires such opening and giving without asking anything from the radically foreign other—not reciprocity, a name, or even a certain behavior. Showing such hospitality is unbearable, Derrida says, but "if, however, there is pure hospitality, it should be pushed to this extreme."[322]

Unconditional hospitality is a limit-concept; due to its extreme nature, Derrida also refers to it as "impossible."[323] In human

---

320 Jacques Derrida, *Of Hospitality: Anne Dufourmantelle invites Jacques Derrida to Respond*, trans. R. Bowlby (Stanford: Stanford University Press, 2000), 77.

321 Derrida, *Of Hospitality*, 77.

322 Derrida, "Hospitality, justice and responsibility: A dialogue with Jacques Derrida," in *Questioning Ethics: Contemporary Debates in Philosophy*, eds. R. Kearney and M. Dooley (London and New York: Routledge, 1999), 70.

323 Jacques Derrida, "Hostipitality," trans. B. Stocker and F. Morlock, *Angelaki: Journal of Theoretical Humanities* Vol. 5, No. 3 (December 2000), 14.

life, the inviting and welcoming of the 'stranger' that defines hospitality always includes a limitation that preserves a certain distance between host and guest. If one says 'welcome,' one is not renouncing one's mastery; the notion of having and retaining the mastery of the house underlies all hospitality.[324] Consequentially, in hospitality, there is an element of hostility, and this doubleness constitutes what Derrida calls a certain *hostipitality*. In order for unconditional hospitality to occur, there must be an absolute surprise, he adds, thus speaking of what it requires for what cannot happen to occur, but also disclosing the impossibility of such occurrence by comparing the radically unexpected other with the Messiah. "The other, like the Messiah, must arrive whenever he or she wants. She may even not arrive. ... I must be unprepared, or prepared to be unprepared, for the unexpected arrival of *any* other. Is this possible? I don't know. If, however, there is pure hospitality, or a pure gift, it should consist in this opening without horizon, without horizon of expectation, an opening to the newcomer whoever that may be. It may be terrible because the newcomer may be a good person, or may be the devil."[325] Unconditional hospitality is thus total surrender to whatever will come, which Derrida categorizes not as an expression of messianism but messianicity.[326] Messianism he considers an example of dogmatism: it attempts to master the divine by subjecting it to expectation and thus also determination. Messianicity, on the other hand, he considers the aforementioned absolute surprise. "If I could anticipate, if I had a horizon of anticipation, if I could see what is coming or who is coming, there would be no coming."[327]

What might Derrida's philosophy of hospitality, including his idea of hostipitality, teach about the hidden host of the *Sympo-*

324 Derrida, "Hostipitality," 14.

325 Derrida, "Hospitality, justice and responsibility," 70.

326 Kevin D. O'Gorman, "Jacques Derrida's philosophy of hospitality," *Hospitality Review* Vol. 8, No. 4 (2006), 53.

327 Jacques Derrida, *Deconstruction Engaged: The Sydney Seminars*, eds. P. Patton and T. Smith (Sydney: Power Publications, 2001), 67f.

sium? If Diotima is the host of the banquet, its guests are strangers invited and welcomed by her, regardless of how parasitic their behavior is. The body they feed on has itself allowed the invasion and exploitation of it by inviting and welcoming its parasites. This interpretation appears equivalent to the well-known male defense when accused of violating a woman: it is her own fault, she asked for it. However, the unconditional hospitality honored by Derrida is a liminal phenomenon and is thus not part of but only on the edge of human life. Among humans, we never experience hospitality of the completely unlimited sort; not even from a woman is one entitled to expect such generosity! The hospitality practiced by humans is always limited, irrespective of how generous it may appear, and it thus always includes the element of hostility leading to hostipitality. However, Diotima is not only a woman but also a priestess and thus closer to the gods. She symbolizes what no woman can do on a daily basis but what all women would do well to strive for, which is not forgiving but bearing with. As the representative of creativity, Diotima is superior to the males she meets, and she knows it. She detests their primitivism—their dualism, hierarchism, and competitiveness—but invests in teaching them the alternative, although she knows that they will never grasp the message. She bears with their minor minds. Without Diotima and the interest she takes in philosophy, Western philosophy would be nothing but yet another expression of bellicosity. Thanks to Diotima's lesson, however, male Western philosophers were destined since antiquity to struggle to integrate the female source of thinking in their thought. They seldom manage, but they never escape this task. That is the bitter gift of messing with a superior woman: it destines you to an eternal attempt to think what you cannot think.

The Beautiful Soul

By the end of the twentieth century, literary studies had embraced early German Romanticism, but philosophy and theology have not yet come that far. Whatever contemporary philosophers and theologians think of Georg Wilhelm Friedrich Hegel's philosophical idealism, most of them share his negative attitude toward his fellow relatives of Diotima, that is, the Romantics. The way in which Hegel treated "the unhappy consciousness" and "the beautiful soul" in *The Phenomenology of Spirit* can be viewed as an example of the previously mentioned struggle between the voices of reason and creativity, respectively.[328] *The Phenomenology of Spirit* is divided into three parts, entitled "A. Consciousness," "B. Self-Consciousness," and "C. (AA) Reason, (BB) Spirit, (CC) Religion, (DD) Absolute Knowing." In the part on self-consciousness, Hegel describes what he calls "the stoic consciousness," "the skeptical consciousness," and "the unhappy consciousness."[329] Historically considered, the unhappy consciousness is Hegel's description of the Christian consciousness of the Middle Ages, which, in his depiction of it, appears split like the stoic and the skeptical consciousnesses of antiquity, but differs from them by being aware of its own disunity. The unhappy consciousness is divided between the present and the past, between the near and the distant, and between the secular and the sacred. Through a series of reflections, the unhappy consciousness tries to maintain and determine its ideal and essence, but it is thrown back on itself and thus remains a captive of the restless flux of appearances. The unhappy consciousness is and remains split between its own appearance as divided and the self-identity it pursues as its essence.

Only later in *The Phenomenology of Spirit* is the reader presented to the beautiful soul, namely in the subpart "(BB) Spirit." While the unhappy consciousness appears just before the chapters on reason, the beautiful soul first appears immediately before Hegel's presentation of the highest spiritual forms, that is, religion, art, and philosophy. Hence, the beautiful soul does not appear until after the initiation of the reconciliation of the particular and the universal, of which the unhappy consciousness is incapable but which reason effectuates and which is a prerequisite for achieving

---

328 Georg Wilhelm Friedrich Hegel, *The Phenomenology of Spirit*, ed. and trans. T. Pinkard (Cambridge, UK: Cambridge University Press, 2018), 123ff. and 381ff.

329 Hegel, *The Phenomenology of Spirit*, 117–135.

absolute knowledge, that is, for becoming transparent to oneself as spirit. According to Hegel's description, reason emancipates consciousness from the concrete by adopting the latter without annihilating it, simultaneously retaining its own autonomy as consciousness and thus maintaining its connection to the essential, that is, the spirituality of consciousness itself. At the level at which the beautiful soul appears, the path to absolute knowledge interpreted as this soul's complete identity with itself is therefore significantly shorter than at the level of the unhappy consciousness. Nevertheless, Hegel's description of the beautiful soul shows that it is also 'unhappy,' albeit in its own way, which means that, even at this stage, there is still a long way to absolute knowledge. The beautiful soul mirrors the unhappy consciousness, as it "lacks the force to relinquish itself, lacks the force to make itself into a thing and to sustain being. It lives with the anxiety that it will stain the splendor of its innerness through action and existence."[330]

The discouragement of the beautiful soul to manifest itself drains this form of consciousness of substance and thus also of spirit. "To preserve the purity of its heart, it flees from contact with actuality, and it steadfastly perseveres in its obstinate powerlessness to renounce its own self, a self which has been tapered to the final point of abstraction. It stably exists in its powerlessness to give itself substantiality, or to transform its thinking into being and to entrust itself to absolute difference."[331] To employ terminology introduced largely by Martin Luther and still used at the time of Hegel, the beautiful soul is a 'fanatic' (*Schwärmer*). Luther used the term 'fanatics' to describe those of his contemporaries who were more concerned with their own inner emotions than their daily life with other people.[332] In Hegel's time, the same term was applied

---

330   Hegel, *The Phenomenology of Spirit*, 380.

331   Hegel, *The Phenomenology of Spirit*, 380.

332   See, for example, Martin Luther, "Smalcald Articles," in *Triglot Concordia: The Symbolical Books of the Evangelical Lutheran Church*, eds. and trans. F. Bente and W.H.T. Dau (St. Louis: Concordia Publishing House, 1921), III, 8, 3–13; http://bookofconcord.org/smalcald.php, accessed October 14, 2020. William H.T. Dau and Friedrich Bente translate 'Schwärmer' as 'enthusiast.'

more widely to characterize contemporary aesthetes, not least the Romantics. The beautiful soul described by Hegel lives in a universe of fantasies produced by itself without real contact with the concrete world. This fanaticism is the result of its longing for spirit; but it is also what makes the beautiful soul unhappy because it keeps the longing of the soul unsatisfied. "The hollow object which it generates to itself it thus now fills only with the consciousness of emptiness. It is a yearning which only loses itself as it becomes an essenceless object, and as it goes beyond this loss and then falls back on itself, it only finds itself as lost.—In this transparent purity of its moments it becomes an unhappy, so-called *beautiful soul*, and its burning embers gradually die out, and, as they do, the beautiful soul vanishes like a shapeless vapor dissolving into thin air."[333]

The beautiful soul lacks "all actuality," which, according to Hegel, is the problem with this form of consciousness.[334] It is "caught in the contradiction between its pure self and its necessity to empty itself into being and to turn itself around into actuality."[335] It dwells in "the *immediacy* of this opposition to which it adheres ... an immediacy which is alone the mediating middle and the reconciliation of an opposition which has been intensively raised to the point of its pure abstraction, and which is itself pure being or empty nothingness."[336] The beautiful soul, which itself is "the consciousness of this contradiction in its unreconciled immediacy, [is] shattered into madness and melts into a yearning, tubercular consumption. It thereby in fact gives up its severe adherence to *its being-for-itself* but engenders only the spiritless *unity* of being."[337]

---

333   Hegel, *The Phenomenology of Spirit*, 380–381.

334   Hegel, *The Phenomenology of Spirit*, 387.

335   Hegel, *The Phenomenology of Spirit*, 387.

336   Hegel, *The Phenomenology of Spirit*, 387.

337   Hegel, *The Phenomenology of Spirit*, 387.

The Motions of the Mind

In Hans Christian Andersen's Christmas tale "The Goblin and the Woman," the eponymous woman receives her guest with an openness that differs radically from the behavior displayed by reason, according to Hegel's presentation of reason in *The Phenomenology of Spirit*.[338] The woman's openness rather resembles what Derrida refers to as 'unconditional hospitality.' As is apparent from Andersen's title, his story includes not only a woman but also a goblin, or more specifically two kinds of goblin. The first goblin presented to the reader—the well-known little gray-dressed goblin with the red cap—is mad at the woman with "the gift of writing and the gift of speech," because she does not believe in his existence. She calls him a notion and fails to give him porridge, and he teases her as punishment for denying his existence. One day, the goblin recognizes, however, that the woman has written a piece titled "The Little Goblin," and he immediately assumes that her narrative is about him personally. "Oh, I'll pinch her! I'll chip her eggs, and pinch her chickens, and chase the fat off her fatted calf!" he says, thinking that she is pulling his leg with her text. Soon, however, it becomes evident that the woman has not ridiculed the goblin but written about "the Goblin's power and glory, and his rule over the Woman." Since the little gray-dressed goblin still assumes that *he* is the protagonist of the woman's narrative, he now also believes that *he* is the one she is praising with it. The goblin's vain belief reveals himself as human, the narrator of Andersen's fairy tale informs the reader, after which it also becomes apparent that the goblin celebrated by the woman is a different goblin. "I love poetry; it haunts me; it jeers, advises, and commands. That's what I mean by my title, 'The Little Goblin,'" the woman tells the assistant schoolmaster before she asks him to read her text aloud. "You know the old peasants' superstitions about the Goblin who is always playing tricks in the house. I myself am the house, and my poetical feelings are the Gob-

---

338 Hans Christian Andersen, "The Goblin and the Woman," in *The Complete Andersen*, trans. J. Hersholt, https://andersen.sdu.dk/vaerk/hersholt/index_e.html, accessed March 27, 2018. All quotations in this paragraph are from this source.

lin, the spirit that possesses me. I have written about his power and strength in 'The Little Goblin.'"

It would be counterfactual historiography for us to consider how Hegel might have judged the woman described by Andersen. Andersen's fairy tale was published in 1867, but Hegel's *Phenomenology of Spirit* was published in 1807, and Hegel died in 1835. There is no harm, however, in categorizing Andersen as a romantic poet, and Hegel had certainly made up his mind about the Romantics of his time. Furthermore, there are similarities between Hegel's description of the beautiful soul and the woman with the gift of speech and writing presented by Andersen. Both the woman and the beautiful soul cultivate poetry rather than striving for the absolute knowledge that, according to Hegel, must be the goal of all intellectual employment. As mentioned earlier, the woman even describes poetry as her 'poetical feelings' and 'the spirit that possesses' her, and she celebrates the emotional power that poetry thus constitutes rather than practicing "the labor of the concept" which, pursuant to Hegel, is the path to true knowledge.[339] Since the beautiful soul described by Hegel can be considered a symbol of the Romanticism from which he departed, we must therefore assume that, even after the woman's statement to the assistant schoolmaster, Hegel would have categorized them both as beautiful souls. However, the narrator of Andersen's fairy tale would have probably abstained from a categorization of this sort. His remark that the goblin reveals himself as human due to his belief, when recognizing that the woman's narrative is favorable toward the goblin it describes, that this narrative praises him personally, does not affirm such a categorization. The narrator's comment rather gives rise to identifying the gray-dressed goblin, not the woman, as a beautiful soul (that is, in Hegel's negative meaning of this term). The gray-dressed goblin's vanity reveals him as a creature who cultivates his own emotional and imaginative life without fulfilling Hegel's expectation of transforming one's inner into something outer for the sake of one's spiritual development. This goblin reveals himself as

---

339   Hegel, *The Phenomenology of Spirit*, 44.

a Romantic or an aesthete in the pejorative sense of these words, which is how they were employed by Hegel and his contemporaries.

By the end of the eighteenth century, early German Romantics challenged the modern notion of the sovereignty of the rational ego, and, in the twentieth century, existential philosophers like Martin Heidegger kept problematizing thought that focused on the subject understood as the ego. Nevertheless, Andersen's fairy tale rests on a subject-philosophical way of thinking, insofar as it is the woman's *mind* and what takes place in this 'house' that forms the focus of the tale. However, the early German Romantic's criticism of the subject-philosophical way of thinking is also reflected in Andersen's fairy tale, insofar as the woman herself is not in control of what happens inside her, that is, in the 'house' constituted by her inner. Poetry storms the woman's mind. It fools her, overwhelming her with feelings, sensations, and presentiments that she cannot control and whose source she calls 'poetry' and 'the little Goblin.' It is this second inhabitant of the house that the woman praises in her narrative; she does not celebrate the gray-dressed goblin but the poetic power of the mind, which disturbs the domestic peace but is also the source of domestic liveliness. Neither the fact that the woman is aware of poetry nor her praise of the power it constitutes suffices as an argument for her being a beautiful soul (in the negative sense). The woman is a Romantic, and her poetic habitus does not empty her of spirit or actual existence. On the contrary, it is precisely spirit that storms her mind, although it rummages in the form of poetry rather than philosophy, and finds concrete expression, namely in the form of the stories she writes and shares with the assistant schoolmaster.

The Condition of Secrecy

The Danish poet Inger Christensen said that "what we sense when we read a poem is *the motions of the mind*. Not only the poet's mind, and not only our own, but both, intermingled in the poem, as if the poem were our minds' common ground."[340] Such motions we only experience, however, if the poem is good, which, according to Christensen, means that it is *beautiful* rather than *banal*. It is the beauty of the poem that is responsible for the motions of the mind, since what is beautiful is not identical to what is pretty, but what is *meaningful*. In beautiful poems, even heavy topics float because each individual word is "so packed with energy that it contains millions of ways to experience things."[341] This poetical floating and thus also the beauty of the poem result from the fact that poems make use of the wealth of meaning with which words are loaded; thanks to this, a poem contains not only the individual poet's private experience of the described object but all possible ways of experiencing it. *Poetic* language hence deals with the whole world at once, whereas *logical-practical* language ignores parts of reality by excluding some ways of experiencing it. Moreover, logical-practical language acts as if "under conditions that we've set in advance, ... it were humanly possible to tell the truth about the world."[342] This is what characterizes the 'methodical' way of thinking, which, according to Hans-Georg Gadamer, dominates modern science, whereas poetry, as demonstrated by Alexander Gottlieb Baumgarten, relates differently to truth.[343] "Maybe poetry can't tell any truths at all. But it can *be* true, because the reality that accompanies the words is true. This secret-filled correlation between language and reality is how poetry becomes insight," Christensen claims.[344]

One can interpret Christensen's description of poetry's relation to 'truths' and 'the truth' as a statement that poems are sup-

---

340 Inger Christensen, *The Condition of Secrecy* (New York: A New Directions Paperback Original, 2018), 37. My emphasis.

341 Christensen, *The Condition of Secrecy*, 37.

342 Christensen, *The Condition of Secrecy*, 38.

343 Hans-Georg Gadamer, *Praise of Theory: Speeches and Essays*, trans. C. Dawson (New Haven and London: Yale University Press, 1998). Alexander Gottlieb Baumgarten, *Reflections on Poetry: Meditationes philosophicae de nonnullis ad poema pertinentibus*, eds. and trans. K. Aschenbrenner and W.B. Holther (Berkeley: University of California Press, 1954).

344 Christensen, *The Condition of Secrecy*, 38.

posed to deliver *insight* rather than *knowledge*. The sciences pursue particular truths about single phenomena and demarcated matters, which does not represent a defect but instead the very idea of modern science, which accomplishes its mission well. However, many people confuse the 'truths' of the sciences with 'truth' as such, and this is the problem. When philosophy takes shape as *philosophia* instead of imitating modern science, it differs from the latter by *not* pursuing 'truths.' Philosophy rather seeks 'the truth,' that is, truth in the metaphysical sense of the word (the *idea* of truth), and this, too, is not a defect but the very meaning of philosophy understood as 'love of wisdom.' Without philosophy's quest for truth and wisdom, it would not be possible to put the scientific way of thinking and its particular 'truths' into perspective. This critical task that philosophy accomplishes is shared with poetry, because poetry and philosophy are closely related. Historically, philosophy originated in poetry; Plato drew on the Homeric sources. Ontologically, philosophy still originates in poetry; when philosophy takes shape as *philosophia* (which contemporary philosophy seldom does, however), it attempts like poetry to *understand* rather than simply *explain* what it describes.[345] Poetry and philosophy both are nourished by, contribute to, and explore language or, strictly speaking, the connection between language and reality, which, according to Christensen, is a *mysterious miracle*.[346] Poetry, and thus also philosophy, are assigned to enter this connection, that is, the mysterious miracle, which "may well be the condition of secrecy Novalis speaks of when he says, 'Das Äusere ist ein in einen Geheimniszustand aufgehobenes Innere.' (The outer world is the inner world, raised to a condition of secrecy.)"[347]

Due to the poet's familiarity with the condition of secrecy referred to by Novalis and Christensen, the poet takes after the child,

---

345   I am referring to understanding in the hermeneutic phenomenological sense of the word, different from the Kantian sense of it; see the chapter "Limit and Threshold," footnotes 265 and 270.

346   Christensen, *The Condition of Secrecy*, 38.

347   Christensen, *The Condition of Secrecy*, 38–39.

that is, the child's way of experiencing the world presented poetically by Andersen in the form of fairy tales and contemplated philosophically by Walter Benjamin in his memorial work *Berlin Childhood around 1900*.[348] In the condition of secrecy, "the poet stands at the center of a universe that has no center," and "we know how things have been connected with each other ever since we were children," Christensen claims.[349] Hence, the condition of secrecy is not an exotic phenomenon reserved for a few of us but a common human experience. One does not have to be a poet in order to know the condition of secrecy, since this condition is the state in which we all encounter the world in the first place. One does not have to be a genius in order to enter the condition of secrecy, unless 'genius' means something other than usually presumed, that is, unless it means actualizing a common human potential rather than being more gifted than other people. Poets are human beings, human beings begin as children, and "poetry is just one of human beings' many ways of recognizing things"—the one that is the most related to the way of cognizing that characterizes children.[350] Many people write no poems, but poetry is alive in all of us, namely as the poetical language we seldom speak in our daily lives but recognize when we encounter it, for example, in the form of fairy tales. Poetry stays alive in adults as a memory of the connection with the world experienced in childhood, which can be aroused by poems written by people who, as poets, have trained themselves to unfold the wealth of meaning with which words are loaded, that is, who have trained in this unfolding in order to linguistically reestablish the connection that is analytically shattered by understanding's way of thinking when understanding performs science and ignores the poet's and the child's poetic way of experiencing the world.

---

348 Walter Benjamin, *Berlin Childhood around 1900*, trans. H. Eiland, in *Selected Writings, Volume 3: 1935–1938*, eds. H. Eiland and M.W. Jennings (Cambridge, MA and London: The Belknap Press of Harvard University Press, 2002).

349 Christensen, *The Condition of Secrecy*, 39.

350 Christensen, *The Condition of Secrecy*, 42.

Some people believe that "we human beings, with our language, are set apart from the world"; other people experience "human beings' use of language as part of the world."[351] This is the distinction Christensen discusses in *The Condition of Secrecy*, whereas, in her poems, she attempts to express the interpretation of the relation between humans and the world according to which human language is a part of the latter, and the world therefore expresses itself along with humans' self-expression. As a poet, Christensen experiences and thinks that the human being and the world are interconnected—that they express themselves by and through each other and that the result of this genuine conversation is *poetry*; not only poetry in the sense of literary works but also poetry in the sense of all sorts of expressions of the condition of secrecy, which the connection between man and world constitutes in a culture dominated by the understanding's technical-scientific and analytic way of obtaining knowledge. The aim of literary poetry is to cultivate the poetry that already sounds in universe in the form of the permanent exchange between everything that takes place as man and world express themselves by and through each other. Poets deliberately attempt to enter this condition of secrecy "where the inner and outer worlds exist together, as if they had never been separated."[352] By way of their 'nonmethodical'—that is, their sensitively attentive—practice, poets consistently strive to suspend the shattering of the original poetic connection between the human being and the world caused by the 'methodical' approach of modern science discussed by Gadamer, which is considered the presupposition for what is now meant by 'scientific' truth.

The Intermediate World

Literary poetry is not hostile to science but protects poetry in times that neglect or even ridicule poetry. The word 'poetry' describes the connection between language and the world referred to by Chris-

---

351 Christensen, *The Condition of Secrecy*, 42.

352 Christensen, *The Condition of Secrecy*, 41.

tensen as the condition of secrecy. Since this state is original, it is constitutive of not only literature but also science, although the latter makes a virtue of suspending the connection between language and the world, which is why it perceives this connection as alien. The condition of secrecy is not secret to anyone but to the understanding's way of thinking, which is the source of modern science's methodical approach and the distance between humans and the world created by this approach. Children and poets, on the other hand, are familiar with the condition of secrecy, this interrelation between everything and everyone that precedes all separation and division. They know the poetic truth that, although we can never get outside the world, we can pretend to do so, which is why we can do science, and that the possibility of us pretending to get outside the world is itself part of the fact that we never do. For precisely this reason, we need not only science but also literary poetry; we need poetry to express and understand the condition of secrecy, which the poetic connection constitutes in a culture dominated by scientific separation. "We can't recognize anything without using recognition itself," Christensen remarks.[353] Not only in literary works but also in scientific cognitions, the world writes itself through the mind of the human being, although it seems that, in science, man only writes about the world, not about himself.

Our potential recognition is already built into the world, "into all the comparisons that the world itself consists of."[354] We are just media for the recognition that is only possible because "we're bound to the forms of nature, in that we ourselves are one of its manifold forms."[355] According to Christensen, although all our cultural forms are something in themselves, they are, above all, forms of nature. They are expressions of nature's writing of itself through us. As our potential knowledge is already present in the world and we 'just' have to discover it, the world is already in the mind and

---

353 Christensen, *The Condition of Secrecy*, 43.

354 Christensen, *The Condition of Secrecy*, 44.

355 Christensen, *The Condition of Secrecy*, 43.

must 'just' find expression. Poets try to promote the latter by deliberately entering the condition of secrecy, which, by being 'original,' already exists, but which we have shut off. Poets open themselves to the condition of secrecy so that it can communicate through them, which translates into surrendering to language and letting language itself speak (about its connection with the world) rather than using it as an instrument (to say something about something other). It is not only researchers who use language as an instrument. We all do. Similarly, it is not only poets who enter the condition of secrecy to let language itself be heard; others do this as well, that is, when they are at play and surrender to language, letting it produce meaning in processes they themselves do not control. According to Christensen, we must know that we are already in the condition of secrecy we seek, which is why she appeals to "our sense of being borne up by an inconceivably huge, already existing foundation of comparisons."[356] We can pretend that there is a distance between us and the world, language and the described, which is something we constantly do; but we must know that the knowledge we swagger about as our own we have extracted from the world; although we perceive the world as distant, we were in fact only able to extract our knowledge because the world is close. Likewise, we must know that the poems we rejoice in as if they were works produced by us are actually the world's writing of itself through us, which is only possible because the mind is not 'closed' to the world but the world is already in the mind.

This condition of secrecy, which, as previously mentioned, is only secret to understanding's way of thinking, which separates mind and world, is similar to what in the metaphysics of experience is termed *the intermediate world*.[357] Secrecy and the intermediate world are both intangible and without borders; the intermediate world is not a geographical space but an experiential realm. It ap-

356   Christensen, *The Condition of Secrecy*, 44.

357   See the chapter "The Dialogue of Experience," last section, for a definition of the concept of the intermediate world. See also the chapter "The Intermediate World" in Dorthe Jørgensen, *Imaginative Moods: Aesthetics, Religion, Philosophy* (Aarhus: Aarhus University Press, 2021).

peared earlier, that, according to Christensen, poetry regarded as the condition of secrecy is an original state in which there is no separation between language and the world. Similarly, the metaphysics of experience describes the intermediate world as a realm in which sensitive experiences occur that are not products of a human mind at a distance from the world but are events occurring to that mind. From a literary point of view, poetic language might be considered the provider of the very possibility of poetic experience. However, from a phenomenological point of view, and thus also from the point of view of the metaphysics of experience, which is inspired by philosophical aesthetics and hermeneutic phenomenology, poetic language presupposes the sensitivity that is the origin of literary poetry (and truly innovative science, as well). Thus, the condition of secrecy and the intermediate world are intertwined in the sense that a condition of secrecy is characteristic of the intermediate world, but this condition and its secrecy are not the only features of that experiential realm.

To us as modern humans dominated by intellectualism, the intermediate world appears as something located between subject and object, which explains the wording of the term. However, in the intermediate world, there is no subject in the sense of a rationally thinking ego; nor is there any object in the sense of something that the subject strives to identify. On the contrary, the intermediate world contains only concrete phenomena and sensitive attentiveness. The term 'intermediate world' thus denotes the experiential level at which those experiences occur that are not products of individual human minds but are events that transform our minds, and which are thus poetic by nature. In these experiences, we sense intimate correspondences between what we normally regard as humans and the world, and as divided and separate; that is, correspondences similar to the comparisons mentioned by Christensen and beautifully described by Benjamin in his depictions of what he termed the 'aura.' I refer in particular to Benjamin's idea of the aura-experiential animation of the inanimate, that is, his idea of a material world provided with responsive eyes, which, like Christensen's poetics, was inspired by early German Romanticism: "Inherent in the gaze ... is the expectation that it will be returned by that on which it is bestowed. Where this expectation is met ... there is an experience [*Erfahrung*] of the aura in all its fullness. 'Perceptibility,' as Novalis puts it, 'is an attentiveness.' The perceptibility he has in mind is none other than that of the aura."[358] Obviously, children are familiar with this animating way of perceiving what we usually consider inanimate objects, but so are poets. This we learned from Andersen and, from Christensen, we learn that anyone is a poet simply by being human, but also that being human means being a sensitively attentive rather than a rational creature.

World Poetry

Due to its multidimensionality, the intermediate world is poetic and characterized by hospitality. Its multidimensionality stems from the sensitive experiences occurring in the realm that the intermediate world constitutes. It specifically stems from the fact that these experiences include not only aesthetic but also religious and philosophical experiences, and that they all originate in *basic experience*.[359] The latter is the experience-metaphysical term for the phenomenological origin of all experience and is thus *not* the designation of a particular singular experience. This origin of all knowledge and culture is sensitive, not just sensuous, and therefore includes comprehension in the sense of insight (not rational understanding). Moreover, it includes faith in the sense of trust (not religious confession), which means that we involuntarily rely on what is sensitively delivered. Therefore, basic experience itself is also multidimensional. In addition to implying that it is the source of various experiences of a both sensitive and rewarding quality,

---

358   Walter Benjamin, "On Some Motifs in Baudelaire," trans. H. Zohn, in *Selected Writings, Volume 4: 1938–1940*, eds. H. Eiland and M.W. Jennings (Cambridge, MA and London: The Belknap Press of Harvard University Press, 2003), 338. Benjamin refers to Novalis, *Novalis Schriften* (Berlin: G. Reimer, 1901), part 2 (first half), 293.

359   Concerning the concept of 'basic experience,' see also "The Dialogue of Experience" in the present volume, and "Fornemmelse, tro og forståelse" (Sensation, Faith, and Comprehension) in *Den skønne tænkning*, as well as several chapters in *Imaginative Moods*.

the multidimensionality of basic experience implies that these experiences are interrelated despite their different categorization as 'aesthetic,' 'religious,' or 'philosophical.' For example, aesthetic experiences deliver insight that is compatible with the understanding delivered by philosophical experiences, and religious experiences are no less sensitive than aesthetic experiences. There are parallels between aesthetic, religious, and philosophical experience, which are explicable due to their common origin and this origin's threefold nature characterized by not only sensitivity but also faith and comprehension.

German Romanticism, to which Christensen referred, rejected modern particularism by presenting alternative universalistic and holistic thought. "*Praying* is to religion what thinking is to *philosophy*," said Novalis. "Praying is *making religion* .... The religious sense *prays*—just as the mental organ thinks."[360] This conception of an essential relationship between religion and philosophy accords with the experience-metaphysical idea of fundamental interrelations between aesthetics, religion, and philosophy, and it anticipates Martin Heidegger's identification of thinking as thanking,[361] which is associated with his idea of thinking as the common source of poetry and philosophy.[362] The thinking addressed by Heidegger obviously differs from the thinking described by Immanuel Kant in his *Critique of Pure Reason*, that is, the intellectual processing of intuitions and concepts performed when we identify what we perceive.[363] Instead, Heidegger's idea of thinking refers to the sensitive dwelling on the phenomena that takes place before we

---

360   Novalis, "[125], Fragmente und Studien 1799–1800," in *Novalis Schriften Dritter Band: Das philosophische Werk II*, eds. R. Samuel, H.-J. Mähl, and G. Schulz (Stuttgart, Berlin, Köln, and Mainz: Verlag W. Kohlhammer, 1983), 573.

361   See Martin Heidegger, *What is Called Thinking?*, trans. J. Glenn Gray (New York: Perennial, 2004), 139ff.

362   See Martin Heidegger, "Postscript to 'What is Metaphysics?'," trans. W. McNeill, in *Pathmarks*, ed. W. McNeill (Cambridge, UK: Cambridge University Press, 1998), 237.

363   Immanuel Kant, *Critique of Pure Reason*, eds. and trans. P. Guyer and A.W. Wood (Cambridge, UK: Cambridge University Press, 1998).

perform any intellectual processing. This thinking is the reflexivity that unfolds in experience regarded as different from both sense perception and intellectual cognition. Interpreted this way, 'thinking' is an adequate term for the preintellectual reflective processes that characterize basic experience and that take place in the intermediate world, that is, in the various sensitive experiences constituting this realm. The dwelling thus performed is the thinking that Heidegger identified as thanking and also characterized as poetizing.[364] Experience-metaphysically translated, Heidegger realized thinking's sensitive origin but without literally acknowledging the aesthetic nature of sensitivity, which was due to his misinterpretation of philosophical aesthetics as traditional metaphysics.[365] As mentioned, however, Heidegger honored poetry as essential to both thinking and thanking. He therefore not only acknowledged a fundamental kinship between thought and prayer (or philosophy and religion) but, despite his rejection of aesthetics, in a sense also acknowledged the aesthetic-sensitive origin of both.

As stated previously, the intermediate world is poetic and characterized by hospitality due to its multidimensionality, as the latter is the product of a state—experience-metaphysically termed 'basic experience'—in which the doors between what we usually categorize as 'aesthetic,' 'religious,' or 'philosophical' are open. In basic experience, that is, at the very outset of human knowledge and culture, a radical hospitality is at work in the form of a simultaneous receptivity and responsivity, which explains the creativity of the reflexivity at work in the various experiences constituting the intermediate world. The poetic quality of this experiential realm, the multilayered nature of the intermediate world, thus goes hand in hand with an open-mindedness, which we unfortunately tend to

---

364 See Martin Heidegger, "The Thinker as Poet," in *Poetry, Language, Thought*, ed. and trans. A. Hofstadter (New York: Harper Perennial Modern Thought, 2013). The word 'poetizing' (*dichten*) is *not* synonymous with 'aestheticizing'; it suggests no affectation. 'Poetizing' denotes a way of relating to Being and beings that results in 'genuine poetry,' which always means more than it utters, and which is produced not only by poets but also by thinkers.

365 For a comprehensive presentation of this critical interpretation of Heidegger's notion of aesthetics, see the part "Heideggers fænomenologi" (Heidegger's Phenomenology) in Jørgensen, *Den skønne tænkning*, 275–357.

leave behind as we grow up, and which got lost in science and society with the introduction of the sharply defined individual modern scientific disciplines. However, according to Andersen, Christensen, and Benjamin, among others, this open-mindedness still characterizes the minds of children and poets. It would therefore be both sensible and possible to initiate a poetization (different from an aestheticization) of our educational systems and research institutions. That is, it would be wise to acknowledge and apply the holism of the state in which human knowledge originates, be it termed a festive banquet, a house inhabited by goblins, a condition of secrecy, or the intermediate world. Furthermore, open-mindedness is both valuable and necessary not only epistemologically but also ethically considered. It takes an open mind to empathize with the other, and it demands radical open-mindedness to include the third point of reference, without which one only pays respect to oneself or the other but not the common good. If we have no eye for the level of ideas constituted by ideas such as the common good, no truly moral conduct is possible. Ideas of this sort are transcendent in the sense that they are ideas of something ungraspable, and, from this, it follows that transcendence is a prerequisite for acting morally. Moreover, this transcendence is itself dependent on openness in the sense of the simultaneous receptivity and responsivity that characterize the origin of human knowledge and culture. Practical hospitality thus rests on ontological hospitality. The hospitality performed in a concrete case rests on the broader and more fundamental hospitality inherent in the intermediate world and thus in human nature.

Bibliography

Adorno, Theodor W. *Aesthetic Theory*. Edited by G. Adorno and R. Tiedemann, translated by R. Hullot-Kentor. London: The Athlone Press, 1997.

Adorno, Theodor W. *Notes to Literature: Combined Edition*. Edited by R. Tiedemann, translated by S.W. Nicholsen. New York: Columbia University Press, 2019.

Agamben, Giorgio. "The Dictation of Poetry." In *The End of the Poem: Studies in Poetics*, translated by D. Heller-Roazen, 76–86. Stanford: Stanford University Press, 1999.

Andersen, Hans Christian. "The Goblin and the Woman." In *The Complete Andersen*, translated by J. Hersholt. https://andersen.sdu.dk/vaerk/hersholt/index_e.html. Accessed March 27, 2018.

Aristotle. *Nicomachean Ethics*. Translated by W.D. Ross, revised by J.O. Urmson. In *The Complete Works of Aristotle: The Revised Oxford Translation, Volume 2*, edited by J. Barnes, 1729–1867. Princeton: Princeton University Press, 1984.

Aristotle. *On the Soul*. Translated by J.A. Smith. In *The Complete Works of Aristotle: The Revised Oxford Translation, Volume 1*, edited by J. Barnes, 641–692. Princeton: Princeton University Press, 1984.

Aristotle, *Poetics*. Translated by I. Bywater. In *The Complete Works of Aristotle: The Revised Oxford Translation, Volume 2*, edited by J. Barnes, 2316–2340. Princeton: Princeton University Press, 1984.

Augustine, Saint. *The Confessions of St. Augustine*. Translated by E.B. Pusey. Auckland: The Floating Press, 2008.

Barthes, Roland. *Roland Barthes by Roland Barthes*. Translated by R. Howard. New York: Hill and Wang, 1977.

Baudrillard, Jean. *Symbolic Exchange and Death*. Translated by I.H. Grant. London: Sage Publications, 1993.

Baumgarten, Alexander Gottlieb. *Ästhetik, Volume 1–2*. Translated by D. Mirbach. Hamburg: Felix Meiner Verlag, 2007.

Baumgarten, Alexander Gottlieb. *Die Vorreden zur Metaphysik*. Edited and translated by U. Niggli. Frankfurt am Main: Vittorio Klostermann, 1998.

Baumgarten, Alexander Gottlieb. *Metaphysics: A Critical Translation with Kant's Elucidations, Selected Notes, and Related Materials*. Edited and translated by C.D. Fugate and J. Hymers. London: Bloomsbury Academic, 2014.

Baumgarten, Alexander Gottlieb. *Reflections on Poetry: Meditationes philosophicae de nonnullis ad poema pertinentibus*. Edited and translated by K. Aschenbrenner and W.B. Holther. Berkeley: University of California Press, 1954.

Benjamin, Walter. "A Berlin Chronicle." Translated by E. Jephcott. In *Selected Writings, Volume 2: 1927–1934*, edited by M.W. Jennings, H. Eiland, and G. Smith, 595–637. Cambridge, MA and London: The Belknap Press of Harvard University Press, 2001.

Benjamin, Walter. *Berlin Childhood around 1900*. Translated by H. Eiland. In *Selected Writings, Volume 3: 1935–1938*, edited by H. Eiland and M.W. Jennings, 344–413. Cambridge, MA and London: The Belknap Press of Harvard University Press, 2002.

Benjamin, Walter. "Eduard Fuchs, Collector and Historian." Translated by H. Eiland and M.W. Jennings, on the basis of a prior translation by K. Tarnowski. In *Selected Writings, Volume 3: 1935–1938*, edited by H. Eiland and M.W. Jennings, 260–302. Cambridge, MA and London: The Belknap Press of Harvard University Press, 2002.

Benjamin, Walter. "Experience and Poverty." Translated by R. Livingstone. In *Selected Writings, Volume 2: 1927–1934*, edited by M.W. Jennings, H. Eiland, and G. Smith, 731–736. Cambridge, MA and London: The Belknap Press of Harvard University Press, 2001.

Benjamin, Walter. "92. To Gerhard Scholem." In *The Correspondence of Walter Benjamin 1910–1940*, edited by G. Scholem and Th.W. Adorno, translated by M.R. Jacobson and E.M. Jacobson, 167–169. Chicago and London: The University of Chicago Press, 1994.

Benjamin, Walter. *On Hashish*. Translated by H. Eiland et al. Cambridge, MA and London: The Belknap Press of Harvard University Press, 2006.

Benjamin, Walter. "On Semblance." Translated by R. Livingstone. In *Selected Writings Volume 1: 1913–1926*, edited by M. Bullock and M.W. Jennings, 223–225. Cambridge, MA and London: The Belknap Press of Harvard University Press, 2002.

Benjamin, Walter. "On Some Motifs in Baudelaire." Translated by H. Zohn. In *Selected Writings, Volume 4: 1938–1940*, edited by H. Eiland and M.W. Jennings, 313–355. Cambridge, MA and London: The Belknap Press of Harvard University Press, 2003.

Benjamin, Walter. "On the Concept of History." Translated by H. Zohn. In *Selected Writings, Volume 4: 1938–1940*, edited by H. Eiland and M.W. Jennings, 389–400. Cambridge, MA and London: The Belknap Press of Harvard University Press, 2003.

Benjamin, Walter. "On the Program of the Coming Philosophy." Translated by M. Ritter. In *Selected Writings, Volume 1: 1913–1926*, edited by M. Bullock and M.W. Jennings, 100–110. Cambridge, MA and London: The Belknap Press of Harvard University Press, 2002.

Benjamin, Walter. *The Arcades Project*. Translated by H. Eiland and K. McLaughlin. Cambridge, MA and London: The Belknap Press of Harvard University Press, 2002.

Benjamin, Walter. *The Concept of Criticism in German Romanticism*. Translated by D. Lachterman, H. Eiland, and I. Balfour. In *Selected Writings, Volume 1: 1913–1926*, edited by M. Bullock and M.W. Jennings, 116–200. Cambridge, MA and London: The Belknap Press of Harvard University Press, 2002.

Benjamin, Walter. *The Origin of German Tragic Drama*. Translated by J. Osborne. London and New York: Verso, 2009.

Boethius, Anicius Manlius Severinus. *The Consolation of Philosophy*. Translated by D.R. Slavitt. Cambridge, MA: Harvard University Press, 2008.

Bourdieu, Pierre. *Distinction: A Social Critique of the Judgement of Taste*. Translated by R. Nice. Cambridge, MA: Harvard University Press, 1984.

Bourdieu, Pierre. *The Rules of Art: Genesis and Structure of the Literary Field*. Translated by S. Emanuel. Stanford: Stanford University Press, 1996.

Calvino, Italo. *Mr. Palomar*. Translated by W. Weaver. San Diego, New York, and London: Harcourt Brace Jovanovich, 1985.

Calvino, Italo. *Six Memos for the Next Millennium*. Translated by P. Creagh. Cambridge, MA: Harvard University Press, 1988.

Cassirer, Ernst. *An Essay on Man: An Introduction to a Philosophy of Culture*. New Haven and London: Yale University Press, 1974.

Christensen, Inger. *The Condition of Secrecy*. Translated by S. Nied. New York: A New Directions Paperbook Original, 2018.

Dante Alighieri. *Purgatorio*. Translated by J. Hollander and R. Hollander. New York: Doubleday, 2003.

Derrida, Jacques. *Deconstruction Engaged: The Sydney Seminars*. Edited by P. Patton and T. Smith. Sydney: Power Publications, 2001.

Derrida, Jacques. "Hospitality, Justice and Responsibility: A Dialogue with Jacques Derrida." In *Questioning Ethics: Contemporary Debates in Philosophy*, edited by R. Kearney and M. Dooley, 65–83. London and New York: Routledge, 1999.

Derrida, Jacques. "Hostipitality." Translated by B. Stocker and F. Morlock. *Angelaki: Journal of Theoretical Humanities* Vol. 5, No. 3 (December 2000): 3–18.

Derrida, Jacques. *Of Hospitality: Anne Dufourmantelle invites Jacques Derrida to Respond*. Translated by R. Bowlby. Stanford: Stanford University Press, 2000.

Dixon, Robert. *The Baumgarten Corruption*. London and East Haven: Pluto Press, 1995.

Eagleton, Terry. *The Ideology of the Aesthetic*. Oxford and Cambridge, MA: Basil Blackwell, 1990.

Foucault, Michel. "On the Genealogy of Ethics: An Overview of Work in Progress." In *The Foucault Reader*, edited by P. Rabinow, 340–372. London: Penguin Books, 1991.

Gadamer, Hans-Georg. "Aesthetics and Hermeneutics." Translated by D.E. Linge. In *The Gadamer Reader: A Bouquet of the Later Writings*, edited by R.E. Palmer, 123–131. Evanston: Northwestern University Press, 2007.

Gadamer, Hans-Georg. *Praise of Theory: Speeches and Essays*. Translated by C. Dawson. New Haven and London: Yale University Press, 1998.

Gadamer, Hans-Georg. *Truth and Method*. Translated by J. Weinsheimer and D.G. Marshall. London and New York: Bloomsbury Academic, 2003.

Greenaway, Peter. *Flyga över Vatten / Flying over Water*. Edited by B. Nordal. Malmö: Malmö Konsthall, 2000.

Gumbrecht, Hans Ulrich. *Production of Presence: What Meaning Cannot Convey*. Stanford: Stanford University Press, 2004.

Habermas, Jürgen. *The Theory of Communicative Action. Volume One: Reason and the Rationalization of Society; Volume Two: Lifeworld and System. A Critique of Functionalist Reason*. Translated by T.A. McCarthy. Boston: Beacon Press, 1984–1987.

Hegel, Georg Wilhelm Friedrich. *Aesthetics: Lectures on Fine Art, Volume 1*. Translated by T.M. Knox. Oxford: Clarendon Press, 1988.

Hegel, Georg Wilhelm Friedrich. "Oldest System-Programme of German Idealism." Translated by T. Carman. *European Journal of Philosophy* Vol. 3, No. 2 (August 1995): 199–200.

Hegel, Georg Wilhelm Friedrich. *The Phenomenology of Spirit*. Edited and translated by T. Pinkard. Cambridge, UK: Cambridge University Press, 2018.

Hegel, Georg Wilhelm Friedrich. *The Philosophy of History*. Translated by J. Sibree. Mineola: Dover Publications, 2004.

Heidegger, Martin. "A Dialogue on Language between a Japanese and an Inquirer." In *On the Way to Language*, translated by P.D. Hertz, 1–54. New York: HarperOne, 1982.

Heidegger, Martin. *Being and Time*. Translated by J. Stambaugh, translation revised by D.J. Schmidt. Albany: State University of New York Press, 2010.

Heidegger, Martin. *Kant and the Problem of Metaphysics*. Translated by R. Taft. Bloomington: Indiana University Press, 1997.

Heidegger, Martin. "Letter on 'Humanism.'" Translated by F.A. Capuzzi. In *Pathmarks*, edited by W. McNeill, 239–276. Cambridge, UK: Cambridge University Press, 1998.

Heidegger, Martin. "Memorial Address." In *Discourse on Thinking: A Translation of Gelassenheit*, translated by J.M. Anderson and E.H. Freund, 43–57. New York: Harper and Row, 1966.

Heidegger, Martin. *Nietzsche, Volume 1: The Will to Power as Art; Volume 2: The Eternal Recurrence of the Same*. Edited and translated by D.F. Krell. San Francisco: HarperSanFrancisco, 1991.

Heidegger, Martin. "On the Question of Being." Translated by W. McNeill. In *Pathmarks*, edited by W. McNeill, 291–322. Cambridge, UK: Cambridge University Press, 1998.

Heidegger, Martin, "Postscript to 'What is Metaphysics?'." Translated by W. McNeill. In *Pathmarks*, edited by W. McNeill, 231–238. Cambridge, UK: Cambridge University Press, 1998.

Heidegger, Martin. *The Fundamental Concepts of Metaphysics: World, Finitude, Solitude*. Translated by W. McNeill. Bloomington and Indianapolis: Indiana University Press, 2001.

Heidegger, Martin. "The Origin of the Work of Art." In *Poetry, Language, Thought*, edited and translated by A. Hofstadter, 15–86. New York: Harper Perennial Modern Thought, 2013.

Heidegger, Martin. "The Thinker as Poet." In *Poetry, Language, Thought*, edited and translated by A. Hofstadter, 1–14. New York: Harper Perennial Modern Thought, 2013.

Heidegger, Martin. *What is Called Thinking?*. Translated by J. Glenn Gray. New York: Perennial, 2004.

Joyce, James. *A Portrait of the Artist as a Young Man*. Edited by J. Johnson. New York: Oxford University Press Inc., 2008.

Jørgensen, Dorthe. *Aglaias dans: På vej mod en æstetisk tænkning* (Aglaia's Dance: Toward an Aesthetic Thinking). Aarhus: Aarhus University Press, 2008.

Jørgensen, Dorthe. "Creativity and Aesthetic Thinking: Toward an Aesthetics of Well-Being." In *Routledge Handbook of Well-Being*, edited by K. Galvin, 243–249. Abingdon and New York: Routledge, 2018.

Jørgensen, Dorthe. *Den skønne tænkning: Veje til erfaringsmetafysik. Religionsfilosofisk udmøntet* (Beautiful Thinking: Pathways to the Metaphysics of Experience. Religio-Philosophically Implemented). Aarhus: Aarhus University Press, 2014.

Jørgensen, Dorthe. "Erkendelsens mirakel" (The Miracle of Knowledge). In *Mirakler* (Miracles), edited by B.H. Callesen et al., 99–113. Aarhus: Aarhus University Press, 2008.

Jørgensen, Dorthe. "Filosofi ved en skillevej" (Philosophy at a Crossroads). In *Tænkningens veje: Et festskrift til Søren Gosvig Olesen* (The Paths of Thinking: Celebrating Søren Gosvig Olesen), edited by P. Jepsen, 135–157. Skive: Wunderbuch, 2016.

Jørgensen, Dorthe. "Forundringsstemt" (Attuned to Wonder). In *Lys og sang: Jørgen Carlsen 60 år* (Light and Song: Jørgen Carlsen 60 Years), edited by H.R. Christensen et al., 181–189. Aarhus: Klim, 2009.

Jørgensen, Dorthe. "Guddommelighedserfaring i en moderne verden" (Experiencing Divinity in a Modern World). In *Interesse for Gud: Ni tidssvarende essay* (Interest in God: Nine Contemporary Essays), edited by H. Brandt-Pedersen and N. Grønkjær, 98–117. Frederiksberg: Anis, 2002.

Jørgensen, Dorthe. *Historien som værk: Værkets historie* (History as a Work: The Work's History). Aarhus: Aarhus University Press, 2006.

Jørgensen, Dorthe. "Hvad skal vi med æstetik?" (Why Do We Need Philosophical Aesthetics?). In *Aglaias dans: På vej mod en æstetisk tænkning* (Aglaia's Dance: Toward an Aesthetic Thinking), 307–323. Aarhus: Aarhus University Press, 2008.

Jørgensen, Dorthe. "Hvordan vi tænker: Om vejen til visdom" (The Way We Think: About the Path to Wisdom). In *Viljen til visdom: En bog om dannelse og uddannelse. En debatbog udgivet i anledning af Odense Katedralskoles 725 års jubilæum* (The Will to Wisdom: A Debate Book on Formation and Education Published on the Occasion of Odense Cathedral School's 725th Anniversary), edited by J.T. Bertelsen et al., 100–109. Aarhus: Slagmark, 2008.

Jørgensen, Dorthe. *Imaginative Moods: Aesthetics, Religion, Philosophy*. Aarhus: Aarhus University Press, 2021.

Jørgensen, Dorthe. "Limit and Threshold: Knowledge and Ethics in the Making." In *Debating and Defining Borders: Theoretical and Philosophical Perspectives*, edited by A. Cooper and S. Tinning, 138–151. Abingdon and New York: Routledge, 2019.

Jørgensen, Dorthe. "Philosophy at a Crossroads." *Philosophy Today: An International Journal of Contemporary Philosophy* Vol. 59, No. 4 (Fall 2015): 611–625.

Jørgensen, Dorthe. "Preface." In *Verdenspoesi: Malerier og tankebilleder* (World Poetry: Paintings and Thought-Images), 73–73. Aarhus: Women's Museum, 2011.

Jørgensen, Dorthe. *Skønhed—En engel gik forbi* (Beauty—An Angel Passed By). Aarhus: Aarhus University Press, 2006.

Jørgensen, Dorthe. *Skønhedens metamorfose: De æstetiske idéers historie* (The Metamorphosis of Beauty: History of Aesthetic Ideas). Odense: Odense University Press, 2001.

Jørgensen, Dorthe. "The Dialogue of Experience." *Trópos: Journal of Hermeneutics and Philosophical Criticism* Vol. 9, No. 1 (2016): 45–62.

Jørgensen, Dorthe. "The Experience of Immanent Transcendence." *Transfiguration. Nordic Journal of Religion and the Arts: 2010/2011* (2012): 35–52.

Jørgensen, Dorthe. "The Philosophy of Imagination." In *Handbook of Imagination and Culture*, edited by T. Zittoun and V.P. Gläveanu, 19–45. New York: Oxford University Press, 2017.

Jørgensen, Dorthe. "Why Do We Need Philosophical Aesthetics?" *Transfiguration. Nordic Journal of Religion and the Arts: 2009* (2010): 17–34.

Kant, Immanuel. "An Answer to the Question: What Is Enlightenment?" In *Practical Philosophy*, edited and translated by M.J. Gregor, 11–22. Cambridge, UK: Cambridge University Press, 1996.

Kant, Immanuel. "Conjectural Beginning of Human History." Translated by A.W. Wood. In *Anthropology, History, and Education*, edited by G. Zöller and R.B. Louden, 160–175. New York: Cambridge University Press, 2007.

Kant, Immanuel. *Critique of Practical Reason*. Edited and translated by M.J. Gregor. Cambridge, UK: Cambridge University Press, 1999.

Kant, Immanuel. *Critique of Pure Reason*. Edited and translated by P. Guyer and A.W. Wood. Cambridge, UK: Cambridge University Press, 1998.

Kant, Immanuel. *Critique of the Power of Judgment*. Edited and translated by P. Guyer and E. Matthews. New York: Cambridge University Press, 2000.

Kant, Immanuel. *Gesammelte Schriften* (Akademie-Ausgabe), I–XXIII. InteLex Past Masters. http://www.nlx.com.

Kant, Immanuel. *Groundwork of the Metaphysics of Morals*. Edited and translated by M. Gregor and J. Timmermann. New York: Cambridge University Press, 2011.

Kant, Immanuel. "Idea for a Universal History with a Cosmopolitan Aim." Translated by A.W. Wood. In *Anthropology, History, and Education*, edited by G. Zöller and R.B. Louden, 107–120. New York: Cambridge University Press, 2007.

Kant, Immanuel. "Lectures on Pedagogy." Translated by R.B. Louden. In *Anthropology, History, and Education*, edited by G. Zöller and R.B. Louden, 434–485. New York: Cambridge University Press, 2007.

Kant, Immanuel. *Religion within the Boundaries of Mere Reason: And Other Writings*. Edited and translated by A. Wood and G.D. Giovanni. Cambridge, UK: Cambridge University Press, 1998.

Kierkegaard, Søren. *Either/Or: Part I–II*. In *Kierkegaard's Writings, Volume 3–4*, edited and translated by H.V. Hong and E.H. Hong. Princeton: Princeton University Press, 1988.

Lichtenberg, Georg Christoph. "[76], Notebook K: 1793–1796." In *Philosophical Writings*, edited and translated by S. Tester, 152–152. Albany: State University of New York Press, 2012.

Luhmann, Niklas. *Art as a Social System*. Translated by E.M. Knodt. Stanford: Stanford University Press, 2000.

Luther, Martin. "Smalcald Articles." In *Triglot Concordia: The Symbolical Books of the Evangelical Lutheran Church*, edited and translated by F. Bente and W.H.T. Dau. St. Louis: Concordia Publishing House, 1921. http://bookofconcord.org/smalcald.php. Accessed October 14, 2020.

Marcuse, Herbert. *Art and Liberation*. In *Collected Papers of Herbert Marcuse, Volume 4*, edited by D. Kellner. London and New York: Routledge, 2007.

Marcuse, Herbert. *The Aesthetic Dimension: Toward a Critique of Marxist Aesthetics*. Translated by E. Sherover. Boston: Beacon Press, 1978.

Negt, Oskar and Alexander Kluge. *History and Obstinacy*. Edited by D. Fore, translated by R. Langston. New York: Zone Books, 2014.

Nietzsche, Friedrich. *Beyond Good and Evil: Prelude to a Philosophy of the Future*. Translated by A.D. Caro. In *The Complete Works of Friedrich Nietzsche, Volume 8: Beyond Good and Evil; On the Genealogy of Morality*, edited by A.D. Schrift and D. Large, first organized in English by E. Behler, 1–203. Stanford: Stanford University Press, 2014.

Nietzsche, Friedrich. *On the Utility and Liability of History for Life*. Translated by R.T. Gray. In *The Complete Works of Friedrich Nietzsche, Volume 2: Unfashionable Observations*, edited by E. Behler, 83–167. Stanford: Stanford University Press, 1995.

Nordal, Bera. "Introduction." In *Flyga över Vatten / Flying over Water*. Text and concept by P. Greenaway, edited by B. Nordal. Malmö: Malmö Konsthall, 2000.

Novalis. *Novalis Schriften*. Berlin: G. Reimer, 1901.

Novalis. "[125], Fragmente und Studien 1799–1800." In *Novalis Schriften Dritter Band: Das philosophische Werk II*, edited by R. Samuel, H.-J. Mähl, and G. Schulz, 573–573. Stuttgart, Berlin, Köln, Mainz: Verlag W. Kohlhammer, 1983.

Nye, Andrea. "The Hidden Host: Irigaray and Diotima at Plato's Symposium." *Hypatia: A Journal of Feminist Philosophy* Vol. 3, No. 3 (Winter 1989): 45–61.

O'Gorman, Kevin D. "Jacques Derrida's philosophy of hospitality." *Hospitality Review* Vol. 8, No. 4 (2006): 50–57.

Ovid, *The Metamorphoses of Ovid: Books VIII–XV*. Translated by H.T. Riley. London: George Bell and Sons, 1893. https://www.gutenberg.org. Accessed October 26, 2017.

Pamuk, Orhan. *Istanbul: Memories and the City*. Translated by M. Freely. London: Faber and Faber, 2006.

Pamuk, Orhan. *The Black Book*. Translated by G. Gün. New York: Farrar, Straus, and Giroux, 1994.

Plato. *Phaedrus*. Translated by A. Nehamas and P. Woodruff. In *Plato: Complete Works*, edited by J.M. Cooper and D.S. Hutchinson, 506–556. Indianapolis and Cambridge, MA: Hackett Publishing Company, 1997.

Plato. *Republic*. Translated by G.M.A. Grube, translation revised by C.D.C. Reeve. In *Plato: Complete Works*, edited by J.M. Cooper and D.S. Hutchinson, 971–1223. Indianapolis and Cambridge, MA: Hackett Publishing Company, 1997.

Plato. *Symposium*. Translated by A. Nehamas and P. Woodruff. In *Plato: Complete Works*, edited by J.M. Cooper and D.S. Hutchinson, 457–505. Indianapolis and Cambridge, MA: Hackett Publishing Company, 1997.

Rancière, Jacques. *Aesthetics and Its Discontents*. Translated by S. Corcoran. Cambridge, UK: Polity Press, 2009.

Rancière, Jacques. *The Ignorant Schoolmaster: Five Lessons in Intellectual Emancipation*. Translated by K. Ross. Stanford: Stanford University Press, 1991.

Rancière, Jacques. *The Politics of Aesthetics: The Distribution of the Sensible*. Edited and translated by G. Rockhill. London: Bloomsbury, 2013.

Rilke, Rainer Maria. *The Poetry of Rilke*. Edited and translated by E. Snow. New York: North Point Press, 2009.

Rosello, Mireille and Stephen F. Wolfe. "Introduction." In *Border Aesthetics: Concepts and Intersections*, edited by J. Schimanski and S.F. Wolfe, 1–24. New York and Oxford: Berghahn Books, 2017.

Said, Edward W. *Representations of the Intellectual: The Reith Lectures*. New York: Vintage Books, 1994.

Santayana, George. *The Sense of Beauty: Being the Outlines of Aesthetic Theory*. New York: Charles Scribner's Sons, 1896.

Schelling, Friedrich Wilhelm Joseph von. *Zur Geschichte der neueren Philosophie: Münchener Vorlesungen*. Edited by M. Buhr. Leipzig: Phillipp Reclam jun., 1966.

Schiller, Friedrich. *On the Aesthetic Education of Man in a Series of Letters*. Edited and translated by E.M. Wilkinson and L.A. Willoughby. Oxford: Clarendon Press, 1967.

Schlegel, Friedrich. "Athenaeum Fragments, 125." In *Philosophical Fragments*, translated by P. Firchow, 34–34. Minneapolis and London: University of Minnesota Press, 1991.

Starobinski, Jean. "L'empire de l'imaginaire." In *La relation critique: Essai* (L'oeil vivant II), 173–254. Paris: Gallimard, 1972.

Stendhal. *Love*. Translated by G. Sale and S. Sale. London: Penguin, 2004.

The Chicago Manual of Style Online. Seventeenth edition. Chicago: Chicago University Press, 2017. www.chicagomanualofstyle.org.

The Merriam-Webster Dictionary. Springfield: Merriam-Webster Inc., 2020. www.merriam-webster.com.

Trías, Eugenio. *Lo bello y lo siniestro*. Barcelona: Editorial Seix Barral, 1982.

Trías, Eugenio. *Pensar la religión*. Barcelona: Ediciones Destino, 1997.

Trías, Eugenio, "Thinking Religion: the Symbol and the Sacred." Translated by D. Webb. In *Religion*, edited by J. Derrida and G. Vattimo, 95–110. Stanford: Stanford University Press, 1998.

Vattimo, Gianni and Santiago Zabala. *Hermeneutic Communism: From Heidegger to Marx*. New York: Columbia University Press, 2011.

Vattimo, Gianni. *The Responsibility of the Philosopher*. Edited by F. D'Agostini, translated by W. Mccuaig. New York: Columbia University Press, 2010.

Wilkens, Claudius. *Æsthetik i Omrids* (Aesthetics in Outline). Copenhagen: Gyldendalske Boghandels Forlag, 1888.

Acknowledgments

Chapter 1: "Attuned to Wonder." Not previously published in English. Published in Danish as "Forundringsstemt," *Lys og sang*, eds. Hans Rubech Christensen et al. (Aarhus: Klim, 2009), 181–189.

Chapter 2: "Philosophy at a Crossroads." Previously published in *Philosophy Today: An International Journal of Contemporary Philosophy* Vol. 59, No. 4, ed. Santiago Zabala (Chicago: DePaul University, Fall 2015), 611–625. Also published in Danish: "Filosofi ved en skillevej," *Tænkningens veje: Et festskrift til Søren Gosvig Olesen*, ed. Per Jepsen (Skive: Wunderbuch, 2016), 135–157.

Chapter 3: "The Relevance of Aesthetics." Previously published as "Why Do We Need Philosophical Aesthetics?," *Transfiguration. Nordic Journal of Religion and the Arts: 2009*, eds. Svein Aage Christoffersen, Martin Wangsgaard Jürgensen, and Nils Holger Petersen (Copenhagen: Museum Tusculanum Press, 2010), 17–34, which was an English translation of "Hvad skal vi med æstetik?" published in Dorthe Jørgensen, *Aglaias dans: På vej mod en æstetisk tænkning* (Aarhus: Aarhus University Press, 2008), 307–323. Both the text and the translation of it were revised for the present volume.

Chapter 4: "Aesthetic Thinking as a Common Humanist Concern." Not previously published in any language. Presented orally at a 2008 conference linked to Copenhagen University's then strategical project "The Humanities in the Twenty-First Century" (Copenhagen University, April 23, 2008).

Chapter 5: "The Dialogue of Experience." Previously published in *Trópos: Journal of Hermeneutics and Philosophical Criticism* Vol. 9, No. 1, ed. Gaetano Chiurazzi (Turin: University of Turin, 2016), 45–62. Presented orally at the conference "Effetti d'interpretazione" (University of Turin, March 16–17, 2016).

Chapter 6: "History as a work." Not previously published in any language. Presented orally at the conference "Presenting the Theatrical Past" (Stockholm University, June 13–17, 2016). Based on Dorthe Jørgensen, *Historien som værk: Værkets historie* (Aarhus: Aarhus University Press, 2006), and *Den skønne tænkning: Veje til erfaringsmetafysik. Religionsfilosofisk udmøntet* (Aarhus: Aarhus University Press, 2014).

Chapter 7: "*Felix Aestheticus* and the Good Life." Not previously published in any language. Presented orally at the conference "Aesthetics in Late Eighteenth-Century Theatre" (Stockholm University, May 31–June 2, 2018).

Chapter 8: "Creativity and Aesthetic Thinking." Previously published in *Handbook of Well-Being*, ed. Kathleen Galvin (Abingdon and New York: Routledge, 2018), 243–249, which was an English translation of "Hvordan vi tænker: Om vejen til visdom," *Viljen til visdom: En bog om dannelse og uddannelse*, eds. Jens Thodberg Bertelsen et al. (Aarhus: Slagmark, 2008), 100–109. Presented orally in both the UK and Denmark, including at the "32nd International Human Science Research Conference" (Aalborg University, August 13–16, 2013).

Chapter 9: "Immanent Transcendence." Not previously published in any language. Based on my three essays: "Guddommelighedserfaring i en moderne verden," *Interesse for Gud: Ni tidssvarende essay*, eds. Henrik Brandt-Pedersen and Niels Grønkjær (Frederiksberg: Anis, 2002), 98–117, "Erkendelsens mirakel," *Mirakler*, eds. Birgitte Haahr Callesen et al. (Aarhus: Aarhus University Press, 2008), 99–113, and "The Experience of Immanent Transcendence," *Transfiguration. Nordic Journal of Religion and the Arts: 2010/2011*, eds. Svein Aage Christoffersen, Martin Wangsgaard Jürgensen, and Nils Holger Petersen (Copenhagen: Museum Tusculanum Press, 2012), 35–52.

Chapter 10: "Limit and Threshold." Previously published in *Debating and Defining Borders: Philosophical and Theoretical Perspectives*, eds. Anthony Cooper and Søren Tinning (Abingdon and New York: Routledge, 2019), 138–151.

Chapter 11: "Hospitality and World Poetry." Not previously published in any language.

The journal editors and publishers who have authorized me to reproduce previously published writings have my deep gratitude.

Poetic Inclinations
© The Author and Aarhus University Press 2021
Cover: Camilla Jørgensen, Trefold
Layout and typesetting: Trefold
Publishing editor: Henrik Jensen
This book is typeset in Chronicle Text and printed on Munken Premium Cream 13, 100 g
Printed by Narayana Press, Denmark

Printed in Denmark 2021

ISBN 978 87 7219 104 1

Aarhus University Press
aarhusuniversitypress.dk

Published with the financial support of Aarhus University Research Foundation

All rights reserved. Except for the quotation of short passages for the purpose of criticism and review, no part of this publication may be reproduced, stored in a retrieval system, or transmitted, in any form or by any means, without the prior permission of the publisher.

International distributors

Oxbow Books Ltd., oxbowbooks.com
ISD, isdistribution.com